THE
WINE
MAKER'S
ANSWER BOOK

THE
WINE
MAKER'S
ANSWER BOOK

Solutions to Every Problem
Answers to Every Question

WITHDRAWN

Alison Crowe

Columnist for

Wine Maker.

Storey Publishing

*The mission of Storey Publishing is to serve our customers by
publishing practical information that encourages
personal independence in harmony with the environment.*

Edited by Lisa H. Hiley and Margaret Sutherland
Technical editing by Daniel Pambianchi
Art direction and text design by Vicky Vaughn
Cover design by Kent Lew
Text production by Jennifer Jepson Smith
Illustrations by Alison Kolesar
Indexed by Susan Olason, Indexes & Knowledge Maps

Printed in China by Regent Publishing Services
10 9 8 7 6 5 4 3 2 1

Library of Congress Cataloging-in-Publication Data

Crowe, Alison.
  The Winemaker's answer book / by Alison Crowe.
    p. cm.
  Includes index.
  ISBN-13: 978-1-58017-656-9; ISBN-10: 1-58017-656-9 (pbk. : alk. paper)
  1. Wine and wine making. I. WineMaker. II. Title.

TP548.C695 2007
641.2'2—dc22

                                                              2006102591

DEDICATION

For my grandmothers, Mary Hartley Crowe
and Bernice Blythe Michel

Ranch managers, world travelers, master gardeners,
expert chefs, and California pioneers, they taught me
a woman's place is doing whatever she sets her mind to.

ACKNOWLEDGMENTS

I greatly enjoy lending my winemaking knowledge and experience to the readers of *WineMaker* magazine, but at the end of the day (sometimes at 2:00 A.M. with grapes in my hair), I live and work as a professional winemaker. I owe heartfelt thanks to many who have contributed to my career. I am grateful for the friendship of Dr. Andy Waterhouse, Dr. Jim Lapsley, Dr. Roger Boulton, Dr. Ralph Kunkee, and Dr. Jim Wolpert at the UC-Davis Department of Viticulture & Enology. I also have had the fortune to log long and hard hours with some of the world's most talented winemakers, including Michael Michaud, Eric Laumann, Don Blackburn, Randall Grahm, Laureano Gomez, and Michel Rolland. Their life lessons, from Mozart's sonatas to Argentine BBQ, go well beyond wine.

I also want to thank my winemaking colleagues and neighbors Jef Stebben, SaDawna McCart-Stebben, Carol Wilson, Sunshine Gladish-Cowgill, Bruce Devlin, Danielle Cyrot, Haydn Wilson, and Nicole Haller-Wilson. Winemakers and wine appreciators, they remind me to stop and smell not just the Cabernet Sauvignon but the roses as well. Elizabeth Hoff, Hope Thrane, Jim Baird, Susan Andersen, and Maureen Foley, as well as editors past and present at the *Davis Enterprise, Vineyard & Winery Management,* and *Wine Business Monthly* have all helped me tremendously. Brad Ring of *WineMaker* and Lisa Hiley of Storey Publishing, along with their staffs, have been the real "superheroes" of this book.

Lastly and most importantly, I thank my husband, photographer Chris Purdy, and the Crowe and Purdy families for their love and support.

CONTENTS

FOREWORD

When will my fermentation stop? Why did my fermentation stop? The one thing I can count on as publisher of *WineMaker* magazine is that my e-mail in-box will have questions each day from winemakers asking for help and looking for answers. Making your own wine is an incredibly fun and fulfilling hobby, but it comes with a host of questions. Some questions are obvious ones we all will face in our winemaking pursuits, while others pop up only when something has gone horribly wrong with our latest batch. And, of course, there are questions that are just plain strange, such as one asking about making wine from Sprite soda. All of these questions are important to ask — and answer — because they help build a greater base of knowledge among winemakers, which results in a more successful and more satisfying hobby for each of us.

When *WineMaker* magazine launched in 1998, we realized from the start the value and importance of seeking out reader questions and answering them in each issue. We were lucky to bring Alison Crowe on board as our Wine Wizard right from the premier issue to answer all those questions. Fresh out of the renowned enology program at the University of California-Davis, Alison brought a wealth of wisdom as well as a sense of humor to her answers. Since then, Alison has answered literally hundreds of questions spanning the world of winemaking.

Winemakers can't seem to get enough of Alison's Q&A department. Each year we send out our annual reader survey and each year readers tell us their favorite department in the magazine is the Wine Wizard because of the variety of questions and the depth of answers it provides each issue. The "Wine Wizard Question of the Week" section of winemakermag.com is among the most visited areas of our Web site. Simply put, winemakers have lots of questions and love reading Alison's answers.

The funny thing is few people knew Alison was the Wine Wizard. Like the identity of most "superheroes," we decided it would be fun to keep her "true" identity as the Wine Wizard a secret. So for eight years, Alison shared her wisdom anonymously with readers on top of her daily duties as a professional winemaker in California. Not even her coworkers and friends in the wine industry knew of her secret double life as winemaker by day and wizard by night. Well, now the secret is out and Alison's best work has been collected here in this book for you.

Eight years' worth of the best questions from small-scale winemakers are in the following pages. These are real questions from real winemakers like you; learn from their mistakes. Alison's answers will expand your understanding of wine and winemaking no matter if you are a first-time winemaker or a knowledgeable veteran with many harvests under your belt.

So enjoy as the "Master of Must," the "Sultan of Siphon," the "Great One of Grapes," the one and only Wine Wizard answers common — and some not-so-common — winemaking questions. You will definitely learn more about making super wine from this "superhero."

— **Brad Ring,** Publisher, *WineMaker* magazine

INTRODUCTION

Winemaking is equally a science and an art. That is really why I ventured, as a 17-year-old college freshman, into the world of winemaking. I wanted to devote my life to a field that would keep me firmly rooted in the sciences — chemistry, biology, agriculture — and yet allow me to channel my love of the arts. Pursuing a winemaking career, starting with a degree from the University of California-Davis Department of Viticulture & Enology while working summers at wineries around California, seemed like the perfect choice.

I already had a few harvests under my belt when an e-mail came through the department asking for contributors to a new magazine called *WineMaker*. Because appending my personal e-mail address to my inaugural Q&A column flooded my in-box with questions from knowledge-hungry readers, we decided to go "underground," routing all questions through the magazine's office and making the mysterious and anonymous Wine Wizard the star of the show.

At nights and on weekends, trying to avoid the busy harvest season by prewriting a column or two, I've had fun being the Wine Wizard (amusingly, many readers assumed the Wizard was a gentleman of a certain age), helping everyday people make better wine and dispensing homeopathic doses of winemaking — and wine enjoyment — philosophy along the way. As better material and equipment have become available (largely thanks to the Internet), I've gently encouraged readers to evolve as well, to apply the same cutting-edge professional techniques to their few barrels that I was employing in my "day job" as a winemaker in California's Central Coast, in Argentina, and now in the Napa Valley.

General interest in wine has never been higher and winemaking remains one of the fastest-growing pursuits in North America. People are more wine-savvy than ever, especially my loyal readers at *WineMaker* magazine. Largely distant from the commercial wine world of glossy magazines, luxury resorts, and touristy tasting rooms, it is the small-scale and hobbyist producer that represents to me the true creative, curious soul of winemaking. Throughout my own seasons in the wine business, the Wine Wizard columns have remained a welcome chance to give back and, perhaps, to look back; being a bimonthly "consulting winemaker" to readers in garages, basements, and start-up cellars across the country reconnects me to my own first harvests and the wonder and excitement I felt as I began learning about this complex and beautiful thing we call wine.

Though many Wine Wizard readers make wine on a small scale, I always try to answer their questions on a level that is not. It is my hope that this book will serve everyone, from experienced winemakers troubleshooting fermentations to connoisseurs looking for an in-depth informational edge. Because every batch is different, every harvest is unique, and each wine has its own particular truths, the Wine Wizard always aims to explore both the science and the art of taking a wine from grape to glass and, most importantly, to share that experience with you.

— **Alison Crowe**
Napa, California

CHAPTER 1

The Basics of the Winemaking Process

Q Is it difficult to make wine?

A Just as a tasty meal is the result of reading cookbooks, buying the right pots and pans, and trekking to the farmers' market to obtain the freshest ingredients, so it is with wine. Anyone can learn to cook up a few gourmet dishes with just a little research and planning, and anyone should be able to learn how to make wine. Only the raw ingredients and the utensils are different.

Wine also requires an attitude adjustment: We have to have a little bit more patience. While our puttanesca sauce can be ready in an hour, a batch of wine made from fresh grapes can take many months, and sometimes years, to become ready for drinking.

Stripped to its essence, here's how to make wine.

◆ Select your starting material with extreme care and get to know it intimately so you'll know where it can go realistically.

◆ Tweak that raw material if need be (and as the law allows, if you're a professional winemaker) to enable a harmonious end result.

◆ Make sure your starting material is only visited by "good" microbes that will do the desired job in a healthy manner.

◆ Give a gentle nudge when necessary, and once the microbes have done their work, protect your new store of ephemeral fermented goodness from oxygen, light, and bacterial scavengers that might harm it.

◆ Sit back and wonder at what Nature has wrought.

■ ═══════ ■

Q **What changes grape juice to wine?**

A The simplest answer is yeast. Yeast cells, either ambient in the environment or purposefully introduced by the winemaker, metabolize the grape's sugar and excrete it as ethyl alcohol and carbon dioxide. In the process, the grape's natural color, flavor, and aroma components are changed and enhanced. Add some action from other microorganisms and a few months' aging, and all of a sudden, simple fermented grape juice starts to become actual, factual fine wine.

Do grapes even need humans to make wine? Some historians believe that we "discovered" wine thousands of years ago when someone stumbled upon the enjoyable and intoxicating effects of a basket or skin bag full of fruit that had sat around for a few hot days.

To truly change grape juice into fine wine, however, one needs top-notch ingredients, the right equipment, and the patient guidance of a winemaker willing to do everything it takes to make the best wine possible.

WINEMAKING TIME LINE

A half-ton (1,020 pounds) of red grapes yields 75–80 gallons (284–303 L) of wine, enough for one full barrel (59 gallons/223 L) and a few kegs or carboys. A half-ton of white grapes yields 80–85 gallons (303–341 L). Yields differ depending on your individual grapes — these are just rough guidelines.

Some small presses aren't very powerful, so you will press out less juice (in the case of whites) or finished wine (in the case of reds). Sometimes you will pick very sweet grapes and so may want to add water to bring your Brix into a safe fermentation range, therefore increasing your yield per ton.

Making a dry red table wine is similar to making white wine, only the grapes are often picked a bit riper, the skins are allowed to ferment with the juice, and the wine is allowed to age a bit longer before drinking. Once you get to know your grapes and specific varietals better, you will no doubt tailor your practices to meet their individual needs.

Here are the basic, universal steps of winemaking.

1. Harvest red grapes at 24–26° Brix (concentration of sugar), or sooner, if they taste ripe and you like the flavors. White grapes should be picked at 22–24° Brix; you can let them hang longer if the flavors are a bit green or too acidic.

2. **Red:** Destem grapes, mix sulfur dioxide into the crushed grapes, cover loosely, and let sit 1–3 hours. Mix grapes again and take initial readings of Brix, pH, and titratable acidity (TA).

   White: There is no need to destem white grapes and better-quality juice is often produced if you take the clusters directly to the press. However, if you destem and crush the grapes first, you may experience higher yields.

   Press grapes gently or until the juice coming from the press is still interesting to you (harder pressing yields higher pH and high-phenolic juice, which you may not want to include) and sprinkle sulfur dioxide into the juice. Take initial readings of Brix, pH, and TA.

3. In an ideal world, your juice or must will not need any adjustment. If you feel the need, however, and for professional winemakers as the law allows, add water if Brix is too high or concentrate or other sugar if it's too low. Add tartaric acid to bring down the pH and raise the TA if necessary.

4. Inoculate with yeast.

5. Monitor fermentation daily by taking a hydrometer reading at the same time each day.

   Red: Mix the cap of skins and pulp into the liquid at least twice a day.

6. **Red:** Once the must has reached dryness, press the liquid from the solids. Let pressed wine settle, covered, for 24 hours.

White: Once the juice has reached dryness, rack into a clean, covered container. Let the wine settle for 24–48 hours.

7. Rack your wine off of the heaviest sediment (gross lees) into a sanitized container that will hold your lot in an almost-topped situation. At this point new red wine may not be completely dry, as pressing will sometimes liberate unfermented sugar "hiding" in raisins or dried grape berries.

   In the first week or two of a wine's life it may be finishing the fermentation of a last 1 percent or so sugar, so don't top up containers completely until you're sure of dryness or you may lose some still-fermenting wine.

8. Fit your containers with sanitized bungs and fermentation locks to exclude air; top them completely when confirmed dry.

9. When dry, inoculate red wine with malolactic bacteria and monitor fermentation. White wines do not need to go through malolactic fermentation (MLF), but can, depending on the style of wine. If MLF is not desired, add SO_2 to achieve the desired level of free SO_2.

10. When MLF is complete, rack into a clean, topped container and add SO_2 to adjust free SO_2 as needed.

11. Every month or so (as wine levels warrant it), top up your containers, monitoring free SO_2 levels every month or so, if possible.

12. When the wine falls bright, isn't spritzy, and tastes ready to you (usually nine months minimum for medium-bodied reds or two months for whites), rack the clear wine off any remaining sediment and adjust the free SO_2 one last time.
13. Rack clarified wine off into clean, sanitized bottles and seal with a cork.
14. Store bottles in a cool, dark place and begin tasting for development a month after bottling. I suggest tasting reds every two or three months to monitor development and to discover when they are nearing their peak.

    White wines are generally ready to drink sooner than reds and have a shorter life due to their lower levels of tannins and other antioxidant compounds, so tasting a bottle every month is a good idea.

Note: This basic time line doesn't include any oak aging, clarification, or stability work, such as using bentonite on your white wines or doing an egg white finish on your reds to round out rough tannins and to help settle the wine more completely. Please refer to chapter 7, "Aging, Oaking, Fining, and Finishing," for more information on these topics. Also see the glossary for definitions of unfamiliar terms.

Q What is the difference between must and wine?

A There are three distinct physiological stages in a wine's life: the grape, the juice or must, and the wine. The first, obviously, is the raw material from which wine is made. White wine grapes are typically pressed before fermentation to separate the grape skins and seeds from the juice. The resulting juice is then turned into wine by the yeast. Red grapes are crushed into a mixture of fresh grape juice, seeds, and skins called "must." Most winemakers don't consider a juice or must to be "wine" until it is dry (no sugar left to ferment) or until the fermentation is arrested (by means of cooling, filtering, or adding sulfites, sometimes all three) at the point desired by the winemaker.

Q What is pomace?

A Pomace is the general term for the solid material that is left over after winemaking, juice production, or cider pressing (*pomme* means "apple" in French). The composition of pomace depends largely on what kind of wine is being made and at what stage of processing the liquid has been pressed out. With white wine, the juice is pressed out of the grapes before fermentation. The resultant pomace is rich in sugar, nitrogen, amino acids, and other goodies that didn't make it into the fermentation tank. Red pomace, which is pressed off after fermentation, is depleted of sugar and nutrients and has given many of its tannins and colored compounds to the wine.

Pomace, even when fermented, contains a staggering variety of chemical components. The skins mainly consist of cellulose, tartaric acid, trace amounts of other organic acids, unfermentable sugars, tannins, anthocyanins (plant pigments), and some aromatic phenolic substances.

The seeds, which remain largely intact during pressing and fermentation, are gold mines of bitter and astringent tannins, as are the stems. The seeds also contain large amounts of nutritious oil that is gaining popularity with chefs due to its high smoke point. If the pomace is pressed from a fermented wine, it will contain water and alcohol.

White or red, pomace varies in moisture content depending on how hard it has been pressed. White pomace, often pressed gently to avoid extracting bitter compounds into a delicate white wine, can end up juicy and sticky with sugar. Red pomace often forms amorphous clumps and can be quite dry to the touch. Anything added during the juice or winemaking process — like enzymes, tannin powder, or yeast — will be present in the pressed pomace. (See page 79 for more on pomace and page 80 for second-run wines.)

Q What are the lees?

A Lees are the solids that are left in the wine after the primary or secondary fermentation is finished, but the term also refers to any sediment that remains in the wine after it is pressed. It is advisable to rack the wine off of these heavy, immediately post-press solids, often called "gross lees," because they can contribute to off flavors or lend a reductive, closed-in character and, in the worst case, hydrogen sulfide (rotten egg smell) if the wine is left too long in contact with them. Taking some of the "fine lees" along into the next container is fine at this stage. This is the sediment that will flow easily down a siphon tube. Some winemakers believe this fine sediment contributes a fatness and richness to the mouthfeel of a wine as it ages. (See page 148 for aging wine *sur lies,* or "on the lees.")

■ ▬▬▬▬ ■

Q What is racking?

A Racking means transferring juice or wine from one container to another, using a siphon line or pump and hose. It is done at many stages of the winemaking process, with the goal of separating liquid, be it raw juice, recently pressed wine, or almost-finished wine, from a layer

of solids. Racking can be a delicate operation and it's important to go slowly. You don't
want to stir up the sediment,
but you don't want to lose your
siphon suction.

How often you rack a wine
before bottling depends on the
wine. White wines are racked several times: after the juice is pressed
and has settled for 24 hours; after
primary fermentation; after fining, if
that occurs; and an additional time
right before bottling. A minimum

*Racking from
bucket to carboy*

racking schedule for reds is after the wine is pressed off;
after malolactic fermentation, if carried out; after settling
out any finings; and sometimes once more before bottling.

White and red wines can also be "splash racked," that is,
racked from one container to another using various techniques to incorporate air into the wine as it pours into the
receiving vessel. This is done to incorporate oxygen into the
early stages of fermentation (necessary for the healthy development of yeast cells) or to help "blow off" unpleasant aromas that may develop in wine during bulk aging. Normally,
however, racking is performed with the goal of not oxygen-
ating the wine needlessly, especially during the latter part of
a wine's life when it has lost a good part of its carbon dioxide and therefore its natural protection against air.

Q Can wine be made out of anything?

A The bottom line is that yes, technically you can "ferment" just about anything organic. When you're looking for a certain end product, however, and you want it to be drinkable to boot, it's important to select the right microbe for the job, give it the proper starting conditions, and carefully control the fermentation to help your microbe deliver the results you seek.

There's a reason the best wines in the world are made from grapes, by the way. The grape is the one naturally occurring fruit that most often has the right combinations of sugars, acids, and yeast nutrients to naturally make a stable, tasty, and healthy beverage.

Other fermented beverages include beer and sake, but cheese, olives, and even some sausages and deli meats are considered fermented, though in a nonalcoholic sense. Cheese results when bacteria turn the lactose in milk into lactic acid, separating the liquid milk into solid curds. The famous dry-cured Felino salami of Parma, Italy, owes its tang to various strains of indigenous molds and bacteria.

In winemaking, when we talk about the "secondary fermentation" or "malolactic fermentation," we really mean the common metabolic process through which certain bacteria eat the naturally present malic acid in wine and spit it out as lactic acid. Even though it's not yeast turning sugar into alcohol, it's still called a fermentation.

This is the academic definition of fermentation, which sometimes gets lost in the shuffle of everyday "winespeak." A general microbiologist will tell you that fermentation is "a metabolic breakdown of a nutrient molecule brokered by microbes through an enzyme-controlled pathway," or words to that effect. In plain English, fermentation occurs when bacteria or yeast eat something, take energy from it, and excrete something else out the other end.

A dear professor of mine at UC-Davis, eminent microbiologist Dr. Ralph Kunkee, used to tease the undergrads by pointing at his podium and saying, "You can technically ferment anything, even this desk here, providing you could find the right microbe to do it." His point was that, according to the technical definition of fermentation, there are "edible" plant carbohydrates out there (even wood) that under the right conditions, will "ferment," or become microbially digested, at least to some extent.

Fortunately for us oenophiles, the conversion of sugar to alcohol, as in winemaking, is a fermentation that tends to have pretty pleasant results. If you present the right microbe (say your typical *Saccharomyces cerevisiae* wine yeast) with the right set of conditions (say a freshly pressed barrel of 23 percent sugar Chardonnay grape juice), you'll end up with an aqueous solution of acid, aromatic compounds, and roughly 12 percent alcohol — in other words, wine.

■ ══════════ ■

Q Is red wine made the same way as white?

A Many steps are similar, but there are some major differences. Red wines are fermented with the skins and pulp; the solids are pressed after fermentation is complete. This is done to extract color, aroma, and flavor from the skins. Red wines are typically picked at a higher Brix (concentration of sugar) than white wines and are made with a higher pH (lower acidity). They are also fermented at warmer temperatures (70–90°F, or 21–32°C) and are almost always subjected to more new oak, whether in the form of barrels or oak adjuncts like oak beans or staves.

White wines are often made in a crisper and more refreshing style; to achieve this, the grapes are picked at a lower Brix and so naturally have a higher level of acid than most reds. White wines are always pressed before fermentation, so only the grape juice winds up in the fermenter. It is rare for a white wine to be exposed to much new oak and, more because of style trends than anything else, fewer and fewer white wines are allowed to go through malolactic fermentation. Whites tend to be fermented in neutral containers like stainless-steel vats or well-used oak barrels. Though late-harvest whites like the famous Château d'Yquem are rare exceptions, most whites are bottled sooner (sometimes within three months of harvest), released to the marketplace sooner, and are not aged as long as reds. (See pages 65 and 66 for more on crushing and pressing options.)

FIVE GOLDEN RULES OF WINEMAKING

1. **Your wine is as good as your starting material.** This is Rule Number One. It's possible to make mediocre wine out of great fruit, but you can't make great wine out of mediocre fruit. An ancillary rule is that you must understand and accept your starting material, both its potential and its limitations. You can ferment with the latest yeast, stir the lees, and use an expensive French oak barrel, but an insipid wine can't grow beyond its roots, even with all the expensive and time-consuming treatments in the world.

2. **Acid is the backbone of a wine.** I learned this at Chalone Vineyard near Monterey, California. Even with blasting 100-degree days, the limestone soils and the chilly nights kept the acid levels in the Pinot Noir and Chardonnay much higher than one would expect. This is one of the secrets to the long ageability of Chalone's wines — they are rich in natural grape acids, modest in alcohol, and rooted in what I would call one of California's only true *terroir* vineyards.

   Lower acid wines historically don't age as well and are more prone to damaging oxidative reactions and microbial spoilage. Fine wines should be made with the true focus being on the pH, titratable acidity (TA), and flavor/texture balance of tannins and acids.

3. **Learn the science behind the art.** Don't just blindly follow a protocol that says to add 30 mg/L sulfur

dioxide. Take classes, read books, learn from experienced winemakers, and do whatever you can to learn *why* you add that 30 mg/L sulfur dioxide. More importantly, you should know when to add 30 mg/L, when to add 50 mg/L, and when to add none at all.

4. **Listen to your wine.** Let the wine tell you what it needs and where it wants to go. Winemaking buddies, current style trends, and market pressure for the commercial winemaker can lead winemakers to use too many new barrels, leave a little residual sugar, or bottle too soon.

    Once the grapes are picked, the path to wine is already laid out before you. A super-corpulent 30° Brix Syrah must will have a hard time squeezing itself into the bottle as a crisp, light rosé. Such ripe, luscious fruit really wants to be the base for a stellar Port-style dessert wine. Don't force it. Go where the wine leads.

5. **Don't take wine, or yourself, too seriously.** Maybe this should be Rule Number One. Even those of us who make wine for a living need to remember that wine is, at its core, supposed to be fun. Whether it's touring wine country with your sweetheart, watching reruns of Lucy stomping messily away, or bringing out a bottle of your finest for the backyard bocce ball team, wine heightens our enjoyment of everyday life, links us to the past, and connects us to the natural world in a very tangible way. If that's not worth celebrating, I don't know what is.

Q Are rosé wines made from a different kind of grape than red wines?

A Most of us are familiar with the three "colors" of wine: red, white, and rosé. The latter is sometimes called blush, *vin gris,* or pink wine and, in the minds of many, not taken as seriously as other wines. Thought to be in some nebulous category that's not quite red and not quite white, rosé wines are often considered as "not quite wine." This lack of respect is unfortunate, however, as these wines are about as serious as you can get, for the drinker as well as the winemaker. Pink wines may be candy-colored and smell of simple fruits, but they are actually more challenging to make than many others and deserve greater recognition from the consumer, trade, and hobby sectors of the wine world.

Perhaps some of the confusion about and mistrust of pink wine stems from the fact that we often aren't speaking the same language when we discuss them. Having all those different names for pink wine certainly doesn't help. In addition, pink wines suffer from the misconception that they are made from inferior red grapes that wineries have rejected or are blends of "scraps" of red and white wines, essentially a dump bucket for second-rate wines that didn't make the quality cut to be bottled.

The true origin of pink-colored wines couldn't be farther from the truth. Rosé wines traditionally are made from freshly pressed red grapes that are not allowed to ferment with the grape skins. They are allowed just enough skin contact to take on a pink (or blush) hue but are separated from the skins early in the winemaking process.

Some of the best rosé wines in the world are made alongside (and from) the best red wines in the world. It's a common practice for premium red producers — traditionally in Italy and France, but also in other parts of the world — to bleed off a portion of juice from freshly crushed red grapes (sometimes called a *saignée*), keeping it separate and treating it in the cellar like a white wine. These wines are usually fermented completely dry, which may come as a surprise to some Americans accustomed to sweet so-called white Zinfandel. Rosé wines generally aren't taken through malolactic fermentation, as their fragile color can turn orange and their fresh aromas run the risk of being negatively changed or lost altogether.

■ ═══════ ■

Q What does *vinifera* mean?

A *Vinifera,* or more specifically, *Vitis vinifera,* is the species name for the European domesticated grapevine, a well-traveled and much-planted fruit from which most of the wines of the world are made. Well-known varieties of *V. vinifera* include the familiar Cabernet Sauvignon and Chardonnay but also include such esoteric and worthy varietals as Torrontés, a delicate white that is a specialty of northern Argentina, and Chasselas, thought to be the oldest known grape varietal still in use today.

Domesticated somewhere around 8500 BCE near present-day Turkey, *V. vinifera* was spread throughout ancient Asia, the Near East, and all parts of Europe. This particular grape species gained wide popularity for making fermented beverages because it was one of the few fruits available to prehistoric or modern humankind that accrued enough sugar to produce sufficient alcohol to ensure stability.

In contrast to wild grapes, *V. vinifera* is monoecious; having both male and female sex organs on the same plant produces higher and more consistent yields. Early winemakers liked the high acid content, depth of color, and sheer flavor variety among the different types of *V. vinifera*. From the days of the Roman Empire to the age of European exploration in the 1500s, the domesticated grapevine followed travelers and adventurers around the globe, taking root in Australia, South America, Mexico, North America, and Africa.

V. vinifera doesn't grow well everywhere, however. It prefers a temperate climate with mild summers and mild winters (although a little frost is okay). In the United States, *V. vinifera* grapes thrive in California and the Pacific Northwest. They also grow well in pockets scattered from the Great Lakes to New York and the mid-Atlantic states.

■ ══════ ■

Q What are the most common "rookie mistakes" to avoid in winemaking?

A Though it's hard to anticipate every possible mistake and take into account every contingency, there are some errors that many beginners make. Here are five.

Picking grapes too early or too late. I can't say this enough — it all starts with the raw material. Pick too early and your Cabernet will never lose that nasty green bell pepper aroma. Pick too late and your delicate Malvasia Bianca will be a flabby, high-pH flop with 15 percent alcohol. Making the pick call is the single most important decision you will make in your wine's life — be sure you do it right. Analyze the numbers (Brix, pH, and TA), but more important, use your taste buds. If you're taking someone's second crop, let it hang on the vine as long as possible to lose some acid and develop the flavor profile you want.

Inappropriate must adjustment. Acid, water, enzymes, nutrients, tannins, sulfur dioxide — the list of things we can add to our freshly processed grapes is too long to enumerate. Many beginning winemakers believe that the more tweaks and additions they make, the better their wine will be. I prefer a minimalist approach that uses additives only when the grapes really call for it.

Not understanding the destructive power of oxygen and spoilage microbes. After the carbon dioxide from the primary and the optional secondary fermentation blows off, your wine is vulnerable to attack by oxygen and spoilage yeast and bacteria. Leaving wine uncovered, untopped, or unprotected with inadequate free sulfur dioxide is asking for trouble. When a wine is actively fermenting, it can be roughed up, left uncovered, and moved around without much worry. Once a wine goes still, it's critical to protect it.

Misunderstanding the constructive power of oxygen and good microbes. Believe it or not, oxygen is critical for a wine's early development. A healthy fermentation needs oxygen, and young red wines in particular can benefit from an aerative racking in the first months of life. Good microbes like yeast and certain strains of lactic acid bacteria are your partners in the fine winemaking process. Learn how to use these tools to your advantage and to actively manage their interactions with your wine.

Keeping inadequate records. So much in winemaking happens by chance — the weather influences the grapes, a cold cellar slows down a fermentation, or a random spoilage yeast invades a perfectly good wine. To maximize control over your wines, keep good records during the winemaking process. Only by logging in dates, treatments, wine analysis, and tasting notes do we learn what works and what doesn't and what we can do to improve.

CHAPTER 2

Choosing and Using Winemaking Equipment

Q What equipment do I need to make wine?

A You should be able to find all the equipment you need at any home-brewing or home-winemaking supply shop. Commercial winemaking supply houses often cater to the small-scale winemaker and are good sources for the most current yeast strains, enzymes, additives, and lab equipment. Purchase cellar equipment through a supplier that specializes in small-batch winemaking.

Here's everything you need to make your first one-barrel batch of wine from fresh grapes.

◆ Hand-crank destemmer
◆ Primary fermenter (a ½-ton plastic MacroBin works great for larger batches; for smaller lots, try food-grade plastic containers or buy a small, stainless-steel variable-capacity tank)
◆ Cover for the fermenter if it doesn't already have one (a tarp with a bungee cord works well)
◆ Punch-down device (if you don't want to use your hands, you can fashion your own from non-toxic wood scraps)
◆ Small basket press

Basket press

- One 59-gallon (223 L) oak or stainless-steel barrel
- Two 10-gallon (38 L) stainless-steel kegs and four 5-gallon (19 L) carboys or other small containers (to store the overflow wine)

Fermentation locks

- One large plastic or stainless-steel funnel
- Four 5-gallon (19 L) plastic buckets with lids
- Hydrometer(s) that read from –5 to 30° Brix
- Plastic 250 mL (1 cup) graduated cylinder
- Thermometer (digital is preferable)
- Acid titration kit
- One 5-foot (1.5 m) length of clear, food-grade, flexible ¾-inch-diameter plastic tubing for siphoning
- One 2-foot (0.6 m) length of clear, food-grade, flexible ½-inch-diameter plastic tubing for siphoning
- Fermentation locks and stoppers to fit your barrel and other containers
- 750 mL (25-ounce) wine bottles
- Corks
- Hand corker (floor-mounted models are easiest to use)
- Assorted brooms, dustpans, and shovels for cleanup

The next items are nice to have if you can afford them (or borrow them).
- pH meter
- Hand bottle filler

- Digital balance that weighs 0.01 g–500 g
- Small cylinder of CO_2 gas

Keep in mind that a half-ton of grapes (1,020 pounds) generally yields one 59-gallon (223 L) barrel with a few 10-gallon (38 L) kegs or 5-gallon (19 L) carboys left over for topping wine. Grapes are usually sold by the ton, but growers who sell to boutique producers often sell them by the pound. Winemakers working with smaller batches can certainly scale down their equipment needs. If, for example, you're making just a few carboys of wine, you don't need a destemmer or a press; you can destem a few pounds of grapes by hand and use a large, sturdy colander or strainer to separate the fermented skins from the wine.

◼ ▬▬▬▬▬▬ ◼

Q How does a hydrometer work?

A As winemakers, we care about the density of sugar dissolved in water — for example, the ripeness of fresh grapes or the sweetness of the juice. The measuring of liquid density is called hydrometry and is based on the principle that an object floating in a liquid displaces an equivalent weight of said liquid. Hydrometers measure the amount of displaced

Hydrometer

liquid with a calibrated scale enclosed within a glass tube that is weighted to keep it upright while floating.

The height at which the tube floats tells us how dense the liquid is or how much it weighs in relation to water. The hydrometer will float much higher in a sweet juice at 20° Brix than it will in a dry wine (with all the sugar turned into less-dense alcohol), which will register on the negative end of the scale. There are many hydrometers with scales in units like degrees Brix, specific gravity, Baumé, Oechsle, and Balling. Luckily there are great calculators that will help you convert between these obscure units if you don't happen to have them floating around in your chemistry book. (See pages 134 for a conversion chart.) However, most hydrometers sold in the United States are in the Brix or specific gravity scale, the latter being favored in Europe.

■ ━━━━━━ ■

Q **Can temperature affect the accuracy of my hydrometer?**

A Since the density of a solution changes with temperature (warming makes it less dense, cooling makes it denser), any hydrometric reading must be calibrated according to the temperature at which the reading is taken. Most scales are calibrated to read a sample at 15.5 or 20°C (60 or 68°F). For an accurate reading, be sure to use the temperature conversion chart packaged with your hydrometer.

Q How do I allow for suspended solids when taking a hydrometer reading?

A Because the hydrometer reading reflects the amount of dissolved solids (density) in the juice, it's easy to see that if you have lots of little bits of suspended pulp pushing the hydrometer above its natural level, you're going to get an artificially high reading. This is why it is so important to measure juice that has as few suspended solids as possible. I don't recommend investing in a battery of strainers, settlers, and centrifuges, because if you follow the tips below, your juice will be just fine to measure. The extra degree of precision that these tools of paranoia could buy you would be minimal indeed and certainly not worth your time or money.

Instead, follow this procedure when checking your sugars: soak, sample, strain, and squeeze. When you receive a load of fresh fruit to ferment, go ahead and crush the fruit for fermentation as you normally would. Then let it soak, which means leaving the fruit and juice to macerate for one to three hours — this step is vital! Freshly breached cell walls take time to release their sugars into the juice.

After you've waited for most of the sugars to be released (but not waited so long that the juice starts to ferment), stir up your container and scoop out a nice, sloppy sample, about 3 cups' worth (710 mL), making sure to include some of the chunky stuff.

Put the whole gloppy mess into a large strainer lined with two or three layers of cheesecloth. Strain the liquid out and give the solids in the cheesecloth a very gentle squeeze, just until the juice stops coming out in a steady stream and begins to drip. Being gentle is the key. If you're forceful, a lot of the solids will squish through the cheesecloth bundle into your sample, which is just what you're trying to avoid!

At this point you should have enough clear juice for a representative sample, so go ahead and measure. If you want to be particularly accurate (for example, if you're going to add sugar or water and you want to know how much to ameliorate), you could let the sample settle for another couple of hours in the refrigerator. We don't want any spontaneous fermentations happening here. Siphon the clearest juice off the top and measure that, adjusting the reading for the temperature (see previous question).

The Refractometer

Another great tool for measuring sugar is the refractometer. Refractometers measure the amount of sugar by bending light through a prism in a way that correlates to the refractive properties of the juice. Refractometers are quick and easy to use but somewhat expensive to buy. They also can only be used on clear, nonfermenting juice and so are best used in the field or on the lab bench to test grapes or just-crushed juice samples.

Q **What's the best way to take accurate hydro-meter readings during fermentation?**

A Since temperature affects density (the colder something is, the denser it is), the temperature of a solution must be taken into account and corrected in order to get an accurate reading. Typically, a fermentation is warmer on top and cooler on the bottom because the warmer fermenting juice tends to rise. Furthermore, if your wine is fermenting on the skins, the floating "cap" of skins will be even hotter than the fermenting juice below and will create its own fermentation "microclimate." The warmer a fermentation is, the faster it will go to completion, so naturally, if you haven't mixed up your container in a while, a top sample will have a lower specific gravity or Brix reading than a bottom sample.

Because density is a measure of dissolved solids, any solid particles in the sample will contribute to the appearance of density. This means if you take a bottom sample out of the valve in your tank, it will most likely be nice and thick, even during fermentation. This extra material will make your hydrometer float higher, giving you a poor picture of what the entire vessel is doing. If you take a sample from the top of a fermenting red wine, you will run into the aforementioned cap, with its thick floaty bits that you will have to strain out to get a good reading.

The solution? Take a sample after punching down your red fermentation and strain it to remove any floating skins that might disrupt your reading. (A plastic or stainless-steel kitchen strainer works fine.) As always, correct for temperature and you should get a pretty accurate density reading.

■ ══════════ ■

Q Can a broken hydrometer be hazardous?

A Arrgghh! The dreaded broken hydrometer! With much gnashing of teeth and tearing of hair, I welcome you to a select international fraternity of the few, the proud, the clumsy. I myself have been known to go through five (count 'em, five) hydrometers in the space of a single harvest.

Check to see what kind of material the hydrometer had in its weighted base. Sometimes the insides of hydrometers, especially old ones, are made of lead. If this is the case, you should not drink the wine for fear of lead poisoning. If you still have it, consult the manufacturer's literature insert to see if that can shed any light on the situation, or try calling the manufacturer directly.

To avoid worries about hydrometer breakage in the future, develop the practice of measuring your densities in a plastic 250 mL graduated cylinder or in a special hydrometer cylinder (it has a collar designed to catch any overflow). These cylinders can be obtained at any winemaking or home brewing supply store.

Characteristics of Oak Barrels vs. Inert Containers

OAK BARREL

◆ Imparts flavors and aromas to the wine, especially if it's a newer one

◆ Can contribute to the "rich and complex" style desirable in many wines like Pinot Noir and Cabernet Sauvignon

◆ Can be harder to control fermentation temperature because wood is a good insulator

◆ Harder to completely clean; barrels build up tartrate crystal deposits, which can be difficult to remove; sanitizing materials can't get underneath these plaques, meaning that microbes have a perfect place in which to multiply

◆ A bit pricey: A 50-gallon (233 L) American oak barrel might cost $500, but an imported French one can easily top $800

◆ Used barrels are a wild card; you don't know what microbes are living in them

◆ The traditional storage vessel of the world's finest wines

INERT CONTAINER (GLASS OR STAINLESS STEEL)

◆ Does not contribute any flavor or aroma to the wine; does not add the classic "oak-aged" or "barrel-fermented" character to wine

◆ Can contribute to the "lean and crisp" style of wine that emphasizes fruit and acidity

◆ Easier to control temperature through ambient air or with conductive method like cold-water bath or glycol cooling coils

◆ Easier to completely clean and thoroughly sanitize

◆ More affordable; often can be bought secondhand

◆ Used stainless-steel and glass containers are more trustworthy than used barrels; you can see most contaminants and can sanitize well to remove the rest

Q Can I use old glass carboys and other items picked up at a flea market for winemaking?

A My response is kindly meant but firm: Don't go there. Though an antiquities enthusiast myself, when it comes to winemaking, I have no trouble putting historical curiosity aside and choosing new equipment instead of charming old bottles encrusted with mysterious matter or "moonshine" jugs of questionable pedigree.

When you can pick up new bottles and new carboys relatively cheaply, there's no reason to jeopardize the quality of your hard-won wine just to save a few dollars. I'm confident in saying that old containers might contain toxic (or just plain smelly) residue that you don't want in your wine and subsequently the digestive tracts of friends or, even worse, customers with friends who happen to be lawyers. When you don't know, it's best not to take any chances.

Use those old jugs, rusty pails, and patina-stained carboys in an antique collection, country cottage, or backyard garden where their beauty will be better appreciated than in the cellar.

■ ══════ ■

Q What is the best way to store plastic fermenters and other containers?

A It is better to clean your fermenting tubs thoroughly and then dry them out for storage instead of trying to use the old-fashioned wet-storage method, where containers are filled with something like a strong solution of sulfur dioxide and citric acid. In my experience, even closely monitored wet-storage solutions lose their potency with time. Forget to add more potassium metabisulfite powder, go on vacation for two weeks, and you'll probably come back to a microbial house party in your tub hosted by those same spoilage organisms you were trying to avoid in the first place. While many strains of bacteria are sensitive to even low levels of sulfites, many spoilage yeasts and other fungi are perfectly happy cohabitating with sulfur dioxide levels at 30 mg/L, especially if the pH of the solution is above 3.0.

The best thing to do is relax and realize that, after all, you're going to clean and sanitize your plastic equipment before you use it again, right? Take a cue from commercial wineries, and don't worry about keeping crush-specific equipment 100 percent sanitized year-round. If it's not going to be used for a few months or until next crush, remove any visible soil, scrub thoroughly (being gentle with stainless steel), rinse, dry, and put the gear away in a safe and dry place. Many wineries even store equipment like large pneumatic presses outside. They simply clean them, let them air-dry, and cover them with a tarp until next crush.

For your tubs, wash them well with any chlorine-free cleaning compound (I've even used dish soap), dry thoroughly, and hang up uncovered so moisture won't accumulate in nooks and crannies and grow any microbial interlopers. If you want to exclude dust, insects, and other pests, use old sheets or large pieces of cheesecloth to loosely cover your equipment. Don't worry about excluding airborne microbes since you'll clean and sanitize before your next crush — it's more important that the tubs be clean, dry, and in a place where they'll stay out from underfoot until next year!

Q **Can I use empty beer half barrels as fermenters and long-term storage devices?**

A By all means, use clean, sanitized, stainless-steel halfbarrels (usually 15–35 gallons/57–133 L in capacity) in your cellar, as long as you know where they came from and are certain nothing toxic has ever been stored in them. I have used beer kegs for storing my topping wines, and as long as they're bunged up tight, are topped, and have SO_2 added when they need it, they're great.

They are easier to clean and sanitize than wooden barrels and obviously don't need as much "care and feeding" as their cooperage counterparts. For the beginning winemaker or for making trial-size batches of experimental wines, they are fine primary fermentation vessels and do a good job aging wine on oak chips or beans. Stainless steel is an inert material, and as long as the vessels are well sanitized, they will not impart any off flavors or aromas to wine.

As with any vessel that has a "past," I suggest a thorough cleaning with hot water and caustic soda followed by a rinse with citric solution and then water. Since one can't see through stainless steel without X-ray vision, I also recommend a good scrubbing (take care not to scratch the surface, though). Get into all the nooks and crannies with a bent-handled brush designed to clean out carboys.

Another method to try (to take a leaf out of the tome of medieval winemakers and brewers) is to add a couple of handfuls of coarse sand or fine gravel to the vessel along with a few cups of water. Agitate the vessel vigorously by rocking it back and forth. This should help to clean up any soil or detritus. Inspect the interior with a flashlight to make sure no crud remains, give it a sniff, and if all appears clean, the vessel is good to go!

Q Is it okay that my variable-volume fermenter leaks gas during primary fermentation?

A If you have the lid on during active fermentation, sometimes the carbon dioxide gas generated by the tank can't all escape through the fermentation lock. It's easy to get this kind of high-pressure gas seepage when the gasket and the tank wall aren't completely flush, especially if there's a grape seed or a piece of skin under the gasket. This can happen if you've let the lid float on the surface of the wine, so be careful when doing that.

A note of caution: Don't ever underestimate the pressure generated by a rolling fermentation — I've seen bungs blown off barrels, tank tops thrown back on their hinges, and geysers of wine shoot 30 feet in the air!

The gas bubbles you're seeing, especially if it's after the fermentation dies down, could be from a leak in the gasket around the lid. If you suspect a leak, deflate the gasket, remove it from the lid, reinflate it, and swab the surface with soapy water. If you see any soap bubbles, you know the gasket has a leak. I make it a practice to check the integrity of my inflatable gaskets every week or two by walking past the tank and making sure that the gasket is tight and the seal still good. Sometimes giving the gasket another good dose of air helps. I keep a bike pump handy for just this purpose.

To avoid leaks, make sure you are treating the gaskets carefully. They are very delicate, especially those made of vinyl. Gaskets made of Desmopan (a thermoplastic polyurethane) are much more durable but still need to be handled gently. The manufacturer's information on these small variable tank gaskets doesn't recommend inflating over 1 bar of pressure. The lid should be raised well above the wine if fermentation is still quite active. This will relieve some pressure and reduce the stress on the gasket. It is critical to always maintain your pumped-up gasket well above the height that a fermenting cap could potentially reach, as contact with the cap can put too much pressure on the gasket.

Better yet, use a tarp, cheesecloth, or fine-mesh screen on top of an active red ferment and only start using the inflated gasket lid to cap off the tank once the fermentation has gone dry and the cap will no longer push up against the inflated gasket and lid. It also helps to use Teflon tape to seal any threaded parts (some gasket air valves have these) and to never raise and lower a lid unless the gasket is completely deflated. Most gaskets can be damaged by extreme heat or cold, ultraviolet light, cleaning chemicals, and SO_2 gas in high concentrations.

■ ══════ ■

Q Why are cleaning and sanitation so important?

A Wine is food. When you're preparing food at home, you use a clean cutting board, wipe the counter, wash your hands, and use clean plates and cutlery. Similarly, it is absolutely critical to have good winery sanitation, as dirty equipment invites spoilage bacteria and unwanted yeast beasties to munch on our wine. There is a point of diminishing returns, however, where you can sanitize too much. I have seen some winemakers go overboard with the microbe killing, so here is some information to help you to make sanitizing decisions appropriate for your unique situation.

First, a vocabulary review: Some winemakers use the terms cleaning, sanitizing, and sterilizing interchangeably, which is a mistake. These terms mean very different things.

Cleaning refers to the physical removal of visible soil, grunge, and muck. Whether done with a scrub brush, a squeegee, or a clean towel, cleaning is as simple as scrubbing down the grape reception hopper or sweeping the floor.

Sanitizing means that you're treating a surface or piece of equipment to reduce the microbial load to an acceptable level, a fancy way of saying that you're killing spoilage microorganisms with heat or a chemical solution.

Sterilizing is another step altogether, and one that goes beyond the scope of anything that is practical in the winery environment. When something is sterilized, it means that it is completely free of bacteria or other microorganisms. As this is a term usually applied to strict laboratory conditions and hospital surgical instruments, no winemaker ever tries to achieve a sterile wine cellar.

Why don't wineries attempt to sterilize, you ask. For one thing, it is practically impossible and for another, it is not necessary. Due to their low pH and high alcohol content, most wines already have some natural resistance to spoilage organisms. As any disgruntled brewer will tell you, most bacteria and even some fungi aren't that happy in wine pHs (3.0–3.75) but will thrive in a higher pH environment like that of beer (4.0–6.0) or water (7.0). That being said, there are some bad guys (the bacteria, not the brewers) that do like to hang around in the wine environment, so it is very important to practice a sensible cleaning and sanitizing program in your winery.

The first step is cleaning, or removing any visible soil, scale, or detritus. This is important because any sanitizing solution you subsequently apply will not penetrate effectively into the hidden nooks and crannies where microbes like to live. Use only gentle plastic scrubbing pads or brushes when cleaning soft stainless steel because it can scratch easily. Simple dish soap can be used, though soda ash is another useful ally in helping you loosen up dirt and grunge. If you do use soda ash, always rinse with a citric acid and water solution to neutralize the base. Follow the acid rinse with a clean-water rinse.

While some would argue that soap or soda ash will suffice, to really be clean and ready to make wine, you have to follow cleaning with some kind of sanitation. The most common sanitizing solution used in small wineries is a strong acidified sulfite solution (see page 54 for recipe). Once a surface is physically clean, rinse with the sanitizing solution, leave it in contact for 5–10 minutes, and then rinse with clear water.

Don't leave strong sulfite solutions in contact with stainless steel, silicone, or some plastic containers for longer than 10 minutes, as they can be damaged. It's also important to protect yourself with an organic-vapor respirator and goggles (the type available at hardware stores) when using strong sulfur dioxide solutions, as the fumes they give off can sometimes irritate the eyes and mucous membranes.

Other sanitizing weapons worth checking into include E-San 205 and PeroxyClean. E-San 205 is a quaternary germicide that cleans and sanitizes and, on previously cleaned surfaces, carries a D-2 USDA rating, which means that it doesn't need to be rinsed with water to be considered food safe (though it has a high pH, so I still rinse with water to protect my wine).

PeroxyClean is a white basic powder, much like soda ash, that produces hydrogen peroxide when mixed in water. Its basic nature helps dissolve soil and scale while the hydrogen peroxide acts as a strong oxidizer, killing microbes as it bubbles in vats, hoses, and barrels. This bubbling action makes it especially good for hard-to-scrub places like the inside of siphon hoses. Though some winemakers feel it doesn't need to be rinsed off, I like to give strong PeroxyClean solutions an acid rinse and a clean-water rinse in order to neutralize the surface and prepare it for contact with wine.

■ ══════ ■

Q When and how often should I sanitize my equipment?

A The answer varies depending on the kind of winemaking you do. My rule of thumb is to always clean and dry equipment that is going into long-term storage. Secondly, always clean and sanitize a piece of equipment before you use it.

If you have to go from red to white wine processing with no storage break, clean all equipment well, making sure no color remains. Rinse off any cleaning or sanitizing solutions with water before allowing contact with your wine.

■ ══════ ■

Q Can I use bleach to clean my equipment?

A I never use any chlorine-containing cleaning compounds in my winemaking and don't recommend it to anyone. Free chlorine molecules can, under the right conditions, contribute to appreciable levels of the swampy or stinky "corked" aroma. There are plenty of alternatives for cleaning; one of my favorites is sodium percarbonate. One brand is PeroxyClean. It also sanitizes clean surfaces as it contains 13 percent available oxygen and is a strong oxidizer.

Sanitizing Solution Formula

◆ 3 grams (0.11 ounce) of sulfite powder (potassium metabisulfite)
◆ 12 grams (0.42 ounce) of citric or tartaric acid (The acid makes the sulfur dioxide more effective.)
◆ 3.78 L (1 gallon) of water

Rinse with clean water after applying to your equipment.

Warning: This solution can be pretty potent if inhaled, so use it out in the open air and wear an organic solvent-grade cartridge mask and eye protection.

People who lack the enzyme sulfite oxidase and are sensitive to sulfites shouldn't use this solution.

CHAPTER 3

From Vine to Vat:

Wine from Fresh Grapes

Q **What are some of the advantages of using fresh grapes?**

A Many hobby winemakers start out experimenting with grape concentrates and winemaking kits. This is fine and dandy, and you can certainly make some good wine this way. In my opinion, however, there is nothing quite like the feel of grape skins between your teeth. Here are my favorite reasons for getting the real goods and going grape.

You're connecting with history and tradition. Humankind has been making wine for more than 8,500 years. How's that for a little living history?

You have more control. You are the one who decides when and how to crush, how much SO_2 to add, whether to press hard or soft, and so on. With kits and concentrates, someone else has already made a lot of decisions for you.

You know exactly what you are getting. Looking at the grapes helps you make better winemaking decisions. How does the rachis (stem) look? Are the grapes completely sound or is there some mold or rot? What temperature are the clusters? It's nice to know the history of your starting material and what you're dealing with up front.

Grapes are where it all begins. The best wines in the world are made at the winery from fresh grapes. Kits can be great, but fresh grapes will always be the gold standard.

■ ══════ ■

Q How do I obtain fresh grapes?

A As the saying goes, "Wine is made in the vineyard." Commercial wineries invest a lot of time, effort, and money in either tending their own vineyards or establishing strong relationships with grape growers. Most beginning winemakers lack those resources, so finding great grapes can be tough.

If you happen to live in a wine-growing area, you may have several fresh-grape options. Try calling some local wineries and vineyards to see if any of them are selling. Be sure to call well in advance of harvest. If you haven't talked to a winery at least a few months in advance, you will probably be brushed off in the rush and bustle of the season.

Sometimes wineries and vineyards allow people to pick "second crop" clusters at a discount. These are the smaller, weaker clusters that are often left hanging on the vine. Because of their weaker color, flavor, and sugar levels, these grapes won't make the best wines of that region, but many small-scale winemakers have made satisfying wines from second-crop grapes.

You might contact a local trade association or winery/grower group to find someone who might have the grapes you want for sale. Local farm advisers or extension agents will also have leads.

Even if you don't live in wine country, you can still obtain fresh grapes. Surf the Internet (or read *WineMaker* magazine) to find companies that ship boxes of just-picked grapes to hobbyists. You can also call your favorite winemaking supply store; many shops order shipments of grapes that arrive in refrigerated trucks each harvest.

■ ══════════ ■

Q What should I look for when buying fresh grapes?

A To make sure your grapes are ripe, squish up a good double handful, strain the juice, and measure the sugar level with a hydrometer or a refractometer. Though ideal parameters will be different across growing regions and varietals, the sugar density should be at least 22° Brix for a white wine and 24° Brix for a red. Target pH ranges are 3.10–3.45 for whites and 3.40–3.65 for reds. Never pick by numbers alone, though. The fruit should taste sweet, ripe, and slightly tart, and the flavors should "pop."

The grapes must be clean, sound, and relatively free of insects and other vineyard debris. Discard any grapes that look rotten or otherwise suspicious. The rachis (the stems of the cluster) should be brown or at least brown at the top of the cluster. Check out the seeds too — for red grapes especially, brown seeds that are crunchy and not too bitter are one sign of ripeness.

Try squeezing a berry or two between your thumb and forefinger; especially in small-berry varietals like Cabernet

Sauvignon, a loose pulp sac that squeezes easily out of the skin is a good sign of ripeness. Some varietals, like Syrah and Zinfandel, especially those grown in warmer areas, have larger berries that naturally become soft as the growing season progresses, which makes this "squeeze test" a less concrete sign of ripeness.

Taste the skins for tannins. They should have some "bite" to them without feeling harsh or bitter. Fresh wine grapes are more sour than your supermarket-variety table grape. They should be tasty and almost savory with a delicious tang of acid. An aggressive, bitter grape is not ripe. An overly sweet grape berry with a flabby taste, very loose or dimpled skin, and deteriorating pulp is probably too ripe for table wine and should be relegated to dessert styles only. More and more winemakers, however, are fans of this super-ripe style and add water (euphemistically called "hydrating") to high-Brix juice or must to achieve the range where yeast can safely ferment to dryness, usually under 25–26°, depending on the yeast strain.

How many pounds of grapes does it take to make a barrel of wine?

As a general rule, you need 800 pounds (363 kg) of fresh grapes still on the stems to make a 59-gallon (223 L) barrel of wine, with some wine left over for the topping up you'll need to do over time. The final volume of wine depends on how much juice you squeeze out of the grapes and whether you press before fermentation for white wine or after fermentation for red wine.

If there are many tiny berries per grape cluster, you can assume that there will be a higher percentage of solids to liquid, both in the form of skins and seeds and in the grape stems that bear each tiny berry. In large, loose clusters where the stem-to-berry ratio is less and the skin-to-juice ratio is less, you will recover more liquid. Similarly, if you add water to ameliorate high-Brix musts, expect your yield to increase.

Winemakers are essentially at the whim of Mother Nature, who one year may grace your Cabernet vineyard with fine, heavy clusters and another year make half the berries too tiny to yield any juice at all. Even with varietal variations on berry size, stem weight, and so on, it's almost impossible to accurately gauge how much juice will come from a certain lot of grapes unless you have years of experience working with grapes and know what volumes they have yielded in the past.

Another monkey wrench to throw in is the year-to-year variation in processing parameters as well as the winemaker-to-winemaker differences inherent in the winemaking process. Your friend down the road may take 100 pounds of grapes and press the heck out of them to yield 10 gallons of wine, whereas your winemaking regimen, with its gentler pressing, may yield only 6 gallons. All we can do is make estimations, gain experience, and go from there.

Q Why is it important for grapes to be ripe when they are picked?

A For quality table-wine production, grapes must be ripe enough to yield a potential alcohol of at least 10 percent and no more than 15–16 percent. Most wine yeast won't ferment above 16 percent alcohol. Grapes that don't have enough sugar to give 10 percent alcohol will have too much acid and not enough sugar and will often display underdeveloped flavors and aromas. Similarly, grapes that are overripe will lack acid (some of it gets metabolized in the ripening process), will have too much sugar to produce a balanced dry wine, and will produce an overabundance of alcohol, putting the fermentation at risk of stopping.

It's important to remember that sugar level doesn't necessarily equate to flavor ripeness. In red wines, especially, it's important to pick when the flavors, tannins, and acids are all in balance. Sometimes using a red grape with over 25° Brix is the only way to accomplish this. You can go too far, however. Some winemakers have been pushing for longer and longer "hang time," letting the grapes stay on the vines until super-ripe to accommodate current red styles.

This may please international wine critics and some consumers, but it can be disastrous for final alcohol content and even long-term ageability. Leaving those grapes on the vine overly long can produce boozy, overblown reds with high volatile acidity, high pH, microbial problems, and shortened longevity. In case you missed your perfect pick window, it is possible to pick super-ripe grapes and then add water to lower the Brix level before inoculating with your yeast strain of choice. Some winemakers fear dilution, but in my experience, the addition of water to juice or must, as long as it's less than 5 percent of total expected volume, does no harm to the end product.

Pick Your Brix

Red grapes are typically picked at higher degrees Brix than white wine grapes, because red grapes benefit from the extra body and mouthfeel that a higher final alcohol level can provide. White wines benefit from a higher acid content, while the riper, sweeter grapes that make nice red wines often provide a good sensory kick.

- ◆ Red wine grapes   24–26° Brix
- ◆ White wine grapes   22–24° Brix

Q **How soon after picking or buying my grapes should I have them in the fermenter?**

A It's important to move your grapes to your primary fermenter as quickly as possible in order to minimize oxidation, microbial ingress, and volatile acidity. VA is a measure of acetic acid, which is produced when certain types of bacteria eat the ethanol in wine and turn it into vinegar. A little VA can be okay, and some people think it contributes to a wine's complexity, but too much is objectionable. High VA is a sign of spoilage (or impending spoilage) and when over 0.05 g/100 mL in the fermenter, may indicate that all is not well with your fermentation. Yeast, when under stress, can produce VA as well, so high fermentation temperatures, high sugar fermentations, and weak yeast can contribute to this off character.

Moving your grapes to the fermenter quickly also helps capture the freshness of the fruit. Pick in the early morning if you can and transport the fruit to the winery in covered containers. If you have access to dry ice, a pound or two in the bottom of a garbage-can-sized container will keep the grapes cool and relatively anaerobic until you are ready to process them.

If you live outside wine country and buy fresh fruit shipped in refrigerated trucks or railcars, the main goal remains the same. Get your fruit to the fermenter as quickly as possible.

When picking up your fruit from the shipper, check that it is cool to the touch and ask the seller when it was picked and if the Brix and acid levels at the time of picking are known. Picking off a few grapes to taste test them for sweetness is also a good idea before loading up your car with fruit. Your clean winemaking equipment should be ready at home so when you pull into your driveway you can begin making your wine right away.

Q What are some options for crushing grapes?

A The easiest way to prepare small batches (less than 50 pounds) of grapes for fermentation, red or white, is to reach in and grab the grapes with your hands and start squeezing. And yes, you can use your feet to crush grapes (at least wash them off before hopping in!). I've done it with 200 pounds of red grapes and have removed the stems by hand later.

For anyone dealing with over a few hundred pounds of grapes, there are mechanical ways to separate stems from grape clusters. The most common machines are called destemmers (or crusher/destemmers, if they also have a set of rollers that squish the destemmed berries as they pass through). Most winemakers I know only destem, because they figure that the process releases enough juice and they don't want to risk chewing up the grape seeds, which can contribute to high bitterness.

Destemmers and crusher/destemmers both consist of a horizontally mounted, motor-driven spindle with paddles inside a hollow drum. The grapes are loaded into a raised hopper above the destemmer. The clusters fall into one end of the drum and as the spindle rotates, the paddles whip the grape clusters against the inside of the drum, which has berry-sized holes through which the berries then drop sans stems.

The stems are moved through to the open end of the drum into a collection bin, where they are disposed of or used for compost. The berries then fall into either another bin or, in mechanized wineries, into a collection sump, from which they are pumped through a food-grade hose to any fermentation vessel in the winery.

If the machine also crushes, the berries then pass through a set of adjustable rollers before falling into the collection sump. The farther apart the winemaker sets the rollers, the less the berries are crushed. Time was when machines focused on roughing up the grape berries instead of gently taking the stems out. These days, even if a winemaker owns a crusher/destemmer (the name of which is a little deceiving as the machine destems first and then crushes), he or she will often remove the crushing rollers or set them as far apart as possible.

Terminology can be a little funny at the wineries; I know a lot of winemakers who refer to the machine that removes stems as a "crusher" out of habit. And the harvest period is still fondly called "crush," even though we don't do a lot of crushing anymore, just gentle destemming.

■ ══════════ ■

Q Are there differences between initial processing for red and white wines?

A Red grapes are usually destemmed before crushing, if they are crushed at all (see above), as grape stems can contribute to excessive tannin levels in the finished wine.

The juice begins to be released in the process, which allows the winemaker to quickly get a grasp on the Brix, TA, and pH of the lot. When both destemming and crushing red grapes, be especially wary of breaking up seeds. These little packets of bitterness will stay with the wine through fermentation, so it's important to keep as many seeds intact as possible.

White grapes don't have to be destemmed or crushed. In fact, excellent juice comes from grapes that have been "whole-cluster pressed." This means the grapes bypass the crusher/destemmer altogether and are dumped directly into the press. Whole-cluster pressing, when done gently, yields white grape juice with a lower percentage of solids, less bitterness, and lower levels of phenolic compounds. However, whole-cluster pressing results in lower juice yields per pound of grape; small "garage-scale" presses have a hard time exerting sufficient pressure, so home winemakers may want to crush their whites first before putting them into the press.

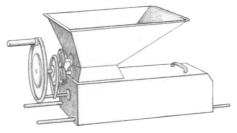

Crusher/destemmer

How Many Stems?

One can destem completely or partially. Stems can contribute some tannins and phenolic compounds to red wines, and some winemakers include up to 20 percent of the stems in a red fermentation. And even though white wines are made by separating the juice from the solids (skins, stems, and seeds) early in the wine's life, a certain percentage of stems can be dumped into the press. The stems help to loosen up the pomace and provide channels through which juice can flow. However, if you are a beginning winemaker, I recommend removing as many stems as possible to avoid the potential for bitterness.

Q Can I destem by hand?

A Destemming by hand is relatively easy if you're working with small amounts of grapes. After you crush, rake your hand through the must and extract a handful of stems. Give it a good squeeze to make sure you've gotten the juicy bits off each cluster, then discard and dive back in until most of the stems are gone. Usually the rachis will stay intact and will be easy to remove by hand.

Some varieties like Syrah don't have very strong stems and may break into pieces, especially if you've picked late and the stems are brittle. If this is the case, you may have to work a little harder to fish out and discard enough stems to make you comfortable. Some folks use "destemming paddles," which are wooden tools that look like Ping-Pong paddles with small nails driven through them at regular intervals.

Q When is a good time to test for sugars with grape winemaking?

A If you're making white wine, you've got it a little easier, as sugar testing can be done immediately after the crushing and pressing (or just pressing, if you've chosen the whole-cluster press option). Once your white grape juice is pressed out of the fruit, you can take a reading and be on your way.

Winemakers dealing with reds can take a Brix reading 1–3 hours after crushing and/or destemming, right when the berries begin to release their juice. However, it's best to take another reading after a 12–24 hour "soak up" period, when the berries, especially any that might be raisined or desiccated, have had a chance to release most of their sugars into solution.

■ ━━━━━━━ ■

Q What is the purpose of a cold soak?

A Some winemakers choose to do a cold soak before inoculating with yeast to attempt to get more color and flavor extraction in the finished wine. The grape must sits in the primary fermenter at a low temperature for a certain period of time — sometimes hours, sometimes days — before inoculation or until the must begins fermenting on its own.

Commercial wineries with huge glycol refrigeration systems have better control over the cold-soak process than do most home hobbyists. It is a risky practice, as keeping the must uninoculated and unprotected by the resulting carbon dioxide could lead to a bacterial bloom and high volatile acidity levels.

However, keeping the must at low temperatures helps discourage the growth of spoilage microbes if one chooses to cold soak. I use 50°F (10°C) for 3 days, which is pretty standard, when I make wine in glycol-cooled tanks. Small-scale fermenters can use 5 pounds (2.3 kg) dry ice/200 (91 kg) pounds grapes to try to mimic the effect.

Q What is maceration and extended maceration?

A Maceration is the time period that your red wine is on the skins during the vigorous primary fermentation. Turn over your must at least twice a day during the active fermentation stage, when appreciable levels of carbon dioxide are still evolving from the must. The goal is to completely submerge the cap (the floating skins and grape material) in the fermenting juice. If you're dealing with a plastic "trash can" drum fermenter, you can easily punch down the cap, either with your hands or by using a 2×4 with a round disk nailed to one end. (Sanitize the utensil in a sulfite solution first.) When the wine is almost dry, you can drop back to one punch down a day.

Extended maceration is a stylistic technique among many winemakers. This fancy term simply means letting the grapes continue to sit on the skins after primary fermentation is complete. (Primary fermentation should take about 5–10 days.) Extended maceration can help extract and fix color and tannin in the wine.

To decide if a wine would benefit from extended maceration, evaluate the must after the wine completes primary fermentation. Chew on a big wad of the fermented must, crunching up some of the seeds. Do you like the flavors you taste? Do the skins taste and feel like they have more goodies to give up? Are the tannins rich, ripe, and brown as opposed to green? As long as the skins have not turned to mush and still taste good (and as long as your fermentation isn't stinky or smelling of volatile acidity in any way), feel free to let the dry wine sit on the skins for another 4–5 days.

Because carbon dioxide is no longer actively coming off the wine during extended maceration, it's unprotected, to a certain degree, from many spoilage bacteria, namely *Acetobacter;* if you can, gas the headspace with CO_2 or argon (some wineries use dry ice pellets to provide CO_2 — about a cup of pellets on a pie tin floated on top of the cap usually does the trick). Moisten the cap and taste the tank every 2 days or so, keeping an eagle eye out for volatile acidity development (most home winemakers need to send samples to a wine lab to monitor VA). Smell the cap with a critical nose — an aroma like nail polish remover or sherry indicates aerobic or microaerophilic bacteria or excessive oxidation.

Punching Down the Cap

Red musts need to be agitated and the cap needs to be moistened to keep mold and bacteria from growing during the fermentation. Punching down the cap is critical for color and tannin extraction. It incorporates a little air into the fermentation. It also cools the fermentation down somewhat, which can be important, because you don't want the temperature to go above 90°F (30°C).

Keep your fermenter tightly covered and continue to wet the cap at least once a day to discourage bacteria. Extended maceration can last from 5–10 days, but I know some winemakers who let it go on for more than a month! I don't recommend this unless you feel that you can properly control your fermenter headspace and prevent spoilage.

■ ═══════ ■

Q Do I have to put my red wines through an extended maceration?

A To macerate or not to macerate . . . and for how long? Most winemakers decide based on the quality of their grapes, their experience with that particular vineyard, the dynamics of that year's fermentations, and the equipment they have on hand to keep an extended maceration tank safe. How long to macerate depends largely on tasting (is the wine improving as the days go by?) and keeping track of potential spoilage parameters.

Extended maceration is not for every wine or every winemaker. The wineries best equipped to attempt it have a great deal of control over the winemaking environment.

The following equipment is necessary to help exclude air and allow the winemaker to monitor potential spoilage.

◆ A tank-chilling system to keep primary fermentation temperatures in check in bigger tanks

- A good lab to monitor volatile acidity
- A good supply of carbon dioxide or argon gas for gassing headspaces
- Tanks with lids that sit on the surface of the must

Home winemakers *can* successfully carry out extended maceration, but it's tricky and requires extreme vigilance. The good news is that extended maceration is not necessary to make an excellent, stylish red wine. In fact, not every red wine will improve with extended maceration — some are decidedly better tasting, more fruit forward, and have more immediate appeal when pressed off and put to barrel warm with even 2 or 3 percent sugar left to go in the primary fermentation.

■ ══════════ ■

Q Should some red grape varieties have longer skin contact time during maceration than others?

A Skin contact time is one of the classic debates among winemakers. In my opinion, the typical Bordeaux varietals, which include Cabernet Sauvignon, Merlot, Cabernet Franc, and Petit Verdot, can definitely take a beating and keep on giving you more.

As long as the grapes were picked with at least 25° Brix, the tannins should be developed and won't taste green, but don't take my word for it. Taste those grapes yourself, squeeze the skins between your fingers, and look at the seeds to make sure they're dark brown. That is my first prerequisite for deciding to take any grape through an extended maceration process.

■ ══════════ ■

Q What are some factors that would counter-indicate trying an extended maceration?

A If you want to put your wine through an extended maceration, be aware of the following situations.

◆ A primary fermentation that is excessively sluggish or even stuck near the end

◆ A fermentation that becomes too hot (higher than 95°F, or 35°C) and releases a lot of hydrogen sulfide

◆ A high VA (more than 0.065 percent)

◆ A high population of fruit flies feeding on the cap once primary is complete

All of the above can indicate microbial instability or high levels of outside spoilage organisms, not a must that you want to try an extended maceration on. These problems also tend to jeopardize the stability and integrity of a wine's character — wines with these issues should be pressed and dealt with sooner rather than later.

It's important that the must finish out its primary fermentation as sound, good smelling, and free of spoilage organisms as possible. Sitting around in the tank, the must is going to be an easy mark for spoilage organisms, so before you decide to go ahead with an extended maceration, think about what happened during the primary fermentation.

■ ══════ ■

Q Can you explain the pressing process?

A Pressing, or separating the solid part of the fruit from the liquid, is a key step in the winemaking process. Without pressing, we'd be drinking chunky grape smoothies — hardly appetizing no matter how much of a grape nut you might be. Pressing is the point of departure for red and white wines. After crushing and destemming (or just destemming), red wines are fermented as must before pressing; white grapes are pressed shortly after crushing (or are whole-cluster pressed) and then fermented as juice.

There are a few different ways for the small-scale winemaker to separate the skins, seeds, and stems from the juice or fermented wine. For those making wine in 5-gallon (19 L) buckets, a large strainer and cheesecloth sack are useful tools. Simply put the sack in the strainer, dump in some must, and let the liquid drain into the bucket. After the majority of the juice has drained through, give the sack a gentle squeeze. Taste the juice or wine as you increase the pressure. If you taste anything bitter or overly astringent, stop pressing or continue squeezing the sack over a different collection container. You can decide later whether you want to include this harsher "press juice" or "press wine" in your final blend.

For winemakers dealing with larger lots, the same principles apply but the equipment used is different. Most home winemakers use basket presses with capacities that range from ⅛ to ½ ton per press load. These presses can be manual, pneumatic, or electric and can press on the grapes from above or inside, if the machine is fitted with an internal inflatable bladder.

The key to pressing is gentleness. Grapes contain many potentially bitter and astringent compounds that can be released into the juice if the press is too aggressive. This is especially true when pressing red must. By draining off as much wine from the red skins as possible before pressing, you maximize your gallons of "free run," which is the highest quality "press fraction" or "press cut."

You can take a press cut with white juices too; this "heavy-press" juice, extracted last in the pressing process, often has a higher pH and more phenolic character than the free-run juice that was produced earlier.

Many winemakers store various press cuts of juice or wine separately in the cellar. This allows the winemaker a variety of blending components to enhance the complexity of the final wine. (See page 78 for more on press cuts.)

■ ══════════ ■

Q What are some tips for pressing red wines?

A Pressing is usually done when the must has completed its primary fermentation; in other words, when the wine is dry. Some winemakers, however, like to press their wines off around 1° Brix and put them to barrel while they're still warm to encourage the quick completion of the malolactic fermentation, which goes more quickly to completion at temperatures above 62°F (17°C).

Watch out for bitterness in the heavy-press wine. Stop pressing once the pomace (the leftover skins) in the press feels dryish when squeezed. Taste any heavy-press wine for harsh tannins, high phenolic content, or bitterness before you decide to add it back to the free run and lighter wine pressings.

■ ════════ ■

Q What are some tips for pressing white wines?

A White wine grapes don't necessarily need to be crushed or destemmed before pressing, though crushing them helps to release their juices better, especially in the small presses many home winemakers own. If your equipment can handle whole grapes, not crushing can yield juices with a lower percentage of solids, higher retention of aromatics, and less browning. If not, simply crush the grapes first — your wine won't suffer unduly.

When pressing whites, keep a nose out for hay or dried-grass aromas. These signify that lower-quality juice is being expressed and may indicate the time to make press cuts. White grape pomace is wetter and slightly gloppier than red grape. There should still be moisture clinging to the insides of the berries and a few drops of juice should appear when a handful of the pomace is squeezed.

■ ══════════ ■

Q What is the difference between free run and press fractions?

A It is always a good idea to taste the free run (the wine that drains out of the must or crush by force of gravity alone) and compare it to the press fractions or cuts that are exuded from the skins and seeds once the material is under some pressure. The free-run wine will almost always be the highest quality portion, while the press fractions, especially as pressure increases, can be exceedingly tannic, have a high pH, or taste bitter, green, and harsh.

If you have enough volume so that it makes sense (or if you have plenty of small containers), try to ferment your white free run and press fractions as separate wines. For reds, try aging your press fractions separately as well. That way, you'll have the option of blending the different batches.

Q What can I do with leftover pomace?

A Whatever its color or characteristics, pomace has always been considered a waste product that winemakers have had to deal with. A myriad of strategies have been developed to utilize this material. Economy-minded home winemakers have historically tried to turn pomace into other grape-based products by simply soaking pressed white skins in water and fermenting the mixture to make a weaker "second wine." (See the next question on second-run wines.)

Modern, large-scale producers sometimes sell their white and red pomace to third-party plants that grind the seeds to extract grape seed oil and mine the skins as a source of cream of tartar. Some wineries sell their pomace to silage processors who turn the oil and fiber-rich grape skins, as well as other agricultural "waste," into feed supplements for cattle.

Many wineries recycle their pomace as compost in the vineyard, which is probably the best option for any home winemaker with a garden or small vineyard.

Q What are second-run wines?

A Myself, I'm content to throw my pomace on the compost pile. However, if you're curious, the easiest way to reuse skins in hobby winemaking is to simply toss the pressings, white or red, into another appropriate fermentation to get more mileage from the grapes. By crushing fresh red must over fermented red pomace, it's possible to extract even more of the colors and tannins and, if the grapes were at all raisined and not completely fermented, sugars.

The most famous (and indeed, delicious) examples of this technique would have to be the Italian "Ripasso" wines, where the sweet, raisined pomace from Amarone della Valpolicella is added to other red ferments of less noble varieties. These wines, having been "repassed" over the sweet, flavorful Amarone skins, are richer and have more depth than they would have had on their own.

However, unless you're looking for an ugly referment or an unbalanced tannin monster, add pomace with restraint. Red or white pomace shouldn't be added to white wine fermentations at all, and it's risky to add fermented pomace to dry wines, as there might be residual sugar in the skins.

Another way to reuse pomace, especially white pomace that has been pressed gently and has quite a bit of sugar left in it, is to make second-run wine. Though not practiced in the commercial winemaking realm, this technique is popular with some home winemakers. To utilize just-pressed pomace to make a second batch, reconstitute the pomace with water to create a slurry not unlike the original must. Stir well, cover, and let this mixture stand at least overnight.

The next day, measure the sugar and acid levels and adjust to normal levels (say, 20–25° Brix and 4.5–6 g/L acid). Add yeast, ferment as you would any wine, and press after a few days so as not to extract too many bitter and tannic compounds. The resultant brew may not taste like a standard wine, but mixed with mineral water and créme de cassis, it might make a great spritzer.

■ ══════ ■

How do I produce a wine that is fruit forward?

Fruit forward is a wine-tasting term that, like so many others, was first spawned by wine critics and writers. It has since trickled down, like it or not, to the realm of everyday wine jargon. Luckily, fruit-forward wine is a more straightforward wine descriptor than many and doesn't take a degree in Enospeak to understand (see page 295 for more on wine terms).

A wine that is fruit forward has fruit as a primary descriptor for the majority of those who smell and taste it. Typical fruit aromas and flavors, for red wines, include cassis (black currant), cherry, blackberry, cranberry, strawberry, and blueberry. For white wines, typical fruit aromas and flavor descriptors are lemon, grapefruit, grapefruit peel, lychee fruit, melon, passion fruit, pineapple, green apple, or pear.

Unfortunately, there's no single specific technique to make a wine that could be classified as fruit forward. A winemaker has to be paying attention every step of the way in order to capture and preserve all of the natural fruit characteristics of the source fruit. That being said, here are some general tips for keeping your wines as fruity as possible.

Use quality starting material. If you don't have fruity ingredients, you won't have fruity wine. Obtain the most aromatic and flavorful material possible.

Ensure a healthy fermentation. Overly warm fermentation temperatures can blow off ephemeral fruit aromas and aromatic precursors. Aim for maximum temperatures of 85°F (29°C) for reds and 65°F (18°C) for whites. Don't let your fermentation get too hot or complete too quickly, or you run the risk of developing off flavors and aromas.

Monitor yeast health. Be sure to feed fermentations up to an initial nitrogen content of 250–300 mg/L (measured as ammonia plus amino nitrogen). If you don't have the lab resources to do so, add a preemptive 2–4 grams (0.07–0.14 ounces) per 5 gallons (19 L) of yeast nutrient before inoculating. Hydrate your yeast exactly according to the directions in order to maximize yeast health and viability.

Don't overoak! Be conservative in your use of oak and taste often while aging on or in wood. If you add too much oak (in the form of chips, barrels, or beans), you will smell oak, not fruit! However, a hint of oak can bring out vanilla, sweetness, and spicy aromas. These flavors are often classified as fruity even though those descriptors are technically not fruits.

Don't wait too long to bottle. Often a wine is most fruit forward when it is young. For whites, you can bottle as soon as all fermentations are done and the wine has clarified sufficiently for your purposes. For a young, fresh, not-so-tannic red, you could bottle as early as eight months after harvest as long as the malolactic fermentation is complete, the wine is dry, and it has settled long enough to attain the clarity you want. If you're going for fruity, fresh, and charming, don't let a red wine get dried out and tired in the barrel. Wines need a little time in the bottle to age, so make sure yours still has some life left when you do bottle it.

All Natural

It's illegal in most countries to add "foreign" fruit flavors to wine and still classify the product as "wine." All commercial wines get their aroma and flavor profiles from the original starting material, and the fruity aromas and flavors present in a bottle of commercial wine are 100 percent natural. Home winemakers, though, are not obligated to adhere to such laws and can do as they wish in regard to both flavor and aroma.

GRAPE VARIETAL FAMILY TREES

All grapes belong to the genus *Vitis*. Some scientists divide *Vitis* into two subgenera, *Muscadinia* and *Euvitis,* because muscadine grapes (of which Scuppernong is perhaps the best known) are so physiologically different

NONHYBRID (NO CROSS-SPECIES GENETIC MIXES)				
EXAMPLES				
Order	Family	Genus	Subgenus	Species
Rhamnales	Vitaceae	Vitis	(Muscadinia)	rotundifolia
			(Euvitis)	labrusca
				aestivalis
				riparia
				rupestris
				vinifera

from other *Vitis* members. All *Vitis* species can technically be made into wine, but it is the European grape species, *V. vinifera,* that is most prized for producing a stable, balanced, and flavorful end product.

Varietal Example	
Scuppernong	(Often applied to any *Muscadinia* subgenus)
Black Beauty	(Female only, not self-fertile)
Sugargate	(Female only, not self-fertile)
Dixieland	(Self-fertile)
Magnolia	(Self-fertile)
Concord	(May also have some slight *vinifera* parentage)
Niagara	(Cross between Concord and Cassady)
Catawba	(Sometimes eaten as a table grape)
	(Native to eastern North America)
	(Native to North America, except the West)
	(Native to southern and western U.S.)
	(Native to the Middle East and Europe)
Chardonnay	
Pinot Noir	
Cabernet Sauvignon	(An early cross between Cabernet Franc and Sauvignon Blanc)

GRAPE VARIETAL FAMILY TREES (Part 2)
HYBRID VARIETAL EXAMPLES

Dioecious varietals (either male or female only) have always historically cross-pollinated to form random genetic crosses, or hybrids. Today most grape hybrids are bred purposefully by plant scientists to take advantage of a certain varietal's characteristics and marry it with those of another. The so-called French-American hybrids are crosses between native American grapes,

HYBRID-GRAPE SPECIES-CROSS FAMILY TREE				
Order	Family	Genus	Subgenus	Species
Rhamnales	Vitaceae	Vitis	Euvitis	labrusca + vinifera
				riparia + vinifera
				riparia + rupestris + vinifera
				labrusca + riparia

known for their disease tolerance and hardiness, and *V. vinifera* grapes, known for their superior flavor and winemaking capabilities.

Crosses can get extremely complicated and family trees very convoluted. Much of the research that went into producing familiar hybrids was never written down, so we don't know where they came from exactly.

Varietal Example	
Isabella	(A Cornell University hybrid)
Delaware	(In use in Ohio since the 1850s)
Winchell	(A Cornell University hybrid)
Baco Noir	(Cross between *vinifera* Folle Blanche and unknown *riparia*)
Vidal Blanc	(Makes fragrant dessert wines)
Marechal Foch	(Developed in Alsace, France)
Beta	(A table grape)

Q What are the keys to making a good Cabernet Sauvignon from grapes?

A Cabernet Sauvignon is actually one of the easiest wines to make. I find that if you purchase the grapes from a climate that is warm enough to ripen them fully (to around 26° Brix) but not so hot as to blast away the aromatic goodies, the wine pretty much makes itself if you follow these simple steps.

- Crush and destem.
- Adjust the pH to 3.65–3.75 (some people don't even go that far).
- Adjust the sugar down to about 25.5° Brix with water.
- Dump in some yeast.
- Let it get going nice and hot (no hotter than 90°F/32°C).
- Punch down at least twice every 2 hours while it's rapidly fermenting.
- Inoculate with malolactic bacteria of choice to ML completeness.
- Age at 20 mg/L free SO_2 with moderate oak levels (3 g/L oak beans or otherwise in a new oak barrel) for at least 18 months.
- Fine with egg whites or casein if the wine is a bit too tannic.
- Settle out any finings, bottle, and taste one month after bottling.

Cabernet is not a persnickety fermenter. It doesn't suffer from extraordinary nutritional deficiencies, and rarely has trouble finishing fermentation if the initial sugar isn't too high and is adjusted down to reasonable levels (commercial wineries do this all the time, by the way). And most importantly, it often turns out smelling and tasting like a champ with very little intervention on the part of the winemaker. Toss in a little oak (Cab can suck it up and still beg for more), age for a while, and hey, presto, if you started with good material, it's almost a shoo-in that you'll have a good wine.

The key is finding that good material. There's a reason why a ton of premium Cabernet Sauvignon grapes can sell for upwards of $4,000. Some of the most popular wines in the world are made from this grape and not all areas of the world can grow it well. Find out if your supplier sells to large wineries or only to small-scale winemakers. Find out what other vineyards are in the region. Is it a wine-growing area you've heard of or one that you know has a good reputation for growing Cabernet?

Some agribusiness companies focus on quantity, not quality. Vines that are forced to produce too many tons per acre make grapes that will become insipid, watery, and uninteresting wines. When grown right and picked ripe enough, Cabernet Sauvignon should make a full-bodied, opulent red table wine.

Q What are some tips for making Chardonnay from fresh grapes?

A First, see page 300 for a discussion of the different types of Chardonnay. Depending on what style you're making, the sugars should be in the range of 23–25° Brix (for a rich style destined for oak and malolactic fermentation) or 21–23° Brix (for a leaner, crisp style).

The pH should be around 3.3–3.55 at the highest, and the titratable acidity should fall between 6 and 8 g/L. The flavor should be full of fresh grapes and the acidity should "pop" in your mouth. It also should be relatively free of suspended solids.

Here are some more tips.

- If you press your own grapes and can chill the juice, cool it to between 40 and 45°F (4–7°C) and let settle overnight.
- Rack the juice off the solids in the morning and let the juice warm to 60–65°F (15–18°C) in preparation for fermentation.
- You can, if you choose, add about 30 mg/L SO_2 to the juice after pressing to discourage oxidation and spoilage organisms.
- Choose a yeast strain like Prise de Mousse that can motor through the fermentation and not leave any residual sugar. (If you want your wine to undergo MLF, you might choose another strain, like D47 Cerevisiae).

◆ Avoid yeasts like Epernay or QA23, which can contribute aromas not normally associated with Chardonnay, such as lychee, licorice, or jasmine.

The decisions you make after fermentation reinforce your choice of one style or the other. Those who have chosen the rich, full-bodied style will embark on a major treatment regimen that includes encouraging malolactic fermentation, oak aging, and stirring the lees. Those who have chosen the lean style will use this post fermentation time to immediately add 30 mg/L SO_2 and store the wine in a neutral container to preserve its fruity freshness.

■ ══════ ■

Q How does the method for making Rhône-style wines differ from other styles?

A Rhône wines, not just Rhône-style, are those that come from the Rhône River region of France. Red, white, or rosé, what Rhône wines have in common is their freshness, expression of *terroir*, unpretentiousness, and restrained use of oak. Rhône-style wines produced in other areas of the world try to capture this same spirit, using many of the same techniques along with the traditional Rhône grape varietals like Grenache and Syrah (reds) and Viognier and Roussanne (whites).

Rhône reds are usually 100 percent destemmed to prevent untoward amounts of green tannins in the fermentation.

However, leaving a few whole clusters, especially in Syrah, will encourage a more red-berry/fruity aromatic profile in addition to the normal pepper, smoke, and earth profile. Fermentations should be cooler for Rhône reds than for Cabernets or Merlots, though whites seem to do pretty well fermenting unchilled in neutral oak barrels. Aim for a maximum fermentation temperature of 85°F (29°C) for reds and no more than 70°F (21°C) for whites.

Rhône reds, especially Syrah, Grenache, and Carignane, don't seem to need as much pumping over or punching down as Cabernet Sauvignon does. Just be sure to get enough air into the fermentation during the first few days of yeast activity and especially at the height of fermentation. Like any wine, Rhônes need to be protected from oxygen once the fermentation is finished and they're no longer producing carbon dioxide.

Extended maceration isn't always the best choice for Rhônes, as they don't seem to improve like Bordeaux varietals can with time (Cabernet Sauvignon, Merlot, Cabernet Franc, or Malbec, for example). Some winemakers have success and see improvement after about a week of contact on the skins, but it's completely acceptable and traditional — and encourages malolactic fermentation to boot — if you press off warm and with about 1° Brix left, and immediately put to barrel.

Post fermentation, most Rhône reds and a few Rhône whites are encouraged to go through MLF after the primary fermentation. While the mouthfeel contributions that MLF can contribute are welcome in most Rhône wine styles, some winemakers halt their whites with 30 mg/L SO_2 in order to keep the floral, fruity, and spicy characters from being lost under gooey gobs of butter and vanilla. Maintaining the initial character of the fruit should be your first priority.

To that end, the single most important thing you can do to make your Rhône varietal wine taste more true to type is to use restraint with oak. Most Rhône Valley wines are aged in neutral barrels that have seen many years of use and don't contribute any appreciable oakiness to the wines. A robust Syrah or a meaty Mourvèdre might benefit from a touch of oak character, but realize that a little goes a long way. Be especially careful when using oak adjunct products like oak chips, beans, or sticks. The small particle size of these additives means they have a large surface area to wine ratio and can easily deliver too much oak to a wine within a matter of days. Conduct scale-model trials in lab beakers or wine glasses if at all possible.

Similarly, fining is kept to a minimum with Rhône varietals. The most that true Rhône Valley or California Rhône-style wineries will do for reds is an egg white fining, and for whites perhaps a little bentonite to pull out extra proteins before bottling. Some commercial whites are cold stabilized, but not all winemakers feel the need to do even that. If the wine has spent at least six months in neutral cooperage, it probably has had enough time to drop out tartrate crystals to an acceptable level.

A Little White Magic

Viognier, a white varietal, is sometimes added to red Rhône fermentations, especially those of Syrah. Originally this was thought to be a quaint country practice that Rhône winemakers followed just because "it's always been done that way." Many an old-timer must have knowingly nodded his head when modern wine scientists discovered that, due to a phenomenon called copigmentation, adding white skins to red fermentations can actually increase the amount and stability of color in red wines. It's not uncommon to see California Syrahs displaying a 1–2 percent Viognier component on the label — and you just thought someone had a blending accident before bottling!

Q How can I identify the mystery grapes growing in my backyard?

A The ancient science of identifying grapevines by their physical characteristics is called ampelography, and you'll be happy to know it is a relatively well-documented field. As you can imagine, in the days before genetic finger-printing and DNA analysis technology, it was pretty valuable to be able to identify a grapevine by its size, shape, color, and other visual characteristics.

Here are some books that might be helpful.

- *A Practical Ampelography: Grapevine Identification,* by Pierre Galet (Comstock Publishing Associates, 1979). This premier tome is recommended by many educational institutions and is often cited by industry professionals. It is straightforward enough for amateur use and has many color plates and drawings to aid in the identification process.

- *Rootstocks for Grape Vines,* by D. P. Pongracz (Barnes & Noble Books, 1985). This text focuses on rootstock but has a solid section on ampelography.

- *Viticulture,* by Bryan Coombe and Peter Dry (Winetitles, 1998). The "definitive text on Australian viticulture," this book is worth buying, even if it is geared toward those who grow grapes south of the equator. This two-volume set covers it all — ampelography is only a small, but detailed, part of the offering. The authors explain planting material, soil, climate, taxonomy, phenology, varieties, and other aspects of operating a vineyard.

What are *labrusca* and *riparia* grapes?

Vitis labrusca and *Vitis riparia* are distinct grape species that are native to this continent. *V. labrusca,* native to the eastern United States, is disease and cold resistant and its varietals (or cultivars) are often described as "foxy," owing to its slightly animal-like or musky smell. The most widely known of its varietals include Concord, Catawba, and Niagra grapes, often used in winemaking, especially in areas where *V. vinifera* (the European grapevine species) do not thrive.

V. riparia grapes are referred to as "riverbank" grapes by some viticulturists and range into more temperate climates across North America, from Texas all the way up to Quebec. They are used to make wine and other fruit products but are also extensively used in hybridizing, because their cold-tolerant genes, when crossed with the European *V. vinifera* species, can yield grapes that are hardy but that have more of the *vinifera* aroma and flavor.

CHAPTER 4

Wine Chemistry 101:

Sulfites, Acid, pH, and More

Q What is sulfur dioxide?

A Sulfur dioxide (SO_2) is one of the most commonly used additives in wine and serves as an antioxidant as well as an antimicrobial agent in musts, juices, and finished wines. SO_2 is mistakenly believed by many to react directly with oxygen itself, thus protecting wine. Instead, SO_2 binds and interacts with negative oxidative products in wine, essentially negating their effect or lessening their impact. It binds to anthocyanin pigments and other color compounds to delay the development of brown colors. It can also bind with aldehydes to produce classic off odors like acetaldehyde. Sulfur dioxide also interacts with the cell walls of wine microorganisms and can inhibit the growth of and even kill yeast and bacteria.

Sulfur dioxide has a long and storied history in wine-making, going back to the ancient Romans, who burned sulfur-containing candles to help keep their empty barrels sound and free from mold and infection. Today, winemakers can introduce SO_2 to their wine by metering in pure SO_2 in a concentrated aqueous solution or gaseous form. More commonly for small-scale producers, however, we can stir in a SO_2 salt such as potassium metabisulfite powder, which delivers about 57 percent SO_2 by weight.

The acidic conditions of the juice, must, or wine help to liberate the SO_2 and make it available for antimicrobial reactions, as long as it doesn't bind up with aldehydes or anything else in the wine as free SO_2. Sulfur dioxide is a critical component of clean, sound winemaking; its judicious use results in cleaner, higher-quality wines with better color stability and better ageability.

━━━━━━━━━━

Q What is free sulfur dioxide?

A Free SO_2 — the portion of sulfur dioxide in your juice, must, or wine that is not bound with aldehydes, sugars, or other substances in the wine — is the form that is available for antioxidant protection and antimicrobial activity. Over time, free SO_2 binds with the above-mentioned substrates, causing a decline in a wine's ability to retard oxidation and microbes.

━━━━━━━━━━

Q How can I measure the level of free sulfur dioxide in my wine?

A One way to measure the amount of free SO_2 in your wine is to use an at-home sulfite measuring kit. You can also send your wine samples out to a laboratory specializing in wine analysis or, if you make a lot of wine or are a true chemistry geek, you can buy an aeration/oxidation setup from an industry supply lab. This is a delicate and expensive piece of equipment, but worth it if you want to measure your free SO_2 accurately.

■ ══════ ■

Q What is the best way to add sulfites to wine?

A Sulfites added at bottling are intended to further protect the wine once you have no more control over it. A high-enough sulfite level — most winemakers say 25–35 mg/L — will retard the growth of most microorganisms in the bottle that could cause off odors, unsightly precipitates, or even secondary fermentation. Much SO_2 gets bound up in the wine during fermentation and racking and thus is unavailable as an antimicrobial agent when it comes time to bottle. So it makes sense that 35 mg/L SO_2 added at the crusher will not result in 35 mg/L free SO_2 before bottling.

However, each batch of wine is different, and winemakers must rely on experience in addition to hard numbers. Twenty-five mg/L may not get the job done, especially if the wine has a high pH, if you don't practice stringent sanitation, or if you use especially moldy or damaged fruit.

Whatever method you use, it's important to measure the amount of SO_2 you have, then do the math and meter a SO_2 solution of the appropriate concentration into your bottles before filling them with wine, or stir in a carefully calculated amount of potassium metabisulfite powder to your storage container, as long as it doesn't kick up any lees.

If you have a way to measure the pH of your wine, you can go one step better and calculate (or use a table, available in professional winemaking books or on the Internet) the molecular SO_2 of your wine, which is related to the pH. The higher the pH, the lower the molecular SO_2 with the same level of free SO_2.

A simple rule of thumb for red wines is to take the decimal digits of the pH value and multiply by 100 to get the amount of free SO_2 required for a specific pH value. For whites, do the same calculation and add 5. For example, for a white wine with a pH of 3.25, I would recommend adding $0.25 \times 100 + 5 = 30$ mg/L of free SO_2 for final bottling.

■ ▬▬▬▬▬ ■

Handy Calculators

There are several Web sites that offer an automatic molecular SO_2 calculator as well as an SO_2 addition calculator that helps you target SO_2 additions based on your starting material, whether potassium metabisulfite powder or a liquid SO_2 solution. Check out *www.fermsoft.com* or *www.winemakermag.com*.

Q I think I'm allergic to sulfites. Can I make a sulfite-free wine?

A It is impossible to make a sulfite-free wine, because wine yeasts produce sulfur dioxide during the fermentation process. Wines with no added sulfites can contain from 6 to 25 mg/L of free SO_2, depending on the yeast and the wine conditions.

Only a small percentage of the population (approximately 0.01 percent) is truly allergic to sulfites. These people lack the digestive enzyme sulfite oxidase and therefore can't metabolize sulfites. A larger percentage of the population, however, may be sulfite sensitive (the FDA estimates around 1 percent) and have a sulfite oxidase deficiency. These individuals should avoid all foods and beverages that contain sulfites, including, but not limited to, lunchmeats, processed salami, processed fruit juices, packaged seafood, and dried fruits, as well as wine. If you have no problem eating any of these foods, you don't have a sulfite allergy. To put this in perspective, a 2-ounce serving of dried apricots (the bright orange ones) contains about 112 mg of SO_2, while a typical glass of wine has only 10 mg.

Sulfur dioxide gets a bad rap because of the government warning label plastered on wine bottles that is targeted at this select group of consumers. Although many people blame sulfites for the so-called wine headache, the symptoms are usually caused by the alcohol or other components in the product. Recent research shows that biogenic amines, like histamine and tyramine, are actually the cause of numerous complaints, ranging from headaches to dizziness to shortness of breath. As these amines are naturally present in foods like wine, beer, and dry-cured salami, it's easy to understand how these symptoms can be confused with a sulfite allergy. Ironically, many consumers trying to avoid headaches turn to drinking white wine, thinking red wines have more sulfites, when actually white wines typically do.

If you want to lessen the amount of sulfites you use in your wine, keep the following things in mind. Sulfur dioxide is used for two reasons: its antimicrobial ability and its antioxidant capacity. If you want to use less of it, you must minimize the amount of microbes and oxygen that contact your wine at every stage. Cleaning and sanitizing effectively are the easiest ways to knock down populations of spoilage bugs. Make sure your incoming fruit, juice, or concentrate is clean and free of visible mold or bacterial colonies before inoculation. Use a strongly fermenting commercial yeast for your primary fermentation in order to outcompete spoilage organisms in the first few weeks of a wine's life. Make sure your wines are fermented to dryness so there is no residual sugar left as a carbon source for spoilage bacteria. Gas your empty containers with carbon dioxide during transfers and rackings to minimize contact with oxygen.

The natural wine components that inhibit organisms are alcohol and acid. High pH (low acid) wines are more prone to microbial attack, so keeping the pH lower than 3.5 will help retard infection. The lower the pH, the more unhappy most sorts of spoilage bacteria will be. Similarly, the higher the alcohol, the more unhappy the organisms. Alcohol levels of greater than 14 percent can help keep bugs at bay, but we may not want to go overboard on the booze because many wine styles, like refreshing whites, don't lend themselves to superhigh alcohol concentrations.

At the end of the day, sulfites in winemaking is not a health issue for most people. Judicious sulfite use can significantly increase the quality of your wine. International regulatory boards usually set legal sulfite levels at around 350 mg/L total, and most commercial wines are bottled with totals between 50 and 100 mg/L. A little bit of SO_2, used wisely, goes a long way and won't hurt 9,999 out of 10,000 of us.

■ ═══════ ■

Q Do I need to add sulfur dioxide every time I rack my wine?

A Most recipes recommend adding liquid or powdered sulfur dioxide to your wine every time you rack because by the time most of us get around to racking a wine (say, every six months), it's time to add some anyway. Do you *always* have to do it? That answer is up to you and your particular wine.

If the wine is throwing a ton of sediment and you find yourself having to rack it every two weeks, it isn't necessary to add SO_2 every time. If your wine is startlingly clear and you haven't racked in two months, your free SO_2 level might be getting dangerously low and you might want to bump it into the 25 mg/L range again.

Never add SO_2 without testing the wine first. There does seem to be a point in a wine's life when the free SO_2 levels off and you don't need to add it as frequently. Once a wine is off its lees and approaching bottling, you should be cautious about adding too much SO_2. Free SO_2 should always be adjusted before bottling. For white wines, typical levels are 30–35 mg/L, and for reds 25–30 mg/L.

Some winemakers use molecular SO_2 (a measure that relates pH and free SO_2) because the antimicrobial properties of SO_2 are best described by looking at the molecular level. The target for complete microbial protection is 0.80 mg/L molecular SO_2, but many winemakers feel that this goal requires that too much SO_2 be added to the wine, especially for reds that naturally have higher pH levels than whites.

Whether they go by molecular or just free SO_2, most winemakers try to err on the low side, because too much SO_2 will be detectable to the nose and it also can bleach color. You can safely lean to the low side if the wine is clean, bright, and dry, especially if it has been sterile filtered before bottling. Don't let the total amounts of SO_2 you're adding get out of control. Adding too much will eventually spoil your wine. In the end, it's best to let a free SO_2 analysis, a molecular SO_2 calculation, and your nose guide you rather than a racking schedule. (See resources, page 368 for Web-based molecular calculators.)

■ ══════ ■

Q Is there a way to make red wine sulfite Titret readings more accurate?

A These test kits, which use an iodine and indicator reaction titrated to a colored end point, are hard to use for red wines because the end point is difficult to see. In fact, the CHEMetrics Titrets Web site says that these kits aren't recommended for red wines for that reason.

Don't despair — or send your samples out to a professional wine laboratory — quite yet. There are two tricks to getting better results, if you don't mind a little wiggle room here and there. First, when you perform the test, try doing it in front of a very bright light (or a yellow light) so that you will be sure to recognize the end point. And second, dilute your wine sample 50:50 with distilled water so there isn't as much colored material in the sample to confuse the color change of the end point. This will only work if you can accurately measure an equal proportion of water and wine. Volumetric flasks purchased from laboratory supply houses are the most accurate, but barring that, graduated cylinders work relatively well, as long as the cylinder's diameter is less than 2 inches (5 cms). Otherwise, it'll be hard to "spot" across the cylinder accurately enough to get equal volumes. Measuring cups just don't cut it.

If you try both suggestions above with fresh CHEMetrics Titrets, you should be able to approach some semblance of accuracy.

■ ══════ ■

Q How do I calculate sulfite additions?

A Most home winemakers use potassium metabisulfite, available in either powdered or solid (Campden tablets) form, to add sulfur dioxide. There's also a sodium form of sulfite (which isn't recommended for use in wine) as well as a self-dissolving effervescent potassium metabisulfite tablet. I recommend using the powdered form.

Many people see Campden tablets as a mysterious "magic pill." For those of you who just want the facts, potassium metabisulfite is 57 percent free SO_2. Most Campden tablets weigh 0.44 g. (Check your package to be sure, because brands vary in weight.) To figure out how many grams of potassium metabisulfite powder to add to your volume to give you the desired concentration (in mg/L) of free SO_2, use the following equation, which turns gallons to liters and adds potassium metabisulfite by weight (taking into account that potassium metabisulfite is only 57 percent sulfur dioxide).

$$\frac{(\text{gallons of wine}) \times (3.785) \times (\text{free SO}_2 \text{ mg/L})}{(1{,}000) \times (0.57)}$$

This equation calculates the total sulfite you want to add, not the free SO_2 you hope to find in your wine after the addition is made. It's impossible to accurately state what the free SO_2 will be in any wine after making an addition. Since SO_2 can bind with any number of wine components, one never knows exactly what percentage of the SO_2 will remain unbound as free SO_2.

Believe it or not, we winemakers just rely on experience with our wines to be our guide as to how much SO_2 will go "free" after any given sulfite addition. Wine scientists have tried in vain to come up with an empirical law of combination that predicts final free SO_2.

One "sort of" rule or guideline indicates that, for dry, aging wines that already have some SO_2 in them, about two-thirds of a supplemental addition will go free, while the other third combines and gets bound up. Again, this depends on the "bindable" substrates in a wine and will differ for different wines as well as for the same wine at different times. Turbid, sweet, aldehydic, very tannic, and very young wines, for example, really bind up SO_2. Your best guideline is to add sulfites and check residual free SO_2 levels a few days later.

Say I've got 5 gallons of wine to bottle. My free SO_2 is sitting at 10 mg/L. I want to get it into the 30 mg/L range. Since my wine is dry, the SO_2 won't get bound up as quickly, so I'll take a stab at adding 25 mg/L.

$$\frac{(5 \text{ gallons}) \times (3.785) \times (25 \text{ mg/L})}{(1,000) \times (0.57)} = 0.83 \text{ grams}$$

You'll have to add 0.83 grams (830 mg) of potassium metabisulfite powder to your 5 gallons of wine to get a free SO_2 level of about 30 mg/L. If you only have Campden tablets or don't have a scale, remember: standard Campden tablets are 0.44 gram of potassium metabisulfite (though they do come in other sizes and some contain sodium metabisulfite instead — read packages carefully!).

The guesswork lies in estimating how much SO_2 will get bound up and not be free SO_2. Sugar, lees, and aldehydes will always aid in the binding process and you'll lose your free SO_2 very quickly. Keep this and the total amount of SO_2 you've added over a wine's lifetime in mind.

■ ══════════ ■

What can I do with an oversulfited wine?

I'm sorry to say that you can't easily remove sulfur dioxide from wine. There is no process, no fining agent, and no additive that removes large amounts of sulfites from wine, except time and the nature of the wine itself. Free SO_2 will decrease in concentration and become less detectable over time. This is because SO_2 eventually binds up with aldehydes, and sugars (among other things) and becomes part of the total SO_2. This is much less volatile and thus much less sniffable. If the free SO_2 levels of your wine are currently under 70 mg/L, there is hope. Give your wine some time. Pop a bottle in a month or two and see what you think. Your wine might grow to be drinkable.

If you have extra wine available, you can also blend wines to lower the SO_2 content. Just blend your high-sulfite batch with a low- or no-sulfite batch and you'll have a total batch with lower SO_2 content. You'll only want to do this, however, if it makes sense for your wine style and winemaking program. Be aware that if you blend heavily sulfited wine with wine that is still going through a fermentation, you will likely inhibit or even kill off the active microbes.

***

How can I adjust acidity?

Adjusting the juice or must of your wine is critical. Luckily, it's also easy. Acid content is measured with a simple titration. Kits are available for single-use titrations, but if you're going to be making a lot of wine, it might be worth it to buy the burets, flasks, and chemicals needed to do multiple titrations. The ideal titratable acidity for wines

Titratable Acidity

Hydrogen ions (protons or H+s) make wine taste sour, and titratable acidity (TA) measures the concentration of all hydrogen ions in juices and wines. TA has a wide range, depending on grape ripeness and desired wine style, but usually falls between 5.0 and 9.0 g/L and is expressed in North America as "tartaric acid equivalents," whereas in Europe it's often expressed as "sulfuric acid equivalents." Tartaric acid was probably chosen as the standard because it is the most prevalent nonmetabolizable (yeast and microbes don't eat it) grape acid.

is hard to pinpoint, and I would argue that pH is actually more important both for how the wine tastes as well as for microbial stability. Nonetheless, depending on wine style of course, there are some titratable acidity targets. A typical range for reds is 5.0–6.5 g/L and 5.5–8.0 g/L for dry whites.

Here's an example of how to adjust your must's acidity. If your must measures 5.5 g/L and you want to bring it up to 6.5 g/L, then you need to add 1 g/L of tartaric acid. Since 1 liter equals 0.2642 gallons (1 gallon equals 3.8 liters), 1 g/L is equivalent to adding 3.8 grams of tartaric acid to your 1-gallon batch.

Always dissolve tartaric acid in a small amount of water first and then distribute it well into your must or juice. It's a good idea to adjust the must or juice before you pitch (add) your yeast so you don't shock the nascent yeast cells by a drastic change in their environment.

■ ══════ ■

Q Why is it important to measure titratable acidity levels?

A Winemakers are concerned with measuring acid levels for a number of reasons. The acidity of a fruit juice or wine is determined by the ripeness of the fruit, which in turn determines a good part of the product's final taste as well as its microbial stability.

The titratable acidity (sometimes called "total acidity", or TA) largely affects how the wine tastes on the tongue and indirectly affects the color stability and the possible ageability of a product. You can make better and more predictable wine if you pay close attention to TA and to pH, which, though measuring different things (pH only measures the free protons floating around in solution), are both ways that winemakers can relate to the acidity of their wine.

The standard industry procedure for measuring TA is cheap, quick, and easy, which makes it a popular analysis among home winemakers. The process involves adding a color-changing indicator (phenolphthalein, which changes color at pH 8.2) to a mixture of water and wine. Drop by drop, a base (sodium hydroxide, NaOH) of known concentration is added to this acidic solution until all the acid in the sample has been neutralized, as indicated by the color of the solution changing from clear to light pink.

By comparing the volume of base used in the reaction, the g/100 mL (multiply by 10 to get g/L) of tartaric acid equivalent present in the sample can be determined according to the following equation.

$$\frac{(\text{mL NaOH}) \times (\text{Normality of NaOH}) \times (0.075) \times (100)}{\text{mL in the wine sample}}$$

$$= \text{g}/100 \text{ mL TA}$$

For example, if it took you 6.10 mL of 0.1 N NaOH to reach the faint pink end point and you used a 10 mL wine sample, the equation would look like this:

$$\frac{(6.10) \times (0.1) \times (0.075) \times (100)}{10} = 0.46 \text{ g}/100 \text{ mL TA}$$

Q When is the right time to add acid to a wine?

A I suggest adjusting your acid before you pitch the yeast for primary fermentation. Primary fermentation typically lowers the TA very slightly (be sure to degas your sample before you run the analysis), so plan for any loss of acid due to this as well as malolactic fermentation (if desired) when you add your tartaric acid.

Some winemakers will adjust acid at many different stages in a wine's life, tweaking it almost up until bottling. I don't recommend this practice, because changing a wine's acidity is overly interventionist and can be dangerous for a wine's long-term stability. A small change in pH or TA can set off whole chains of chemical reactions whose effects

TA AND pH RANGES

While you should never make wine by numbers alone, there are some general ranges to aim for in the initial juice or must, always keeping your own wine style in mind.

Measurement	Range for Reds	Range for Whites
TA	5.0–6.5 g/L (0.50–0.65%)	5.5–8.0 g/L (0.55–0.80%)
pH	3.40–3.65	3.10–3.45

may not be felt until after the wine has been bottled, resulting perhaps in hazes, precipitations, or potassium bitartrate crystals. Big changes like adjusting a wine's acidity are best done early in a wine's life.

■ ══════════ ■

Q Can I use grape juice concentrate in place of acid blend?

A If you're looking for a way to boost acid without adding extra sugar to a grape wine, stick to acid blend, or better yet, use tartaric acid alone. Using grape juice concentrate as an additional fermenting agent in nongrape fruit wines, on the other hand, is a good way to add extra acid, sugar, flavor, and yeast nutrients.

Acid blends can be any combination of citric, tartaric, and malic acids. They add tartness to wine but also add acids of types and proportions that may not be naturally present in the grapes. Using citric acid in winemaking is a little risky, as some spoilage organisms can metabolize it as an energy source. I usually stick to tartaric acid alone and only add a bit of malic when I'm making a non-malolactic fermentation white or rosé wine.

Grape juice concentrates pack a lot more than tartness, including water, carbohydrates, amino acids, nitrogen, tartaric acid, malic acid — lots of stuff that grapes naturally possess. If you want to add sugar and grapey flavors to your wine, use the juice concentrate. To boost tartness without adding anything else, go with tartaric acid or, if you prefer, a packaged acid blend. Just read the label carefully so you know exactly what you're adding to your juice or must.

■ ══════ ■

Q Is there a more accurate way to test red wines for acid levels than using a phenolphthalein indicator?

A It can be hard to titrate to the correct "faint pink end point" when testing red wine, even if it's diluted. The problem, of course, is that diluted red wine is "faintly pink" to start with, so it can be hard to tell when the correct end point has been reached! Some reds turn gray-green when diluted, which makes it easier. But in general, testing red wines for TA using the same phenolphthalein-indicator procedure that's used with white wine can be tricky, and it's possible to overrun the end point and arrive at erroneous results.

What's an accuracy-seeking winemaker to do? Use a pH meter, of course! The TA standard end point is pH 8.2, which is precisely the pH at which your little white or red wine titration, stained with phenolphthalein, will start to turn the rosy pink color that indicates you've added enough solution. What this means is that you could eschew the phenolphthalein-indicator procedure altogether and just do all of your TA titrating with NaOH, adding base until your pH meter reads pH 8.2.

You measure whites and reds with the pH meter exactly the same way; they both come to the 8.2 end point and are "done." Many wineries do just that, though using the phenolphthalein indicator for whites is pretty accurate. Models perfect for the home winemaker cost from $150 to $350. I realize that this may sound like a lot of money, but if you make wine or beer every year and plan on continuing to do so, it might be a good investment.

What Is pH?

The pH level indicates the ionic concentration of H+ ions, as well as the extent to which they dissociate, and it is directly involved in many physical-chemical reactions and microbiological stability. It is measured on a logarithmic scale, with 0 being the most acidic and 14 being the most basic.

Neutral is pH 7. (The pH of water is commonly accepted as 7.) Anything between 7 and 0 is increasingly acidic, while anything between 7 and 14 is increasingly basic. pH = $-\log[H+]$, or pH is a measure of the negative log of the concentration of dissociated H+ ions in solution.

Q What is the role of pH in my wine?

A The answer to this question fills entire chapters of technical winemaking books, as pH is much more than just another way of expressing acidity. Suffice it to say that after the sugar concentration, pH is the single most important analytical parameter in winemaking. The pH level affects flavor, color, aroma, physical stability, microbial stability, ageability, and a myriad of other quality indicators. It plays a role in the majority of chemical reactions and equilibria in juice, which means that if you know your pH, you know a lot about where your wine is and where it might go.

■ ══════════ ■

Q Can I fix a wine that has too much acid?

A Achieving the right acid balance is an art in winemaking. The total acidity in a must or juice can be increased easily by adding tartaric acid powder, but it is much more difficult to remove. Excess acid can make a wine taste harsh or too sour and can exacerbate the sensation of bitterness and alcohol.

If your goal is to make a wine with perceptible sweetness, a high acid content (or a low pH) can make the wine's sugar level seem lower than it actually is. A lot of acid can keep a wine from going through malolactic fermentation, as the malolactic bacteria prefer an environment with a pH around 3.5. Extremely low pHs, under 3.2, can inhibit most malolactic bacteria strains.

Many winemakers deacidify their wine by making sure it goes through malolactic fermentation (MLF), which naturally is a deacidifying reaction. Malolactic bacteria metabolize malic acid (two protons, H++) into lactic acid (one proton, H+), losing a net proton in the process. I've seen reds go from a pH of 3.45 to 3.60 after MLF is complete. The pH change is hard to predict, however — where the pH goes after MLF depends largely on the initial malic acid content.

If malic acid makes up a large part of the juice's or must's total acidity, when the malolactic bacteria eat it and spit out lactic acid, you could see a really big rise in pH. Ironically, even though MLF is a convenient and natural deacidification process, most malolactic bacteria won't be happy unless the pH is above 3.2 and will have a hard time surviving in pH levels much lower than that.

There are other ways to deacidify. In commercial settings, blending a high-acid wine with a lower-acid one is usually the best way to go. Blending may not be as feasible for the home winemaker, whose entire cellar might consist of 5 carboys and 3 1-gallon jugs.

Deacidifying chemically is seen as a last resort, even among professional winemakers. If not done carefully, it can wreck a wine by causing the pH to rise too much, irreparably compromising the flavors and mouthfeel.

Calcium carbonate ($CaCO_3$) is recommended in some older winemaking texts, but I feel you shouldn't use it because while it can lower acidity, it also forms solid salts that can precipitate out of a wine over its life span, even after filtering. I achieve better results with potassium bicarbonate; using the powder at a rate of 1 g/L will result in an estimated TA reduction of 1 g/L. Dissolve the powder directly into your wine and let settle for six to eight weeks as potassium and tartrate solids will precipitate out (solids settle best once fermentation is complete). Once you've achieved good settling, you can rack the deacidified wine off the solids.

In the case of acidic juice, it's always best to deacidify before pitching your yeast or after primary and any malolactic fermentation is complete. Adjusting acid during a fermentation makes it harder for the microorganisms to do their job; yeast will actually slow down and can stick a fermentation if the acidity of their environment is drastically changed mid-ferment.

However, adjusting acid before they do their job can help them out as they can struggle in high-acid situations (below 3.0 pH). Similarly, ML bacteria will complete their jobs faster and more completely if the pH of a wine is higher than 3.30.

Q How do I adjust sugar levels?

A Adjusting sugar levels in must and juice is one of those winemaking parameters heavily regulated in most countries. In the United States, commercial winemakers may legally add only grape concentrate to bump up their initial sugar levels. Home winemakers can use anything they feel adds sugar and marries well with their winemaking style and goals.

Before you adjust your sugar, you need to have an accurate picture of your starting point. This can be measured with a hydrometer or a refractometer. Like any major change in juice or must composition, sugar should be adjusted before

---

Chaptalizing

Adding sugar, or *chaptalizing,* is generally legal in France, where low summer and fall temperatures can sometimes put a whole harvest's ripeness in jeopardy. Each region specifies its own laws of use. For example, in Burgundy one can only add up to 2 percent alcohol with added sugar. The right to *chaptalize* is only granted if a wine won't reach a certain minimum alcohol on its own, usually 10 percent.

fermentation. As to what to use to increase the amount of sugar, I've seen small-scale winemakers use fruit juice concentrate, table sugar, powdered fructose, honey, or even dried fruit. It depends on what kinds of flavors, if any, you want to add to your final wine. To lower the sugar level, simply dilute your must or juice with water, mixing well and measuring as you go.

* ════════════ *

Q How can I increase the sugar content and body of my juice without using refined sugar?

A If you've seen a lot of home winemaking recipes that recommend pounds upon pounds of refined sugar, it's because refined sugar is the cheapest agent available to home winemakers who want to raise specific gravity. If you happen to be a beekeeper or know one with whom you could trade a few bottles of wine for a few pounds of honey, then your chances of getting cheap honey (which is a great sugar source for wines and meads) are pretty good. Or you could just buy a few pounds of honey at a local health food market.

Other sources of fermentable sugars that won't necessarily cost you an arm and a leg are beer malt syrups, grape concentrates, fruit juice concentrates, and dried fruits. However, on a pound-for-pound average, all of these sugar sources are likely to cost more than a 5-pound bag of sugar from your local supermarket. If you have a good source of any of the above, however, go ahead and replace some or all of the refined sugar in your recipes. Just be aware that you'll be imparting the flavor of that sugar source to your wine.

Since honey, concentrates, and dried fruits all vary in the amount of sugar they contain, it's difficult to say how much you'll need to use. Just add more or dilute until you get the desired Brix you're looking for. For a table wine, you'll want to start off with a Brix between 21 and 26 degrees.

Q What is the relationship between TA and pH?

A Wow — that's a question that my college chemistry professor took almost a whole quarter to explain adequately, or adequately for her purposes, I suppose. For our purposes (we just want to make some good wine, right?) I'll keep it as simple as I can. Titratable acidity (sometimes called total acidity), is the measure of total hydrogen ions that are and will ever be present in a wine, while pH is the measure of dissociated hydrogen ions present at any given moment.

Their relationship is not cut-and-dried, because any given adjustment in the pH will not necessarily be correlated exactly to any given change in TA, and vice versa. They aren't even measured in the same units. TA is usually expressed in grams per liter (g/L) or grams per 100 mL (g/100 mL), a weight-over-volume concentration, whereas pH is a negative log of the concentration of hydrogen ions in solution (pH = −log[H+]).

Almost any commercial winemaker will say that, after sugar concentration, pH is probably the most important winemaking parameter. Even though TA is certainly an important number, and a key factor in the way a wine will taste, adequate pH numbers are even more critical to the microbial and chemical stability of wines. However, analyzing and predicting TA are a little easier to do, so many of us also use TA as a key parameter.

Incidentally, the pH cannot be manually adjusted without affecting the TA. Since they both rely on the hydrogen ion concentration in the wine (the stuff that makes acids acidic), they are completely interconnected. Wine is what's called a "buffered" solution in chemistry, meaning that sometimes the pH does not change even when incremental amounts of acids are dissolved into it. This is part of the reason why it's impossible to calculate what a certain tartaric acid addition will do to the pH of a wine.

We know pretty well that a 1 g/L tartaric acid addition will raise the TA 1 g/L, but because of the crazy hodgepodge of weak and strong acids and bases hanging out in wine (which predicts its buffering capacity) interacting with that added 1 g/L, we can't accurately predict where the pH will end up. Bench trials combined with experience are the best tools to work within predicting pH shifts.

To raise the TA and lower the pH (make the must or juice more acidic), most winemakers add acid in the form of purchased tartaric acid. Tartaric acid is one of the naturally present grape acids and is not consumed by yeast or by any other microorganism in the winemaking process. What you add is what stays in the wine, unless it precipitates later with age or with cold stabilization.

Q What could cause a red wine's acid level to rise during fermentation and aging?

A Though most titratable acid levels go down slightly (due to potassium bitartrate precipitation probably), in my experience, it's not uncommon for a red must's TA to climb during fermentation. My viticulturist friends tell me that in some varieties, and especially in specific years, the grape tissues will selectively sequester and then release some compounds before others during fermentation.

I have had Cabernet Sauvignons from California's Paso Robles area that came in with a TA of 4.0 g/L, but as the fermentation progressed, the TA climbed up to 6.5 g/L, a more typical number. The acid was there all along, it just took a little while before it was released in the juice.

Q What factors might skew the results of a titratable acidity assay?

A There are many sources of error in a typical titratable acidity assay, which is usually done by titrating a diluted wine sample with a base of sodium hydroxide (NaOH). We all learned in high school chemistry that water has a pH of 7.0, which is totally neutral, neither acidic nor basic, on the pH scale. When measuring the pH of water in the real world, however, or even of distilled water, the pH can range from 5.0 to 8.0, a far cry from "totally neutral."

The problem is that pure water is extremely rare in the natural world. The pH of water is affected by many things, from dissolved minerals and organic matter (like waterborne microorganisms) to dissolved gasses. Gasses, in fact, are the main source of acidity in distilled water, which can have a pH of 5.0–6.0. Distilled water reacts with carbon dioxide in the ambient environment at typical atmospheric pressure levels and will trap CO_2 molecules, dissolving them and essentially turning "pure" distilled water into a weak solution of carbonic acid.

Before you panic about adding CO_2 with your dilution water, let me reassure you by mentioning that boiling your distilled water helps drive out most of the dissolved CO_2. To be even surer that you're starting your titration free of interference from acidified water, it's important to add a few drops of dilute NaOH to the 100 mL or so of water that you use to run each TA analysis. If you're using a phenolphthalein indicator, add your indicator to the water and add the dilute NaOH until you barely see the water turn pink.

This is now your end point — when you add the wine sample, be sure to titrate back to that same pink color. If you use a pH meter to indicate when your titration has reached the end point of 8.2 pH again (which I recommend, especially since red wine is almost impossible to test using the phenolphthalein method), add dilute NaOH to get your water to read 8.2 pH. It's all right to overrun this end point in the water, as the solution at this juncture is unbuffered, and a reading of 8.2–8.7 won't significantly affect the final answer.

However, when you add the wine sample to the 100 mL of your adjusted water and then titrate it, it is critical to try to get back to 8.2 (or your colored end point) as accurately as possible. This is important because the solution is now buffered by acid and small errors in the amount of titrate added will greatly affect the final reading.

Make sure that your distilled water and your wine sample are thoroughly degassed, as dissolved CO_2 in the wine sample will give an erroneously high TA. Wine samples are usually degassed using a vacuum aspirator — if you don't have access to a lab with this setup, the best way to degas at home is to let the sample come to room temperature (CO_2 is more soluble at cooler temperatures) and shake vigorously, "burping" your sample bottle repeatedly. If your wine is fermenting, you must freeze the sample to knock down any yeast activity before you degas.

Another thing that may contribute to a bad TA result is an old chemical reagent. It's normal for the NaOH solution with which we titrate to weaken over time, so it's important to standardize the reagents yourself or buy fresh, prestandardized ones from a reputable laboratory supply company. If you're using an NaOH solution that is weaker than you think it is, this could explain a high TA reading — it takes more of a weak NaOH solution to titrate the same wine to achieve the target end point.

Q What can cause faulty pH readings in wine?

A Most errors come from a few common sources. One culprit is failure to calibrate the pH meter often enough. You really ought to calibrate your equipment daily, or at least before each time you use it.

Another source of error is calibrating the pH meter with old, off-concentration buffers. The pH 4.0 and 7.0 buffer solutions for calibration will chemically change and become unusable in two to three months, so always make sure you have fresh buffer. Storing the buffers covered away from light and heat, as well as never pouring any buffer you've used to calibrate the pH meter back into the mother storage bottle, will go a long way toward keeping the buffers sound and contaminant free.

Another big source of pH meter fallacy is not following the specified use and storage instructions for your particular instrument. A pH probe is one of the most delicate pieces of equipment in the lab and needs exacting care and attention in order to function at its best.

■ ══════════ ■

Q How can I boost the final alcohol content of my wine?

A Non-commercial winemakers can either add sugar at the beginning of the fermentation and hope that their yeasts are strong enough to ferment to dryness, or they can ferment to dryness and then add alcohol (or fortify) at the end of fermentation. The method you choose depends upon your aim and what you're trying to correct by bumping up the alcohol.

Most table wines are in the 12 to 14 percent alcohol range. No sugar was added to these wines nor were they fortified at the end of the fermentation. The final alcohol levels correspond directly to the initial sugar levels in the grapes. As alcohol is very important for the final flavor and mouthfeel balance of a wine, grapes for table wines are usually picked between 22 and 26° Brix.

If your starting material isn't sweet enough and would produce a wine that needs a few more alcohol percentage points, your grapes aren't ripe enough. It's better to correct under-ripeness in the vineyard rather than in the fermentation vat, so my first bit of advice would be to buy riper fruit. If that is not possible, then you certainly could oomph up the sugar before fermentation is complete. I strongly recommend *chaptalizing* (adding sugar) with grape concentrate. This will give the wine more character than if you used table sugar, which has a neutral aroma and flavor.

The big caution for adding sugar before fermentation is that if you want a dry wine, make sure that (1) you're not adding too much sugar and (2) your yeasts can handle the amount of sugar you give them. You run the risk of a stuck fermentation if the initial sugar level is much more than 26.5° Brix. Similarly, if you use any yeast strain other than Premier Cuvée or some other "super fermenter," your yeast might poop out with a few degrees Brix remaining in your wine, leaving you with a sweet, stuck fermentation.

Because of these dangers, I actually recommend "setting" your initial Brix at the desired level before you pitch your yeast. Yeast can be persnickety about major sugar level changes once they get their cell walls and mechanisms accustomed to a certain concentration.

If your aim is to make a dessert wine or simply to have a table wine with a little kick, then by all means dose in a measure of distilled alcohol at the end. Fortification is an ancient and time-honored art, and it wasn't always done just to get a little tipsier a little faster — often "distilled spirits of wine" (brandy) was added as a preservative. Many traditional liqueurs and dessert wines got their start in history that way. I suggest fortifying with the most neutral kind of grape brandy that you can find. You don't want to waste the fine aromas of expensive Cognac on a sweet Zinfandel dessert wine. (Well, maybe you do.)

And don't forget, if you have a higher alcohol wine kicking around in your collection, you can always blend to achieve your desired results. (See pages 216–220 for more on blending.)

■ ══════════ ■

Q When should I add enzymes?

A In the world of chemistry, enzymes are classified as proteins that catalyze chemical reactions. In the winemaking world, there are many different commercial enzyme preparations, usually in liquid form, that one can use in various stages of the winemaking process. Some are added to destemmed red grapes to help them release color during fermentation, some help white juice to settle out more quickly, and some assist in getting a higher yield from grapes being pressed.

As you might guess, enzymes are more often than not the realm of commercial winemakers, who year after year have to achieve stylistic consistency or hit high gallon/ton yield projections. They are always entirely optional for the small-scale or home winemaker. However, if included in a kit they should be utilized, as kit wines turn out the best when you follow the directions to the letter.

If you do want to try using enzymes in your fresh-grape winemaking and aren't sure when to add them, here's a simple rule of thumb. Enzymes are proteins, and proteins don't mix well with bentonite or with sulfur dioxide. Always wait at least 12 hours between using sulfur dioxide and an enzyme product.

Enzymatic activity can also be inhibited by high alcohol and low or high temperatures, so try to avoid these situations. If you can't, it's generally all right to use a little more enzyme than you normally would. Commercial winemakers, of course, must pay attention to legal limits for certain additives and home winemakers, just to be "street legal," might want to be instructed by these rules as well.

Q **Is there a point of diminishing returns when adding acid and sugar to must or juice to balance the final product?**

A This is an excellent point, one that many of us who make our own wine and advise others probably don't think about often enough. Sometimes we concentrate so much on which additives to add and when, that we aren't as engaged when it comes to making the decision to *not* add stuff to our wine. As you might guess by my direction here, I do think there is a point of diminishing returns. No matter how much we tweak those acid and sugar levels, no matter what "magic" malolactic culture or special yeast strain we use — we still must accept our initial starting material for what it is. This is as true for home winemakers as it is for the most celebrated Grand Cru wineries in the world.

Adding acid and sugar (or anything else) just to hit target numbers is a poor way to make wine. A winemaker needs to take many things into consideration when making addition decisions, and it's critical to "listen" to your grapes. Don't think about what you're going to try and make them do, but how you're going to let them do what they want to do.

Focusing on what a must or juice is will help clue you in to what it is not. In other words, a ton of 30° Brix Zinfandel with raisined clusters practically falling off the rachis really doesn't want to be a white Zinfandel, it wants to be a Zinfandel port. Too bad if you had visions of a limpid strawberry-hued tangy summer sipper, we all must change course midstream sometimes. However, it is the right decision if your Zin wants to grow up to be a wintertime hearth-warmer instead.

For my part, I find that intervening as little as possible in order to capture the qualities inherent in the fruit is crucial. It's easy to overdo it in an attempt to hit a target that is inappropriate for the fruit's capability. I promise that if you get the best fruit you possibly can and you handle it in a way that is true to its character, rather than just trying to hit a number, you'll craft a better wine every time.

Specific Gravity or Baumé and Balling and Brix, Oh My!

Specific gravity and degrees Brix, Baumé, Balling, and Oechsle are all scales developed to measure the density of liquids. (Note: Balling and Brix are different names for the same scale.) This variety of scales leaves us with a plethora of different equipment, techniques, and recipes, all of which operate on different measurements! It's maddening.

No matter what hydrometric tools you may have in your home arsenal, and no matter what scale an interesting recipe may read in, here are the equations you will need to convert one density reading to another.

BAUMÉ AND BRIX (BALLING)

1.8 Baumé = 1° Brix (1° Balling)

Example: I have a solution that measures 20° Brix on my hydrometer. I multiply it by 1.8 to get the reading in Baumé, which is 36. To go the other way, divide by 1.8.

SPECIFIC GRAVITY AND BRIX

SG = 1.0 + [(x° Brix) x (0.00414)]

Example: I have a solution that measures 20° Brix, so x = 20. Multiply 20 by 0.00414 and add to 1.0. You get 1.0828 specific gravity. To go from specific gravity to Brix, use this equation: x° Brix = [(SG – 1)/0.00414].

Since Brix and specific gravity carry different significant digits, these equations will give you conversions that are "good enough for government work" but that aren't 100 percent accurate.

For total accuracy, refer to the conversion chart on page 136.

OECHSLE

The Oechsle readings are simply the digits after the 1 on a specific gravity reading. For example, 1.82 specific gravity equals 82 Oechsle.

HYDROMETER READINGS/ BRIX EQUIVALENTS

Specific Gravity	Brix	Percentage Potential Alcohol
1.040	10.4	5.4
1.045	11.6	6.1
1.050	12.8	6.8
1.055	14.0	7.6
1.060	15.2	8.3
1.065	16.4	9.0
1.070	17.6	9.7
1.075	18.7	10.4
1.080	19.8	11.1
1.085	20.9	11.9
1.090	22.0	12.7
1.095	23.1	13.4
1.100	24.2	14.2
1.105	25.3	15.0
1.110	26.4	*
1.115	27.5	
1.120	28.5	
1.125	29.6	
1.130	30.6	

*At about this point, the alcohol concentration becomes sufficient to kill remaining yeast, and any residual sugar will remain unfermented.

CHAPTER 5

Choosing and Using the Right Yeast

Q What should I look for when choosing a yeast strain?

A Many winemakers make a big deal about selecting different yeast strains for different varietals, and, of course, the yeast catalogs make a huge deal about the supposed organoleptic and sensory differences each yeast strain imparts to wines. Do different strains really affect wine more than, say, the type of grape used or the temperature of the fermentation? The answer is not so clear; though some winemakers do have favorite "magic" yeasts they love, in my own experience the answer is "No."

The single most important factor I use when choosing a yeast strain is making sure it can ferment easily through the level of sugar in my juice or must. High-sugar musts can be difficult for some yeast strains to ferment to dryness, and like all winemakers, I hate a stuck fermentation. To avoid this speed bump, I always check the manufacturer's specifications before selecting yeast for a particular job. If you want to avoid the hassle, choose a yeast strain that best fits most of your winemaking needs and become familiar with it on an array of wines.

Q What is the shelf life of dry yeast?

A Yeast cells, even those that have been freeze-dried, do have an expiration date. Using yeast that is more than six to eight months old greatly enhances your chances for problems such as stuck fermentations and off odors down the road. I recommend that winemakers purchase yeast from a reputable source (a home-winemaking store with high turnover or a commercial-winemaking supply company) before every harvest. If you use kits, make sure that the yeast that is included hasn't been sitting on a shelf for more than six to eight months. If it has, then you might want to buy a fresh packet just to be sure.

■ ══════════ ■

Q Why do I need to rehydrate dry yeast before using it?

A Rehydrating yeast before pitching (adding) it to juice or must is an important step in assuring a healthy fermentation. Adding dry yeast to a high-sugar solution such as grape juice is like giving a presentation to the boss without preparing a good outline — you're just not ready. Dry yeast cells are dormant and must be awakened before they can be called on to perform their best for you. Rehydrating them is like lubing them, revving their cellular mechanisms, and giving the poor guys a chance to get their heads screwed on straight before they start chewing away at the sugar.

■ ═══════ ■

Q How do I rehydrate dry yeast?

A I always follow the package directions. Companies that sell yeast know the best way to activate their product and usually include directions.

If there are no instructions, calculate about 0.7–1.0 g of dry yeast for every 1 gallon of juice or estimated yield of must. Remember, a half ton of grapes yields about 85 gallons (322 L) of wine.

Follow these steps.

1. Dump your measured yeast in 105–110°F (40–43°C) water (about 15 mL water for every gram of yeast) and gently mix in until just suspended. It's okay if the mixture is a little lumpy.
2. Let sit for 15 minutes and mix again before stirring it directly into the juice or must to be fermented.
3. Add an equal volume of juice from your fermenter and let stand 10 minutes more.
4. Mix once more and then pitch into your fermenter.

■ ═══════ ■

Q Can I do anything to help my yeast get a head start on a healthy fermentation?

A Perhaps the most important thing is to make sure you hydrate them according to the manufacturer's directions. In addition, ensure that your must (or juice) is at a reasonable pH (3.10–3.65); that your pitching temperature is between 55 and 65°F (13–18°C), depending upon how quickly you like your wine to ferment; that they have enough available nitrogen (use a yeast food like Fermaid K or Superfood); and that they don't get too hot or too cold as they ferment.

Some winemakers are turning to a new line of yeast nutrients that are added at the time of rehydration. These products contain various vitamins, micronutrients, and other proprietary ingredients that the manufacturers claim help yeast better adjust to any harmful minerals or metals in the water and give them a head start before they even hit the fermenter.

Q What are yeast nutrients, yeast extract, and yeast hulls?

A Yeast need micro- and macronutrients to carry a healthy fermentation to completion, so supplementing the grape must with a good mix of vitamins and nitrogen sources should be standard procedure in the cellar. It's important to add the yeast nutrients to the juice before you inoculate with yeast.

Ideally, you should check your yeast-available nitrogen (YAN), a number that reflects the concentration of free amino nitrogen and ammonia (another source of nitrogen) levels in the juice. Samples can be sent to commercial wine laboratories for analysis. Once you know your mg/L YAN, make up any difference (I usually shoot for a total of 300 mg/L) using your nutrient of choice. Nutrient manufacturers should include product specifications with their products that tell you how much nitrogen you're adding if, say, you add 1 g/L of their nutrient.

Yeast hulls (sometimes called "yeast ghosts") are essentially yeast skeletons. They're the freeze-dried empty shells of yeast cells that have had the water and other liquid elements sucked out of them. Sounds a little gruesome, but yeast hulls can provide extra nutrients helpful to a fermentation.

Yeast extract, in contrast, is a concentrated mixture of dead yeast cells. It is sold as a wet slurry or in dehydrated form, which should be reconstituted before use. Yeast extract is rich in vitamins, minerals, nitrogen, and other elements, some of which yeast can use and some that they'll simply excrete unmetabolized.

It's up to each individual winemaker to decide which additives, if any, to introduce into a fermentation. I like to add yeast nutrients to my musts and juices before pitching the yeast. In the event of a stuck or sluggish fermentation, sometimes I'll add in about 0.5 g/L of yeast hulls. They supply extra micronutrients and also help retard the effects of alcohol toxicity in the fermentation environment.

Always scrutinize labels and be aware of what you're adding to your wine. Yeast nutrients are dense in vitamins, minerals, and especially nitrogen. It's never a good idea to add more nitrogen than you need to a fermentation. Most musts and juices do just fine if you adjust your initial YAN to 250–300 mg/L and no higher. If you add more than you need, you'll just be feeding spoilage organisms (*Pediococcus* and *Brettanomyces,* for example) with the leftover nitrogen your yeast won't consume.

■ ══════ ■

Is it possible to add too much yeast?

A rule of thumb that's always worked for me is to calculate my yeast and all other additions based on my expected liquid yield, not on pounds of grapes. The yield will vary depending upon how hard you press your grapes, what variety they are, and so on, but in general you can expect 150–160 gallons per ton (568–606 L) of grapes for reds and 160–170 gallons per ton (606–644 L) for whites. Once you know your yield, follow the manufacturer's directions on how much yeast to use.

For yeast, 0.70 g/gal (about 0.185 g/L) is a good starting point, and yes, you can add too much, but adding too little is worse. The concentration level of the yeast cells should be high enough to complete the fermentation healthily; if they're spread too thinly, you might be left with a sluggish or stuck fermentation. It's hard to add too much yeast as long as you're paying attention to your measurements, but your wine might taste yeasty if you add too much. There's no reason to add more than 0.70–1.0 g/gal (0.185–0.264 g/L). Err on the high side only if you anticipate fermentation challenges.

■ ══════ ■

Q Does adding more yeast give the finished wine a higher alcohol content or just a yeastier taste?

A If you use more yeast than you need, it is likely that your fermentation will proceed a bit faster, possibly have a more yeasty aroma, and go dry more quickly. It's also likely that the fermentation will occur at a higher temperature, because yeast generate a lot of heat when they're working fast and furiously. When concentrated in a small volume — in 5 gallons as opposed to 55 — the density causes the temperature of the wine to rise. As long as you ferment to dryness, more yeast in the solution won't cause a higher final alcohol content because that's determined by the initial sugar concentration of your juice, regardless of volume.

However, if you're starting with a very high initial sugar (more than 26° Brix), adding more yeast may give you a higher sugar-to-alcohol conversion rate. This works because a stronger, healthier fermentation will result, and the yeast may be able to ferment the sugar to dryness. If you had a high-sugar must or juice to begin with, the yeast may be stressed by the sugar level (and by the resultant increased alcohol concentration) and might die before the fermentation is complete. This shortcoming would leave you with residual sugar as well as a lower alcohol level.

If you have a challenging fermentation and dryness is your aim, I would suggest using 1.0 g/gal or even 1.5 g/gal (0.264 or 0.40 g/L). Conditions that can contribute to a less-than-ideal fermentation include: high initial sugar (more than 26° Brix), cold temperatures (below 55°F or 13°C at inoculation), damaged fruit, and moldy or infected fruit or juice.

Q Can I blend yeast strains before fermentation in the same way wines are blended after fermentation?

A It's such fun to read yeast catalogs in the summertime and, with one eyebrow skeptically cocked, imagine mastering my Merlot with M-394 or taming my tannins with TPS-25. But it is never a good idea to randomly mix yeast strains in the same batch of must or juice.

Think about yeast cells as if they were animals living in a rain forest jungle. Yeast cells need food to eat, air to breathe, and an appropriate environment in which to live and reproduce. Yeast cells form colonies, adapt to their environment when necessary, and actually communicate using primitive chemical signals. Yeast cells, like wild animals, compete for resources. When foreign yeast cells of different types invade, the competition can get ugly. Eventually, the stronger yeast type will win out and its offspring will dominate, taking over whatever resources (sugar, nutrients, amino acids) remain.

While this Darwinian struggle for dominance is going on at the intercellular level, you, the winemaker, are asking, "Hellooo down there, can you guys please stop fighting and get on with your job of turning this grape juice into wine?" When yeast cells are warring with invading yeast or bacteria, are distressed by colder-than-optimal temperatures, or are repressed by a lack of a certain vitamin in their environment, they slow down, or even shut down, or they might produce stinky waste products like hydrogen sulfide (that classic rotten egg odor we all try to avoid.)

Though the above example may be a little simplistic, it is instructive in reminding ourselves that yeast thrive and perform best when they have everything they need to keep them warm, fed, and happy. Blending different yeast strains prefermentation can result in sluggish or stuck fermentations and microbial off odors.

That being said, there are some recently engineered hybrid yeast strains being sold that are a combination of

Saccharomyces cerevisiae (your garden-variety wine yeast) with non-*Saccharomyces* yeast like *Kluyveromyces thermotolerans* and *Torulaspora delbrueckii* (try saying that five times fast). There are commercial yeast blends that were specially chosen because of their ability to work together, so it's probably not that much of a risk to give these yeast blends a try. I would still caution against making your own off-the-cuff yeast blends. I, for one, am perfectly happy to leave the serious microbe wrangling to the experts.

■ ════════ ■

Q Are there risks with using "wild" yeast for fermentation?

A I'm not a big fan of so-called natural fermentations, in which a winemaker relies solely on ambient yeast and fungi to find their way into the fermenter, gain a dominant foothold, and have the oomph to take a fermentation to dryness. Commercial yeast strains have been bred specifically for the purpose of eating 20–30 g/100 mL of sugar before they are poisoned by the 11–17 g/100 mL of resultant ethanol that they inevitably excrete as waste into their environment.

Relying on whatever type of yeast or fungi we happen to have floating around our cellar can result in the bane of the winemaker's existence: sluggish or stuck fermentations and microbial off odors. I'm not plugging for commercial yeast suppliers here. Rather, I'm plugging for good, sound, and fermentation-finished wine with minimal headaches. And why not call inoculated fermentations "natural?" All fermentations are natural, whether conducted with a specifically chosen strain or with whatever muck happened to be at the bottom of a barrel of the last batch.

However, I do give certain winemakers the "go feral" dispensation. If you've been successfully making non-inoculated wine in the same place for years, practice good sanitation, don't have high-pH musts, and are assiduous in your yeast nutrient protocol, you must be blessed with a nice, strong indigenous yeast population that can go forth and multiply with nary an inoculation. Just remember the possible pitfalls, because one year or another you'll run into a fermentation challenge your house yeast can't handle. For example, wild yeast are particularly sensitive to sulfur dioxide.

■ ══════ ■

Q What does *sur lies* mean and what are its benefits?

A In French, *sur lies (soor-lee)* means "on the lees." The lees are the gooey, sludgelike deposit of dead yeast solids and other small particulates that collect on the bottom of a fermentation vessel after the alcoholic fermentation is done.

Aging a wine on the lees is traditionally used in Chardonnay production (though I've also seen it in the making of Sauvignon Blanc, Chenin Blanc, and Gewürztraminer, all white wines). Many winemakers feel it gives the wines more mouthfeel, body, and aromatic complexity. The dead yeast cells, assisted by weekly or biweekly stirring in barrel, break down over time, releasing amino acids, proteins, and other biological compounds into the wine. It is currently being employed more and more in fine red winemaking — I've had great luck using *sur lies* aging with Pinot Noir to enhance mouthfeel and body.

Q **What is *Brettanomyces* and how do I avoid it?**

A The *Brettanomyces* genus, which is often not-so-affectionately abbreviated to "*Brett*," is a particularly nasty yeast. Its foul by-products, which can be detected in very minute quantities, are frequently described as smelling like a barnyard or mouse pee. Since it's a non-*Saccharomyces* (the good yeast we choose to conduct primary fermentations) yeast, it's sometimes called a spoilage yeast. Though some winemakers say a small amount is appealing, it's wise to avoid *Brettanomyces* contamination at any cost.

Brettanomyces yeast are especially dangerous for the winemaker because unlike most good winemaking yeast, they can survive on 5-carbon and other unfermentable sugars naturally present in wine. What that means is that even after your primary fermentation is over, certain sugars remain that your winemaking yeast can't digest but *Brettanomyces* can.

The really bad news is that a lot of these unfermentable sugars also happen to be present in wood. Oak cells (and, ergo, barrels) are rich in these carbohydrates and can become the perfect breeding ground for this especially hard-to-eradicate yeast. Add an inadequate barrel sanitation regime, a high-pH wine (3.65 plus), and extra leftover yeast nutrients — not to mention a little residual sugar because you picked your grapes too late and your yeast pooped out during primary fermentation — and you have the perfect recipe for *Brett*.

* ═══════════ *

Q Can I fix a wine that has developed *Brett*?

A As Dr. Roger Boulton, winemaking professor at University of California-Davis puts it, "You'd better just burn the whole winery down." I *think* he is only kidding. What the good doctor is referring to is the fact that *Brettanomyces* are very persistent little microbes. They thrive in wines and can even survive in empty barrels, feasting on sugars and other lovely leftovers, hiding in the cracks that your cleaning system missed. They're usually transmitted from winery to winery via shared barrels or purchased bulk wine.

Once the spoilage yeasts are in a wine, it's wise to isolate the wine from other wines or winery equipment.

There's no way to erase the barnyard smell in your wine. Because some consumers and wine producers (particularly in France) actually like a small percentage of *Brett* smell in their wine, many winemakers blend small portions of objectionable wine into a larger portion of sound wine. According to some, small amounts of these wild yeast can actually make a wine more complex.

The problem is that once you have *Brett*, it's extremely hard to get rid of it. Even worse is that *Brett*, once bottled, can continue to thrive in the bottle, producing carbon dioxide gas, turbidity, and even more of that famously noxious barnyard aroma.

Here are a few keys to preventing *Brett* in your winery.

Beware of used barrels as they may be harboring *Brett.*

Practice scrupulous barrel sanitation. Remove all scale and crystals from inside of barrels and if you can rent or have access to an ozonator, rinse with ozonized water before using or storing them.

Avoid high-pH musts. Initial pH levels higher than 3.65 make your final wine more susceptible to *Brett*.

Inoculate your musts promptly. Use a commercial strain of yeast in order to outcompete the ambient wild yeast population, of which *Brett* could be a member.

Add the right amount of nutrients. Only add enough yeast nutrients to get your starting YAN (yeast-available nitrogen) to 250–300 mg/L, or, if you can't send a sample out to a lab to get a measurement, consult the manufactur-er's instructions for what would be a conservative dose. Any nutrients left over after your primary fermentation just pro-vide food for spoilage organisms.

Monitor your free sulfur dioxide levels. Keep white wines around 28–30 mg/L and your reds 25–28 mg/L (bear in mind that SO_2 loses its effectiveness as your pH increases, so it's best to monitor molecular levels of SO_2 and keep molecular SO_2 above 0.8 mg/L).

Do I Need an Ozonator?

Though ozone is an excellent sanitizer, the short answer is that unless you're making more than 50 barrels of wine that you plan to sell, you're probably better off leaving these expensive machines to larger producers.

Ozone generators use UV light to zap air or piped-in oxygen gas (O_2) into ozone (O_3). The ozone gas is then dissolved into a stream of water, which exits as ozonated water and can be used to rinse tanks, barrels, etc. Ozone is a powerful oxidizer and can attack microbial cell walls, disabling microbes.

Ozone biodegrades by quickly turning back into water or oxygen (if it doesn't attach to organic mat-ter like microbes), and if ventilated properly, it is safe to use.

CHAPTER 6

Fermentation:

Bubbles without Troubles

Why is fermentation temperature so important?

Fermentation temperature is important because you want your yeast warm enough to be healthy but not too warm so that your fermentation will get too hot, blowing off aromatics and stressing the yeast. Heat-stressed yeast can produce elevated levels of VA or hydrogen sulfide and can even die off due to an increased permeability of the cell wall to alcohol, which is toxic to them.

Fermentations that are too cold are equally problematic. Most yeast strains become sluggish (some even start shutting down) if the ambient temperature of the wine drops below 55°F (13°C). Cold fermentations, while good for preserving aromatics in some wine styles, especially whites, aren't as beneficial for red fermentations, which need heat (around 80°F, or 27°C) to extract the most color, tannins, and phenolics.

Each yeast strain is unique in its ideal temperature range. It's a good idea to check with the manufacturer for the specific characteristics of your yeast strain, but most commercial yeast strains are happiest in a 60–80°F (16–27°C) temperature range. Temperatures much below those will contribute to a slowdown and the eventual sticking of your fermentation.

Q **What temperature should the must be before the yeast is added?**

A Recently rehydrated yeasts are delicate and can easily be shocked by temperatures that are too warm or too cold. The ideal temperature to pitch your yeast for white wines is between 58 and 62°F (14–16°C); for reds, the ideal is around 65°F (18°C). You don't want the yeast to have a sluggish start because they are too cold, nor do you want — especially in your white ferments — to have the yeast super-activated in a warm environment and run away from you with a hot and too-rapid fermentation.

■ ═══════════ ■

Q **How do I restart a stuck fermentation?**

A Restarting a stuck fermentation is a lot of work, so of course my first suggestion is to avoid one in the first place. Restarts are notoriously fiddly operations and often don't work — sometimes the juice or must is past the point of resuscitation. Essentially a restart involves hydrating a big slug of new yeast and adding your stuck wine to it in batches. It works best if your potential alcohol is less than 16 percent, as even strong yeast may have a hard time pushing beyond that high level of alcohol.

If you want to try restarting a stuck ferment, here's a procedure that's worked for me in the past.

◆ **In warm (~100°F/38°C) water, hydrate** about 5.7–
7.6 g/L (1.5–2.0 g/gal) of yeast using the whole volume
of your stuck lot to calculate for a yeast that can toler-
ate high alcohol. Add a yeast nutrient to the rehydration water.

◆ **Add yeast hulls** to your stuck wine at 0.5–0.75 g/L
(1.9–2.8 g/gallon). After the hydrated yeast has set for
about 15 minutes, mix in some unsulfited juice — grape
if you have it — or use organic apple juice, honey, or
plain table sugar. The goal is to add just enough to get
the yeast eating the sugar and producing a bit of alcohol. If I had 1 gallon (3.785 L) of rehydration water, I'd
add in about 3 ounces (100 mL) of grape juice.

◆ **Let the yeast chew** on the sugar for about 30 minutes.

◆ **Add about 5 percent** of your stuck wine to the yeast
mixture. It's critical that you not drop the temperature
of the yeast mixture more than 10 or 15°F at a time, or
you could subject the yeast to temperature shock. The
yeast will be very warm, and your wine is probably sitting at a much lower temperature, perhaps 65–70°F
(18–21°C). If your wine is very cold (below 60°F/16°C),
you may need to add less of it to avoid dropping the
temperature of the yeast culture.

◆ **Wait about an hour** for the yeast to acclimate to the
alcohol.

- **Take a temperature reading** of your yeast-wine mixture. Add about 10 percent of your volume of stuck wine to the yeast-wine mixture; again, do not drop the temperature by more than 10°F. Wait 60 minutes.
- **Test the temperature** and add another 10 percent every hour until you have added the entire volume of your wine to the yeast culture.
- **Maintain the wine temperature** between 70 and 78°F (21–26°C). Measure Brix and temperature twice daily. If the Brix gets below 0.5° by hydrometer, start using Clinitest tablet kits. If you have access to a commercial wine lab, you can send out samples for residual sugar analysis. I consider bone-dry to be 0.1 percent (0.1 g/ 100 mL) residual sugar or less. Many wineries are happy with 0.2 percent (0.2 g/100 mL) or less.

Clinitest Tablets

These little tablets are usually used by diabetics to measure glucose in a test tube of urine, but if used according to the directions that should be packaged with them, they can be used to test the approximate amount of residual sugar left in a few milliliters of your wine.

Note: These tablets are poisonous and must not be added to a wine batch or eaten — only use them in a test tube.

PREVENTING A STUCK OR SLUGGISH FERMENTATION

If you wanted your wine to be dry and it ended up sweet, it means that your yeast, for whatever reason, could not ferment the sugar completely to alcohol. Here are some potential causes of a stuck or sluggish fermentation and some ideas on how to prevent it from happening again.

PROBLEM	SOLUTION
Initial Brix of juice too high; yeast died due to alcohol toxicity.	Measure your Brix carefully before inoculating. Pick grapes when they are less ripe. Water down must or juice.
Yeast bred to ferment in a lower sugar concentration.	Choose the right yeast for the Brix level. Most yeast strains are sold with information about their alcohol tolerance or ideal Brix levels.
Yeast did not have adequate nutrition.	Unless you send samples to a lab for nitrogen analysis, it's impossible to know how much food your yeast have. Feed your favorite yeast nutrient blend before pitching.
Yeast died due to cold fermentation temperatures.	Monitor fermentation temperatures and keep above 55°F (13°C). At the end of the fermentation, when yeasts are at their weakest, keep temperatures between 70 and 80°F (21–27°C).

PROBLEM	SOLUTION
Yeast died due to high fermentation temperature.	Monitor fermentation temperatures and keep below 90°F (35°C); if the yeast seem to be sticking between 1 and 0.5° Brix, do not let the temperature rise above 80°F (27°C), where yeast cell membranes are more sensitive to alcohol toxicity.
Yeast were inhibited by too much SO_2.	Carefully measure prefermentation SO_2 additions. Levels above 70 mg/L free may inhibit yeast. Check levels of SO_2 in the must stage (30–50 mg/L total addition is sufficient for must and juice) and buy commercial *Saccharomyces cereviseae* yeast that are bred to withstand SO_2.
Yeast had too much competition from other microbes.	Pick and process only sound, mold-free fruit. Fruit fly infestations or a vinegary odor during fermentation are warning signs of high microbial load. Add 30 mg/L SO_2 at the must or juice stage and inoculate at 0.5–1.0 g/L (1.9–3.8 g/gal) *Saccharomyces cerevisiae* yeast that is appropriate for your initial sugar content. Keep your pH for red must below 3.65.

Q How long should a fermentation of a red wine like Cabernet Sauvignon take?

A Many premium Cabernet Sauvignon producers finish out their fermentations in five days or so, especially if the temperature gets up to 80–90°F (27–32°C). Many red fermentations take longer, however. Time to the completion of fermentation depends on a lot of factors, but in general, the higher the initial temperature, the higher the yeast dose, the higher the amount of oxygen introduced during fermentation, and the more nutrients in a juice or must, the faster a fermentation will go.

It actually is good for the production of Cabernet and other red wines to have higher fermentation temperatures to help extract color. Just make sure that your yeast have been correctly hydrated and that they stay healthy during this rapid fermentation.

Supplementing the must before inoculation with some yeast nutrient, as well as adding about 0.5–1.0 g/gal (0.13–0.26 g/L) DAP (diammonium phosphate) on the second day of fermentation might not be a bad idea. Be careful, however, as fermentation temperatures that are too hot, like over 90°F (32°C), run the risk of sticking.

Q What could cause a yellow ring to form around the edges of my fermenting wine?

A Sounds like ring-around-the-fermenter to me! Don't worry, it's common, though rings of vibrant yellow slime are not. Your yellow ring is probably a deposit of post-fermentation residue, especially if your wine hasn't finished fermenting to dryness. Winemaking is not a sterile process, and wine tends to leave lots of lovely residue in the form of thick layers of lees, skins, and other winemaking detritus in fermenters, barrels, and bottles, as well as on the periphery of carboys or stainless-steel tanks.

As your yeast cells sputtered through their last degree or two Brix, they probably — with the help of evolving carbon dioxide gas — spattered minute particles of suspended solids (which aren't necessarily red) and stirred-up yeast lees onto the sides of the fermenter. Add the time it takes for newly fermented wine to clear up and the small amount of evaporation that can occur in a carboy with a fermentation lock, and the wine level will sink ever so slightly, revealing the debris, which is entirely harmless albeit ugly. Just rack into a clean container when you're ready and continue to enjoy your wine. If you're really unhappy about the residue, carefully examine every step of your procedure and find out what you did differently this year.

Q What is the best way to cool my fermenter down if it's too warm?

A Cooling your wine is important if your fermentation is getting out of control. Otherwise, the fermentation may give off hydrogen sulfide (indicated by a rotten egg smell), develop high volatile acidity (because the yeast are stressed), and become susceptible to slowing down or stopping altogether. In addition, an overly vigorous ferment can blow off the primary fruit aromas and have other deleterious effects on your wine. Most commercial wineries have temperature-controlling glycol lines attached to their tanks, but few small-scale producers have this luxury. If you're fermenting in half-ton or smaller bins, the cheapest, easiest, and fastest way to cool a small, primary fermenter is to freeze gallon-sized jugs full of water and add them to the fermenting wine. Use containers that can be sealed tightly.

The number of jugs you'll need will vary, depending on how much cooling power you need and the size of your fermenter. A 50-gallon (189 L) can that's gently simmering might need a single jug, while a 200-gallon (757 L) batch that's peaking at 8° Brix and 90°F (32°C) might take six. Once you've added the jugs, punch down the fermenter,

Immersion coil

mixing thoroughly until the desired temperature is reached. Then put more jugs in the freezer, as you'll probably have to toss in some new ones eight hours later.

Needless to say, this technique is a little labor-intensive. If you don't have an extra freezer, or just want to try something a little more automatic, you might want to buy an immersion cooling coil. This is a stainless-steel coil that you place in the fermenter and run cold water through to cool the juice or must. I first had the pleasure of using one of these coils when I was working at a little winery up in the Santa Cruz Mountains of California and I have never been without one since. They are available at most home-winemaking and homebrewing retail shops, as both hobby winemakers and homebrewers use this gadget.

Once you hook up the coil to a water source and turn the water on slowly, you will have a constant source of cool, warm, or hot water traveling through the tube and cooling or heating your juice or must — sort of like a tank-cooling jacket but on the inside! Try to recycle the water by having the outlet end of the tube go out to your garden, yard, or vineyard. Sanitize this device (and the frozen gallon jugs) just like you would anything else in your winery.

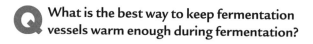

Q **What is the best way to keep fermentation vessels warm enough during fermentation?**

A If you feel the need to heat the fermentation or if you sense that the yeast are cooling down too much with a number of degrees Brix left to go, you may want to warm them up a tad.

An immersion coil made of stainless steel is an easy way to keep your must warm. These coils are available at most home-winemaking supply shops and are easy to hook up to a faucet. Just throw the coil into your bin and flow warm water (100°F, or 38°C) through the pipe while stirring the must with your arms or punch-down tool. This technique can raise the temperature in a bin of must by 5°F in about 30 minutes.

Another trick that works well with smaller volumes is to take out a soup pot full of fermenting juice and gently heat it on the stove to about 95°F (35°C) (watch for foam-over and stir frequently). You run the risk of making the yeast in those few gallons a bit unhappy, but if you return the juice to the fermenter promptly and mix well, you'll minimize stress and warm up the rest of the must.

A third option is to put an electric blanket over or around your container. This method is probably the least effective unless you have a metal or glass container, because you really can't conduct much heat through a plastic or wood fermenter (like a barrel). At best you'll be warming up the ambient air, which still can be effective. Most winemaking supply shops sell electric heating bands designed to wrap around carboys to keep them warm. These do a better job than the blanket method.

Q What should the fermentation temperatures be when making red wine from grapes?

A Even though a warm fermentation temperature (85–90°F, or 29–32°C) is common in Europe, the United States, and Australia, home winemakers shouldn't feel that they have to follow this (or any other) trend just because they read it in a recipe somewhere. Warm fermentation temperatures are often used to extract the most color and tannins out of the must. Those who didn't fall asleep in high school chemistry class will remember that, in most cases, the warmer a system is, the faster and more complete a chemical reaction will go. This means that a warm fermentation temperature can extract more color and phenolic goodies from the skins.

Even though this is one of the road rules of the chemistry world, however, we can't apply it wholesale to every winemaking situation. If you've got a fermentation temperature higher than 95°F (35°C), you are probably going to disrupt the yeast cells' collective ability to function properly when their cell membranes become more permeable to ethanol toward the end of the fermentation. When this happens, there is a good chance that the fermentation will stick, because the yeast die out before they can turn all of the sugar into alcohol. You also run the risk of developing cooked-fruit aromas or a more Portlike character in the aroma and flavor — something you may not want for your wine style.

Another danger of a high fermentation temperature is the extraction of too many goodies, like tannins, which in large doses can make a wine bitter and overly astringent. The flipside is that if you ferment too coolly (for red wines, that's cooler than 60°F, or 16°C), you may not get the extraction of color and tannins that you want. On top of that, your yeast might not be as happy and healthy. I always inoculate my red ferments with must temperatures hanging around 65°F (18°C) and get the peak fermentation temperature around 80–85°F (27–29°C).

Q Is it a problem when small flies buzz around the must during primary fermentation?

A The ever-present *Drosophila melanogaster*, or common fruit fly, is a prolific and pesky little insect that is the bane of not only the winemaker, but anyone who has ever left peaches or bananas out too long, or forgotten to take out the trash or to turn the compost pile.

Fruit flies are attracted to the aromas of fruits and vegetables, especially those that are rotting or fermenting. Their small size means that they might slip your notice for a day or two, until your winery has suddenly become the *Drosophila* Dating Game. Your primary fermenter is where they all go to raise their little fruit fly families and live happily ever after for their short but annoying lives.

What can the conscientious winemaker do? I suggest you first try to stop them from entering your winery. Install tight screening on windows and doors and make every attempt to keep doors closed. Remove other sources of fruit fly attraction from your winery environment. Keep garbage, recycling, and compost well away from your cellar. Pick up and remove windfall fruit from nearby trees or vines.

In addition to large barrier tactics, use more "fruit-fly-excluding" materials to seal off your fermentations. I use cheesecloth or simple fine-weave fabric. Muslin works well — simply attach small squares of it with rubber bands around the openings of jugs and carboys. For bigger fermenters, secure a larger piece of cloth with bungee cords or some other elastic. When a cloth cover becomes soiled or damp, replace it with a clean one and launder the other.

A plastic tarp might also work, but it must be tightly bungeed or tied to the rim of the fermenter. I've had problems with plastic tarps; the flies can worm their way under the ridges and wrinkles around the edge. Muslin works well because it's easier to cinch up tightly against the fermenter edge. The carbon dioxide is heavier than air, so enough of it will stay on top of the must and protect it during active fermentation. When the fermentation is no longer producing CO_2, it's a good idea to switch to a hard top to keep stray air currents from disturbing the CO_2 layer. Commercial wineries often use wide-mesh fabric screens cinched tightly around the openings on top of their fermenters for the "open top" fermentation scenario.

MEASURING VOLATILE ACIDITY

Most winery labs have a small still, called a cash still, that boils off a known sample of wine to capture the distillate, which is then titrated with a base to calculate the g/L of volatile acidity (VA). Though a VA analysis will also ferret out other minor acids such as formic, butyric, and proprionic, acetic acid makes up the lion's share of a VA measurement.

Some large wineries, as well as most of the commercial wine labs open to the public, employ enzymatic assays, gas chromatography, or high-performance liquid chromatography (HPLC) technology to get faster, more accurate results. Since acetic acid production can be a sign that something is wrong with a wine, diligent winemakers monitor VA levels monthly and keep an eye out for sharp increases that might signal a problem.

Legal limits for VA in the United States are 1.2 g/L (4.5 g/gal) for red wines and 1.1 g/L (4.2 g/gal) for whites. A small amount of VA is produced naturally in all wines, because yeast and malolactic bacteria excrete a small amount in normal fermentations.

VA can be controlled by practicing good sanitation, maintaining free SO_2 levels at an appropriate level (at least 28 mg/L for a dry red wine, less for lower-pH wines), and keeping vessels covered and topped to exclude air and microbes. High VA levels won't harm you, though they definitely affect your appreciation of a wine's aroma.

If a batch of wine is invaded by the winged masses, however, I wouldn't necessarily throw it away. No human pathogen can survive in wine, so it's impossible for the wine to make you sick from anything the flies carried. The only problem you might have is that the wine itself might "get sick" from bacteria such as *Acetobacter* that fruit flies may carry in. These bacteria can metabolize alcohol into acetic acid or vinegar. In high enough concentrations (600–900 mg/L being typical sensory thresholds), acetic acid or volatile acidity is seen as a definite defect.

■ ══════ ■

Q What is malolactic fermentation?

A Malolactic fermentation (MLF) is a series of metabolic reactions carried out by a group of bacteria that breaks down malic acid into lactic acid. MLF can and often does happen spontaneously at any time during a wine's life. For most homemade red wines, actively encouraging MLF by adding a commercial ML culture can add some flavor complexity and stabilize the wine against postbottling MLF by preemptively ridding the wine of malic acid. By depleting the supply of malic acid early on, you lessen the chance of malolactic fermentative spoilage later, when you may not be ready for it and when the carbon dioxide spritziness it produces may not be welcome.

If not controlled properly (planned inoculation with a known ML strain to a complete fermentation), MLF can contribute several unhappy-smelling by-products that may spoil a bottle of finished wine. The most noticeable by-products are carbon dioxide gas and diacetyl, a compound that many people say smells like artificial popcorn butter. MLF can also create some aromatic characteristics that are desirable for certain styles, namely the buttery, oaky New World reds that are still popular with some consumers and wine critics. Spontaneous or uncontrolled MLF, especially in a bottle of finished wine, can cause spritziness, cloudiness, and off odors classified as leathery, sweaty, mousy, or cheesy.

Q What grape varieties traditionally go through a malolactic fermentation?

A Historically and stylistically, wines that are almost always encouraged to go through malolactic fermentation are Merlot, Cabernet Sauvignon, Pinot Noir, and almost any dry, red table wine that will be aged for more than six months for consumption at least a year after it's first fermented.

Among whites, Chardonnays make good candidates for MLF for stylistic reasons. Other whites (Riesling, for example) usually aren't allowed to go through MLF because such wines show best when they retain their fresh, fruity character and zingy acidity. Sometimes, however, white wines can gain a little mouthfeel or roundness by going through a partial MLF.

It is always up to each winemaker to decide to what extent he or she will allow a wine to go through MLF.

Q How can I prevent malolactic fermentation?

A MLF is usually arrested by chilling, adding SO_2, and eventually, filtering. If you don't like the characteristics that MLF contributes to your wines and want to actively discourage MLF, you can do the following.

◆ Keep the pH below 3.30, keep the wine relatively cool in the cellar (below 62°F, or 16°C).
◆ Rack your wine carefully (avoid transferring sediment or picking up too much air).
◆ Keep sulfur dioxide levels at 25 to 30 mg/L free SO_2.
◆ Bottle as cleanly as possible, meaning sanitizing well and minimizing the chance that wine microbes or ambient bugs in the air get in contact with the wine. A 0.45-micron nominal filter can cut out a large portion of the bacterial population.

Q What conditions will encourage malolactic bacteria and ensure a successful MLF?

A To promote MLF, you must avoid conditions that inhibit malolactic bacteria. These include the following.

♦ **Cold temperatures.** Malolactic bacteria don't thrive in cold cellar temperatures, so keep your storage temperatures between 62 and 77°F (17–25°C).

♦ **Low pH.** Maintain a pH above 3.30.

♦ **High alcohol.** Keep alcohol levels at less than 14 percent.

♦ **High SO₂.** Keep free SO_2 levels at less than 10 mg/L.

♦ **Compromised inoculum.** Buy fresh culture from a reputable lab, follow directions to the letter, and inoculate with care.

♦ **Low inoculum.** Don't spread too little culture among too many barrels. Use the recommended dose.

♦ **Microbial competition.** It's always best to inoculate with your malolactic bacteria after the yeast have done their job on the primary fermentation. Similarly, a high level of any other kind of bacteria in your wine will compete with your selected malolactic bacteria for resources.

Do not rack the wine during MLF, because the lees in the carboys can actually help the bacteria finish their job by providing them with the micronutrients and other goodies they need to survive. Racking will also aerate the wine and inhibit the anaerobic malolactic bacteria. Try to keep your containers topped up in order to stave off any microaerophilic spoilage organisms (like the vinegar-producing *Acetobacter*).

You can test for the completeness of your malolactic fermentation by using a paper chromatography kit, available through most home-winemaking supply stores or mail-order catalogs. If you have a commercial wine lab close by, I recommend getting an enzymatic analysis done. I consider the MLF to be complete with less than 0.1 g/L malic acid, though some wineries will accept 0.3 g/L.

Once malolactic fermentation is complete, wait for the lees to settle out, rack the wine off the lees, add sulfur dioxide as required, and, after your chosen aging regimen, bottle as usual when the wine falls bright. One of the reasons that winemakers actively encourage malolactic fermentation is that it lessens the need for prebottling filtration. Bottling a wine with residual malic acid is risky unless you plan to filter with a 0.45-micron pad or membrane filter prior to bottling.

If you've fulfilled all of the above requirements and are still having issues, your low malic acid conversion rate could be due to the fact that you've got a type of malic acid in there that just can't be metabolized by malolactic bacteria. Malic acid, as naturally present in grapes, is only found in the L-Malic acid format. Its mirror image, evil twin D-Malic acid (remember chiral molecules in high school chemistry?), is never found in grape juice and only will get there if added by an accomplice — a winemaker armed with a bag of "acid blend." Synthesized in labs and factories, D-Malic acid is often sold in these popular powders, and wouldn't you know it, malolactic bacteria just can't convert it to lactic acid.

■ ══════ ■

Q What can I do with a wine that won't complete a malolactic fermentation?

A The quick answer is: Don't throw that wine down the drain! If you like it as it is, by all means don't try to force it through malolactic fermentation. If there's ever a time when a wine is loudly and persistently trying to tell you something, it is now. Since your wine cried uncle and just won't go through malolactic fermentation, your first option for finishing the wine is to rack cleanly, adjust free SO_2 to about 25–30 mg/L, filter to exclude any microbes that might get by, and bottle normally.

Option two is riskier, but if you don't have access to a filtration setup and can't filter before bottling, merely racking cleanly to minimize organisms and bumping up the free SO_2 at bottling will give you some protection against a future refermentation in the bottle. If your wine happens to have a lower pH, it'll help the SO_2 in the wine be more active (SO_2 is more antimicrobial at lower pH levels) and will aid in keeping spare bacteria in check, as they are generally happier living at pH levels well above wine pH.

Option three is to blend the wine in with a batch that has completed malolactic fermentation. This will either dilute the malic acid concentration such that it's under the radar (less than 0.1–2.0 g/L), or the other wine may have enough MLF-beneficial characteristics (higher pH, lower alcohol, etc.) that MLF may start back up again on its own. If the blending wine already has SO_2 added to it, however, a spontaneous referment isn't too likely as ML bacteria are very sensitive to sulfites.

* ━━━━━━━━━━ *

Q Are there ways to decrease the chance of malolactic fermentation without bumping up sulfite levels?

A Lysozyme is gaining popularity among winemakers as a tool to use to retard malolactic fermentation early on in a wine's life. Lysozyme, a naturally occurring enzyme isolated from egg whites, has been in wide use in the wine industry over the last 10 years or so. Prior to that, it became popular in other food-processing fields, namely the cheese and dairy industries.

It degrades the cell wall of gram-positive bacteria like *Leuconostoc oenos* (the guys responsible for malolactic fermentation in wine) but doesn't harm yeast or gram-negative bacteria like *Acetobacter* (the bacteria that make wine into vinegar).

Lysozyme comes in a liquid or powder form, is virtually odorless and tasteless, and has been used successfully by winemakers to inhibit malolactic bacteria and lessen the amount of sulfur dioxide needed to be added to a wine for stability. Its anti-MLF effects don't last, however, so it's not a permanent solution like sterile or 0.45-micron nominal filtration. After using lysozyme in finished wines, allow for adequate reaction time (until flocculation occurs) and then rack the clean wine off the sediment before bottling. Lysozyme is a useful wine additive, but be aware that it will bind with tannins and some color compounds and can cause sediments and flocculants.

■ ══════ ■

Q How can I tell if malolactic fermentation is complete?

A Malolactic fermentation is over when all of the malic acid has been transformed into lactic acid by the malolactic bacteria. For the small-scale winemaker, the easiest way to detect whether MLF is complete is to use a chromatographic kit to test for the disappearance of the malic acid.

You drip a tiny dot of the wine to be tested on a special piece of paper and immerse one end of the paper into a tray containing the chromatographic developer solution. The solution wicks through the paper and separates out various

Use Your Ears

If you prefer doing things the old-fashioned way, perk up your ears — literally. You can actually listen for the completion of MLF. If a wine is still fermenting, you will hear little "pinpricks" or bubbling when you put your ear to the bunghole. Similarly, if you have an ML fermenting wine tightly bunged up, you'll hear a distinctive "pop" or "burp" when you gently and slowly release the bung. Once the bungs no longer "pop," the bacteria probably have finished off their job.

Of course, this is a tool best employed by an experienced winemaker. The sounds of gas can be confused with many things unrelated to the completion of MLF. A bung "popping" or "burping" can be a sign of spoilage organisms other than malolactic bacteria. The sounds could also be caused by an incomplete primary fermentation giving off gas or the ambient temperature in the cellar warming up and causing the wine and its dissolved gasses to expand. This is called "degassing" or "off-gassing" and is easy to confuse with MLF activity.

Be aware that a "stuck" MLF can occur. If the gas noises cease, it might be because your malolactic bacteria have all died!

compounds, like organic acids, by virtue of molecular weight. After the paper dries, you look for a colored spot where the malic acid should have been deposited. If there is no spot, then the malic acid has been metabolized by the bacteria.

Even though a chromatography kit is yet another thing to buy for your home wine lab, it is an important tool for monitoring the completion point for malolactic fermentation. You can also send wine samples to a lab for an enzymatic assay. ML completion is indicated if your malic acid content is less than 0.1g/L, though some wineries consider under 0.3 g/L "complete."

Q Is oxygen good or bad for wine?

A Oxygen is one of the most reactive elements in our everyday environment. It causes iron to rust, cut apples sitting on your countertop to brown, and our blood to become red after it passes through our lungs. Though we need it to survive, its oxidizing capabilities are so powerful that our doctors advise us to eat a diet rich in antioxidants to avoid cellular damage by free radicals — highly unstable single molecules of oxygen.

Because of oxygen's amazing powers, a large part of our winemaking hours are occupied with keeping our wines away from it. When a wine stops producing CO_2 gas during primary and malolactic fermentation, it becomes susceptible to over-oxidation, especially if it doesn't have a high antioxidant load to protect it. That means that because red wines are higher in colored and tannic compounds (natural antioxidants) than white wines, they are better able to withstand the effects of oxygen. This is the primary reason why white wines may be browned and undrinkable after five years in the bottle whereas a red might be just hitting its stride.

Slightly aerating your wine at the right time, such as racking a young red, can be a positive. However, when a wine is aged and bottled, oxygen becomes more destructive than beneficial.

Before we get too carried away here, though, understand that some oxygen is necessary for a healthy wine, especially during fermentation. Yeast need a little air to develop healthy cell walls, and in the later stages of fermentation, lightly aerating the must sometimes helps the yeast survive as they ferment to dryness. Oxygen, particularly in the first six months of a red wine's life, helps it form the polymerized tannin and other polyphenolic molecules that stabilize its color in the long run as well as create better and rounder structure.

Q **Can I use fresh juice instead of sugar to sweeten a wine and still avoid a referment?**

A Adding new juice to finished wine to sweeten and generally freshen things up is an age-old technique practiced by winemakers around the world. However, as you suspect, there is the problem of refermentation. Introducing any kind of fermentable substance gives the microbes present in the wine a new food source. If you have yeast in your carboy (or worse, in your corked bottles) and you add sugar or new juice, there's a good chance the yeast will wake up, start to eat the sugar, and begin producing sediment and carbon dioxide gas.

If this is fine with you, then don't worry about it. If, however, you were envisioning a sweetened, still, clear wine, you'll have to add potassium sorbate, which retards yeast growth, or sterile filter your wine to take out the yeast and bacteria. Even under the most stringent of practices, however, it is difficult to completely remove or incapacitate all of the microbes that might cause refermentation. Potassium sorbate doesn't retard bacteria, and it also has an annoying tendency, in malolactic-complete wines, to create geranium-like off odors.

As for filters, there are increasingly better choices available for small-scale producers, though some, especially those made of flimsy plastic, are perhaps of dubious quality.

So what's a winemaker to do? My advice is to throw a lot of things at the wall and see what sticks: Keep your free

SO_2 levels above 30 mg/L, rack your wine well using a filter to knock down the microbial population, and bottle with 150 mg/L potassium sorbate as an added precaution. Taken together, these steps will decrease your chances of having a refermentation in the bottle or carboy.

■ ═══════════ ■

Q How do I stop a fermentation early to leave some residual sweetness in the finished wine?

A To arrest a fermentation, it's best to chill the wine below 40°F (4°C) if you can, then add 50 mg/L sulfur dioxide, stirring shallowly so as not to kick up the lees on the bottom of the fermenter. Then rack the wine off the sediment as soon as possible to separate it from as many yeast cells as you can.

Be aware that residual sugar in a wine is like handling a ticking time bomb. As long as there are viable microbes in that wine, they will almost always attempt to keep eating the sugar, causing an imbalance in your desired final sugar levels, carbon dioxide spritziness, and microbial sediment.

For people who insist on sweet wines, I suggest immediately rough filtering at this point to knock down your microbial population and maintaining free SO_2 levels around 30 mg/L to inhibit yeast activity. You may also want to add potassium sorbate when bottling to avoid bottle refermentation.

It Takes a Lot of Good Beer to Make Good Wine

Work a harvest at any small winery in California and you will usually see a six-pack (or even a tiny keg) of microbrew tucked in the lab fridge next to settling juice and wine samples. Though I'm not advocating drinking on the job or storing food next to lab chemicals, the reality is that I've worked several harvests where the winemaker always capped off a good day's work by passing around a few cold ones to the thirsty crew.

Whether it's the camaraderie after a hard day of crushing together, the fact that we're sick of wine after making it all day, or just that a cold, hoppy beer tastes so good as the sun sets over a California vineyard, any winemaker will tell you that it takes a lot of good beer to make good wine.

CHAPTER 7

Aging, Oaking, Fining, and Filtering

Q Why are oak barrels so popular in winemaking?

A The answer is part tradition, part style, and part consumer expectation. Barrels have served as containers for all sorts of goods for more than a thousand years. Herodotus describes wine from Armenia being shipped in palm-wood barrels to Babylon in ancient Mesopotamia. The early Roman Empire learned about cooperage technology from the European Celts, discovering that these durable and easily transported containers held oil, tar, grains, and other goods without breaking as frequently as the Roman clay amphorae.

As the Romans spread viticulture and winemaking throughout their burgeoning empire, the technology of barrel making took firm hold. In medieval and Renaissance Europe, coopered containers held ale, cheese, water, meat, almost anything. Oak, with its tight pores, straight grain, and mild flavor, lent itself well to barrel making and food storage. Oak vats, puncheons, and barrels, which when full of liquid swell up and create a tight seal, became the obvious choice for making, storing, and transporting wine.

Oak cooperage and a tradition of winemaking (and wine consumption) traveled to South America, California, and South Africa with European settlers. In areas where the right kinds of oak trees didn't grow, such as the west coast of California, early winemakers used whatever kind of wood best fit the bill — there are 10,000-gallon redwood tanks from the 1800s still in use today at the Wente Vineyards winery in Livermore. No matter how creative New World winemakers got, though, early North Americans still had a powerful thirst for imported French wines, and the gold standard for a wine's style and taste remained with barrels from the European oak species *Quercus robur.*

Today, even though American oak *(Quercus alba)* and oak from Hungary and other parts of Europe are becoming popular, we still have that legacy. Though stainless-steel tanks have pretty much made expensive, heavy, and hard-to-clean oak cooperage all but obsolete from a wine storage point of view, we still are enamored with the flavor profile oak gives a wine. There is no doubt that, for certain wine types, the unmistakable stamp of being aged in a fine French oak barrel is a critical component of style and personality.

The most exclusive and expensive wines in the world are still made with a large percentage of French oak barrels, though recent industry surveys have shown that this trend is flagging. While large wineries have always had to limit their barrel use due to cost and/or storage logistics, even medium-sized and small wineries have started buying fewer barrels.

More and more winemakers are discovering that American oak barrels and even noncoopered oak alternatives like oak beans, chips, and staves can add plenty of character to their wines. As the quality of these products has improved over the years, many of us have had fun experimenting with them in the fermentation and aging of our wines.

Small-scale wine producers will probably always be fans of the traditional barrel; I know I am. It's great to be able to buy half a ton of grapes, ferment it in a half-ton picking bin, and press it off into a conveniently sized barrel with just enough wine left over for topping. And one of my favorite smells in the winemaking process is the toasty, caramel-spicy aroma that wafts up from a freshly rinsed barrel being filled for the first time. Despite the cost, the current trend toward less oak, and the increasing quality of noncoopered oak, traditional barrels still form an important part of winemaking tradition and style.

Q Can I impart oak flavor to my wine without using an oak barrel?

A Absolutely. If you like a little oak for your wine styles but don't want the expense or the hassle of keeping barrels, noncoopered oak, or "oak adjuncts" (industry jargon for nonbarrel oak) are an option. Easy to buy in small quantities, much cheaper than barrels, and convenient to add to wine in measured doses, these adjuncts can be wonderful tools for the home and commercial winemaker alike; I encourage everyone to experiment with them.

Oak can be purchased in the form of staves (think of a deconstructed barrel), chips (similar to landscape chips), beans (3 cm cubes), and powder. These are all made from different oak (French, American, Hungarian) and toast levels (light, medium, medium-plus, heavy), just like barrels. They can be tricky to use, however, as many winemakers have no point of reference for how much to add or how to utilize them in their winemaking protocols.

Here are some tips for incorporating oak alternatives into your winemaking.

- The best oak products, just as the wood for the best barrels, come from wood that is aged and air-dried for three years before being fire-toasted.

- Buy from a reputable producer or a winemaking supply store with high turnover, which helps guarantee freshness. These small oak pieces, especially chips or powder, can lose much of their aroma and flavor compounds if stored in the open air or exposed to sunlight.

- Generally, the darker the toast of the chip, the darker the aromas you'll get (coffee and burnt toast versus hazelnut and vanilla).

- American oak products typically contribute more vanilla notes than French oak.

- Inspect oak products carefully. Don't purchase any that are damp or moldy or have a musty or dank aroma.

- Use them conservatively: Put oak beans or chips in the fermenting container at a starting rate of 1 g/L for primary fermentation and, if more oak is desired upon tasting, again during the first few weeks of bulk aging.

- Taste often for development and add more oak as you think necessary. Staves, with their unwieldy size (some are more than 4 feet long) are best left to the larger wineries with their big tanks. Try 3- to 4-inch stave pieces as a compromise.

- The smaller the particle size, the faster the extraction. Stave pieces are a nice choice for long-term aging (5–12 months). Since chips and beans have a higher ratio of surface area to wine than barrels do, overoaking can happen overnight!

- Taste at least every week for flavor development during the first month, then every other week after that.

- Oak powders (sometimes called "granular oak") are best approached with conservative experimentation. I don't use them in my wines as I find the tannins too harsh. Of all the noncoopered oak, powder seems to be the one that people can always pick up in the wine later on — that rough mouthfeel is pretty obvious.

■ ═══════ ■

Q When should I add oak beans, cubes, or chips during the winemaking process?

A As you might guess, there is no one correct answer except this: You must go by taste and have patience. Remember that fermenting wine is warmer than wine that has completed the primary fermentation. Adding oak cubes, chips, or powder during the active fermentation might cause you to overextract before you realize it.

Old Oak Never Dies . . .

. . . but it does lose its flavor after a few years. As oak barrels get used for subsequent batches of wine over time, they lose their strength. Many of us use neutral or used-up barrels in our white winemaking programs because you don't get the obvious oak aromas/flavors you did when the barrel was new, and the barrel becomes just a storage vessel.

With oak adjuncts there is a point of diminishing returns where you've sucked up all of the goodness that is available. At this point, they have no more value than as barbeque wood and smoke chips — a great tip, by the way. I know a lot of winemakers that make killer BBQ and smoked meats with their wine-soaked oak chips!

This is why, especially if you're new to winemaking, I suggest you add oak adjuncts after the primary fermentation is complete and you've racked the wine off its gross fermentation lees, when the wine is about four weeks old. This way, you don't have any weird fermentation aromas, a bulky cap, and lots of chunky lees (in addition to high temperatures) to get in the way of determining when you've added enough oak to your wine.

Similarly, because alcohol is a better solvent than water, wine that is high in alcohol will absorb oak flavor and aroma more quickly. It's easier to mistakenly overoak higher-alcohol wines than those that are hovering around a moderate 11.5–13 percent. Wine that's more than 13 percent alcohol may need to be tasted more frequently in order to avoid adding too much oak character to the wine.

In my experience, it's safe to add oak chips to bold, big red wines at the rate of 1–3 g/L. The oak bits can simply be floated on the surface (as long as you stir them occasionally), but it's best if they're tied up in a small cheesecloth sack, tea bag-style, and submerged in the liquid by means of a food-safe weight. (See directions on next page.)

Sample the wine at least once a week to determine when it's done according to your taste. Depending on the wine in question and the toast level of the oak, this could be anywhere from 2 to 20 weeks. Ideally, the effects will be subtle, and the oak aromas and flavors will serve as a grace note on top of all the other wonderful things already present in your wine. When you're happy with the amount of oak, rack the wine off of the chips into another container or, if you've made a tea bag, simply remove it from your storage container.

Keep in mind the surface area of the oak product you're using. Smaller pieces of wood, when added at the same weight-to-liquid ratio as larger pieces, will impart wood aroma and flavor more quickly. The good news is that you can always add more later. That's the beauty of using oak products; the danger is that you can never go back once you've added too much.

MAKING OAK CHIP TEA BAGS

Rather than floating handfuls of chips on top of your wine, try using this handy method, which works well with narrow-necked fermenters like carboys.

1. Cut a few layers of cheesecloth into strips measuring 12 x 4 inches.
2. Fold a strip in half lengthwise, creating an even narrower strip.
3. Sew up one of the shorter ends and most of the long side.
4. Stuff a bunch of chips into this cheesecloth "burrito" and finish sewing up the long side.
5. Tie off the open end with sturdy thread, leaving a length to hang outside the vessel.

Hey presto! You've got oak chips that are easy to remove!

Note: For a larger container, add a few sanitized marbles or stainless-steel weights to submerge the bag into the wine.

Q Why are there different toasting levels of oak?

A Barrels and oak adjuncts are often sold at different levels of toasting. Heavily toasted oak imparts more burnt aromas like coffee and chocolate, while medium and medium-plus toasted products contribute mellower scents on the caramelized scale like allspice, *dulce de leche,* toasted bread, and vanilla.

Lightly toasted barrels offer some oak aromatics like the medium and medium-plus barrels and are great for winemakers who want some of the benefits of oak aging (added oak tannin for mouthfeel and astringency, compounds that enrich the mouthfeel, etc.) without having an overwhelming oak character. Lightly toasted barrels can be great for white wines as well as for lighter style reds like Pinot Noir.

■ ━━━━━ ■

Q Do I need to soak or prepare oak chips before adding them?

A Like so many things in the winemaking world, there are no hard-and-fast rules. Some winemakers boil or soak their chips before use and others toss them into a fermentation without any sort of preparatory ablutions. If you buy your chips from a reputable supplier with sound storage conditions and a high inventory turnover, you shouldn't have to worry about mold, bacteria, or fungus. Most companies stock clean chips that can be tossed in directly.

However, if you or someone you know has had problems, and you feel that the extra step is justified (or if you suspect the chips might be old, moldy, or stored in a damp place), boiling could potentially help kill off any ambient microbes, and tossing the resulting "tea" in with the oak chips will ensure that you are retaining most of the oak goodies that might otherwise get lost in the rinse water.

Subjecting the chips to a spin in boiling water will extract some of the tannins, polyphenols, and the like that can add structure to and may help the color stability of most red wines. Boiling also drives off some of the more volatile, ephemeral aromatic compounds that you may want to capture in your finished wine. If you are trying to retain that vanilla, clove, and spice grace note that good oak chips can add to a wine during the aging process, I'd avoid the boiling step. If you feel that you need to boil a batch of chips to sanitize them, you probably shouldn't use them.

■ ━━━━━━ ■

Q Can using an oaking alternative cause a haze to develop?

A The tannins imparted by oak adjuncts bind to the proteins naturally present in wine, which may cause them to fall out of solution as the tannin-protein complexes become too large to remain soluble. This results in visible (though still tiny) particles floating in your wine. With time, these might eventually settle out, but using a fining agent like Kieselsol (a silicon dioxide product) will help. Used in conjunction with gelatin, it's particularly good at settling out protein-tannin complexes that have formed a haze in the wine. Normally you would add the gelatin first to the whole batch, then add the silica agent a little later. Each product is different, so follow the manufacturer's instructions.

The mechanism of settling is not 100 percent understood, but it seems that the added gelatin precipitates out the tannin while the silica prevents an excess of gelatin from remaining in the wine. What results is a layer of sediment on the bottom of one's carboy, keg, or, if the tannin is added too close to bottling time, in the bottle. The good news is that this sediment is expected, natural, and easy to rack off. Predicting when tannin-peptide hazes will occur, however, is difficult; each situation must be evaluated individually as it happens.

■ ══════ ■

Q Which is better for wine, a toasted or charred barrel? And can I use bourbon barrels?

A When in doubt, stick with tradition. Toasted oak is the way to go when you want the benefits of attractive storage, proper aging environment, and toasty aromas and flavors. The distilled beverage industry, like the wine industry, uses heat-treated wooden barrels and kegs as storage vessels in which liquors are aged. In the process of making brandy or whiskey, the distillate that comes out of the still is entirely colorless. It is actually the toasted — or charred — aging barrel that imparts a golden brown color to the beverage.

Likewise, toasting methods are chosen so that the finished product will benefit from the natural aromatic compounds present in the wood. The insides of barrels to be used for distilled spirits — bourbon especially — are usually exposed to a very hot flame and will be entirely black on the inside, what some folks call an "extremely high toast" level.

Bourbon barrels are really too toasted for fine winemaking, in my opinion. Barrels used in winemaking can be ordered from wine-specific coopers at low, medium, or high toast, and sometimes only the heads (the flat ends) of the barrels will be toasted. Wines pick up some spicy, vanilla, and clovelike notes from being kept in toasted wood, assuming the supplier you're working with recommends these barrels for wine storage.

Q Is there an easy and cost-effective way to frame a stand for my oak barrels?

A Make like a Burgundian and find some triangular pieces of wood about 3 × 5 × 5 inches on the sides and about 2 inches thick. I use these simple chocks all the time to keep barrels from rolling around in my cellar. You need four per barrel. All you do is position your barrel (bunghole up, of course) on the floor where you want it and then shove your handy wooden chocks under the barrel between the floor and the bilge, two at either end. With a little prodding and nudging, your barrel will lay contentedly on its side, completely stable and ready for filling.

If you want to be fancier and keep your barrel off the floor, find two 2 × 4 boards about 2–3 feet long and put them down first, one on either end of the barrel (perpendicular to the staves) so that the barrel is balancing on them and not on the floor. Then stick your chocks under the barrel where it meets the 2 × 4 and you've created a cheap stand!

If this sounds a little hokey and homespun, take heart in the fact that wineries the world over rely on this system and stack hundreds of barrels, pyramid style, using just 2 × 4s and chocks. It is quite stable, especially when the barrels are filled with wine, and make a neat, aesthetically pleasing display of barrels in a cellar, rather than those fussy metal racks that invariably lose their metal coating after five years. To raise the barrel to a height convenient for racking, you could take it a step further and build a sturdy platform about a foot high.

Barrel on chocks

Q What are some different ways of fining wine to help clarity?

A Fining agents are compounds like bentonite clay or egg whites that are introduced into wine to bind with one or more wine components. The added fining agent gloms on to its target wine molecule and forms larger, heavier complexes that settle to the bottom of the container. The treated wine can then be drawn off and moved to another container. The goal of fining is to pull something out of the wine that you find undesirable; the side benefits are usually increased clarity and stability.

Wines are frequently fined with added protein like egg whites to remove excess tannins and with bentonite clay to pull out excess proteins. All wines contain at least a little protein. A protein instability usually makes a wine look hazy; in extreme cases, it can look like wispy pieces of cotton (called flocculation) at the bottom of a bottle. If a wine isn't protein stable (sometimes called "heat stable" because heat experienced during aging can cause protein hazes), it means the proteins that are naturally in the wine don't want to stay in solution; the denaturing and condensation of wine proteins turns them opaque. This can happen either before or after bottling.

I like bentonite, a naturally occurring clay that has been used in winemaking for centuries, especially when fining proteins out of white wines. Most commercial wineries use bentonite to help wines achieve heat stability, a state where enough proteins have been removed from solution that they won't form an unsightly haze later in the bottle. Bentonite is added to the wine in the tank and allowed to settle, which can take up to a week.

Meanwhile, the lab filters and "cooks" a 100 mL sample of the treated wine in an incubator at 100°F (37.7°C) for 24–36 hours. The sample is then visually analyzed by the winemaker and if no flocculation or protein haze is observed, the wine is confirmed to be heat stable. This test is thought to simulate the worst case scenario a bottled wine will ever face during its initial storage, transport to the marketplace, and any subsequent aging once it's been purchased by the consumer. The high temperature and short time frame force out any proteins that may come out of solution and allow the winemaker to get a relative idea of whether or not the wine will throw a protein haze later in its life.

Most small-scale winemakers are probably pretty safe adding 3 g/gal (780 mg/L). The treated wine, when settled, is ready to be racked into another container and will have a much lower protein content, enabling it to be stored with less of a chance of throwing an unsightly protein haze.

Kieselsol is another additive to try for hazes and proteins. Kieselsol is a proprietary name for a silicon dioxide product that works in the same way as bentonite. Silicon dioxide electrostatically binds with positively charged proteins in wine to initiate flocculation and settling.

It's always best to rack your wine off the primary fermentation lees first and then add your agent according to the product instructions. Fining agents must be stirred well into a wine, given time to absorb into the wine, and then settled out again (adding another week or three onto your bottling time line) before you proceed with filtration and bottling.

Fining agents should always be used conservatively (after doing small-scale bench trials beforehand), as their effects can sometimes strip a wine of flavor, aroma, color, mouthfeel, or all four.

Q How are egg whites used as a fining agent?

A Egg whites, usually employed to precipitate excess tannins and smooth out the mouthfeel of red wines, are by far one of the most traditional and natural products used to finish off wine. The technique is a sine qua non of Burgundian Pinot Noir production. Egg-white fining is affordable, easy to administer, and doesn't require special chemicals. All you need are egg whites, salt, and water. If you want to be superfanatical (as some winemakers, certainly of Pinot Noir, are), you could insist on organic, free-range eggs, French *sel de mer,* mineral water, a copper bowl, and a stainless-steel whisk with which to make your fining solution.

Fining with egg whites is quite simple. What isn't simple, however, is deciding how much to add for your particular wine. A typical addition level is one-half to three egg whites per 59-gallon (223 L) barrel. That's all well and good, but what about those of us who want to fine 5 or even 205 gallons of wine that doesn't happen to be in a barrel at all? Fortunately, I've done the research for you and, many omelets and batches of crème brûlée later, have concluded that an average North American, free-range, grade AA large egg has about 28 mL of egg white. So, if we're talking about two-and-a-half egg whites per barrel, we are adding 2.4 ounces of egg white per 59 gallons (70 mL/223 L).

In order to figure out the best level of addition for your particular wine, I suggest conducting small-scale bench trials first, using small jars or containers that hold 50–375 mL (2–12 ounces) of wine (baby-food jars are perfect). If you have pipettes or similar volumetric measuring devices with small enough increments, you can try different rates. Don't forget to include a control, or untreated sample, and be sure to make your bench trial egg-white solution the same way you would to treat the larger batch. Wait a week and then evaluate all the samples. Then, simply pick your favorite and proceed with treating the whole lot.

So where do you start if you don't have the equipment or patience to do lab trials? I find that one egg white per barrel (28 mL egg white per 223 L of wine) is a safe addition level to start. I'm going to pretend you have a 10-gallon (38 L) fermenter of red wine. A rate of 28 mL egg white to 223 L of wine gives us 0.12 mL egg white per liter. Multiply 38 by 0.12 to figure out the total amount of egg whites you need to measure, and the result is 4.6 mL (0.16 ounce).

- Break your egg and separate the yolk from the white.
- Measure out 4.6 mL of egg white (if you don't have a beaker small enough, estimate as best you can; a little more won't hurt because egg whites are gentle) and put it in a medium-sized bowl with a pinch of salt and enough water (a few milliliters) to make a liquid solution.
- With a whisk (or even a fork), gently dissolve the egg white in the water, taking care not to incorporate too much air into the whites. The idea is to make a liquid, not a meringue.
- Dump the entire solution into your fermenter and stir gently with a long stirring rod for 15–30 seconds.
- Leave your covered fermenter alone for about three weeks.
- Rack carefully to another container, leaving any deposit behind.

You can wait longer if you want to, but be sure to rack within two months as the protein-tannin globules formed by the interaction between the egg white and the wine components can start to break down and redissolve into the wine. This can be difficult to remove.

Fish Bladders to Clear Wine?

Yes! Isinglass (a very pure protein isolated from the swim bladder of fish) is one of the most effective fining agents available.

Q Why do I need to top up my wine?

A Topping up (sometimes just called topping) containers with wine, preferably of the same lot, varietal, and vintage, is necessary to limit air exposure and microbial infection in wine containers. This practice is critical immediately after primary fermentation has completed (when the wine is put into its aging vessels). When a wine is fresh from the fermenter, it still carries quite a bit of carbon dioxide, which it will lose over time, along with a noticeable amount of volume.

When the wine volume shrinks, you must add wine to fill the container again or air will creep in, leaving the wine vulnerable to oxidation and microbial attack. During extended bulk aging, especially in barrels where alcohol and water can evaporate through the pores of the wood, it's important to keep adding wine at least once a month (some wines in some containers may need it more often) to keep the containers full. Topping up eliminates the air space and reduces the danger of spoilage.

Q What are some good tips on topping up and managing my headspace?

A Finished wine and air don't mix. Oxygen can oxidize aroma and color components, while air-loving bacteria (especially *Acetobacter*) will inevitably infect unprotected wine. During bulk aging, when a wine's aromas and flavors are developing, it's critical to exclude air. Headspace in containers must be managed in order to avoid exposing our wine to excess air while aging.

We can do this in one of three ways: by keeping our wine in containers appropriate for the volume, by adding wine to fill or completely top up our containers, or by blanketing the wine's surface with a gas heavier than air.

It's usually a challenge for winemakers to always have the perfect-sized storage vessels on hand for completely topped batches. This is why topping up, or filling any spare headspace with wine, is so important. I always try to use the same wine when topping because there's a much lower risk of introducing foreign or unstable agents. Such instabilities can cause refermentation, bacterial infection, or precipitation. Similarly, if you top a wine that's going through malolactic fermentation, you must not top up with previously sulfured wine — even a tiny amount of free SO_2 from another lot could inhibit or halt the malolactic fermentation of your current batch.

Gassing empty headspace with a gas heavier than air is another way to manage your headspace. In this case you carefully lay a "blanket" of gas on top of the surface of your wine. If you have a source of CO_2 or argon (welding-supply stores and, increasingly, winemaking supply stores will carry small gas cylinders), gas a slightly smaller container well and siphon the wine into it, being careful not to aerate the wine any more than is necessary.

To do this, take the empty container and stick the nozzle or hose of the gas can as far as possible into the bottom. Dispense the gas slowly. The goal is to create a blanket of gas on the bottom of the container without creating turbulence and mixing oxygen into the layer.

Then take a small siphon hose and place one end in your container of wine and the other end in the very bottom of the empty container into which you've just placed the gas. Siphon the wine very slowly so as not to mix in any air. Be careful not to splash.

■ ══════ ■

Q How do I prepare ahead of time to have enough wine on hand for topping up my barrel or fermenter?

A This is one of the classic challenges faced by small-scale winemakers and is often the reason recipes for the ubiquitous 5-gallon (19 L) batch aren't always useful. When making wine for any volume, whether a 5-gallon (19 L) carboy or a 59-gallon (223 L) barrel, it's always best to make a bit extra for topping up.

The topping wine can be made in a container that fits the proportional size of what you're doing. Allowing an extra 20 percent for topping up usually works. Use the same winemaking practices with this small batch as you do for the main batch. Use it to top up the main batch about once a month or whenever you notice your containers getting low.

■ ═══════════ ■

Q **What is cold stabilizing and when in the wine-making schedule should I do it?**

A Cold stabilizing — in commercial winemaking at least — involves chilling the wine down to 30°F (–1°C) for a minimum of 36 hours. This reduces the chance that the wine will precipitate harmless but unsightly potassium bitartrate crystals when it is later bottled, purchased, and chilled down in someone's refrigerator.

Once the wine becomes cold enough, some of the naturally present potassium and tartaric acid molecules solidify into sandlike grains that fall to the bottom of the chilling vessel. Sometimes extra potassium bitartrate is added as "seed crystals" to facilitate this reaction. The wine must then be filtered or racked off while still cold. If the wine is allowed to warm up before the full removal of the potassium bitartrate crystals, some of them may be reabsorbed into the wine and precipitate later when the bottle is chilled again.

Cold stabilization is not a flavor- or sensory-quality issue, just a visual one — no one wants to serve a wine that seems to be contaminated with glasslike shards, no matter how harmless they actually are. Red and white wines alike will throw precipitates, usually during the bulk aging process. Because many white wines are "soon-to-market" products and don't have the extended barrel time that most reds do, cold stabilization is necessary to force the precipitation. Cold stabilizing isn't necessary for reds that will throw these precipitates out on their own (most reds in my experience are done with this in a year or so). However, if you have a "soon-to-bottle" red, by all means go ahead and cold stabilize it.

Small-scale wine producers, especially those not putting their wines out in the marketplace, usually don't bother with cold stabilization. This is convenient, as most non-commercial winemakers don't have access to the chilling tanks and equipment needed to perform an effective cold-stabilization procedure. Storing your wines in a cold place, like an uninsulated garage over the winter, will probably increase the wine's cold stability.

Don't be surprised if you do see some precipitation crop up later on in the wine's life, especially if it is stored in the fridge for a week or two. Without the proper equipment, it's probably not possible to reach temperatures cold enough to really make your wines commercially cold stable and to really drive the crystalline condensation reaction to completion.

If you do have access to a chilling system and want to incorporate it into your winemaking practices, it's best to

The Angel's Share

In olden times, the wine that evaporated from storage barrels was called the angel's share. In reality, much more volume is lost during primary and malolactic fermentation. Sure, some wine is absorbed by the wood and some wine (usually the alcohol) evaporates through the wood over time, but the main cause of the empty space encountered after putting new wine into barrels is the loss of CO_2 as the wine settles.

The age of the barrel has little to do with this process, but the moisture content of the barrel does to a certain extent; a very dried-out barrel will suck up more wine as the wood becomes saturated. To avoid losing more wine than you have to, soak your barrel with a water-and-potassium metabisulfite solution overnight and make sure there are no leaks before you fill it. Always keep relative humidity between 60 and 70 percent to minimize evaporation over time.

save cold stabilizing as the last step before the final racking or filtering. This enables you to filter just once, to both exclude the potassium bitartrate crystals and prep the wine for bottling.

Q What are some tricks for keeping bacteria out of wine as it ages?

A Keeping containers of finished wine full to the brim in airtight containers is the key to keeping ambient bacteria from finding ingress. This is part of the reason why topping up and breaking down partial containers into smaller, full ones is so critical. However, whether you make 10 gallons or 10,000, it's difficult to either have enough wine on hand to keep your containers topped up or to collect a sufficient variety of different-sized tanks, barrels, and carboys for storing your various batches and styles of wine. It's an age-old winemaking dilemma.

Here is an unorthodox trick I learned from a Burgundy-trained winemaker who swears that this technique is still used in the "old country." He called it the Olive Oil Trick, and the basic premise is to float a layer of oil on top of the wine surface, forming an impermeable barrier that air can't get through and therefore in which yeast and aerobic bacteria can't survive.

While the principle is sound and olive oil *was* used in ancient days, I don't recommend it today. Olive oil is expensive and can oxidize and spoil just like wine, though not so easily. Spoiled oil may eventually contribute off flavors to your wine. Food-grade mineral oil from the digestive aids section of drugstores is the best type to use. It's colorless and odorless, so it won't flavor your wine. Here's how to use it.

- Say you've got a 5-gallon (19 L) carboy that has only about 3 gallons of finished wine in it. (Perhaps you had to break some out for that dinner party you threw last weekend.) All you need to do is buy a 500 mL bottle of mineral oil and lay a layer about ⅛-inch (0.3 cm) thick very carefully over the surface of the wine.

- Tilt the carboy as low as it will go and pouring the oil slowly from the bottle at a similar angle. If the mineral oil doesn't have a nice pour spout, use a container that does. Slowly tilt the carboy up as needed until it's finally sitting upright again, and presto, a topped carboy that is 2 gallons down!

- When you want to get to the wine again, get out your siphon hose. Put your thumb over the end of the hose, lower the other end below the surface of the oil, start your siphon, and decant away.

- If you want to completely empty the container, decant as much wine as you can using the above procedure.

- Pour the remaining wine and oil mixture into a tall, small-diameter container, like a 1 L measuring cylinder. The small diameter makes it easier to separate the oil and wine.

- Decant again using your siphon hose, sucking from underneath the oil (kind of like a backward racking!), and you should be able to recover just about all of your wine. The oil can be reused if it is racked cleanly off of all wine droplets and sealed tightly in a clean container.

Even though this is a fun and useful trick, it does have its limitations. I never store wine like this for longer than one month and even then, I keep the larger container covered tightly. Just because you've got a layer of oil on top that air can't get through doesn't mean that bacteria and other nasties will not enjoy living on the sides of the carboy, just waiting to get mixed into the wine the next time someone gives the carboy a jostle. I also don't recommend it for wooden containers, as the oil is hard to wash out.

Your containers obviously need to be washed with lots of hot water and a surfactant agent before you use them again. Common dish soap works well for small containers. Note also that a layer of oil on top of a fermenting wine, or wine that is going through malolactic fermentation, will result in a turbid top layer that'll be harder to collect. This technique, consequently, is much more effective for finished wines.

Q How can I tell if there is enough CO_2 on top of my wine to protect it while it ages?

A It is a good idea to test for the presence of your gently laid CO_2 blanket. Too many people make the mistake of thinking that if they quickly squirt a little bit of CO_2 into their container, their wine will be protected, but

CO_2, like any other gas, can be dissipated by air currents or high temperatures and, especially with repeated opening and closing of bungs, can eventually disappear to the point of ineffectiveness.

Rather than spend hundreds of dollars on an accurate oxygen meter to ensure that your wine is protected, the time-honored (though not 100 percent scientific) flame trick is a quick-and-dirty one that French winemakers have used for centuries to indicate the presence of CO_2. Hold a lit match near the surface of the wine. It will extinguish due to the lack of oxygen if a CO_2 blanket is present.

■ ══════════ ■

Q What is the aging potential of homemade wine? Is it true homemade wines go bad after two years?

A It is an absolute falsehood that homemade wine always goes bad after two years. Losing a batch of wine is probably due to inexperience and poor winemaking practices more than anything else. If home winemakers use the same quality raw material as the "big guys," their wine has just as much potential for staying power as some of the best wines in the world. It's just a question of building quality and stability into every stage of wine production.

Even though there's no magic bullet that works wonders across all wines, many winemakers find that the key to longevity is a balance between adequate acidity (some like pHs of 3.3–3.6), alcohol content (12 percent and higher), tannin and phenolic content (they act as antioxidants), and microbiological stability.

Proper storage is also key. Heat, light, oxygen, and microbes are some of wine's worst enemies while aging. All care should be taken to store wine bottles on their sides in a cool, dark, and relatively humid environment. Being a conscientious winemaker who pays attention to all of the above factors and isn't afraid of putting in some long hours is the first step on the road to making great wines.

How long should I bulk and bottle age my wine?

It really is up to you. Each wine (and wine drinker) is different, and there are no hard and fast rules that dictate how much of each type of aging a wine will need. It all depends on your wine and your tastes. It's safe to say that every wine that ends up in a bottle goes through both stages, at least nominally. Bulk aging can be as simple as letting your wine settle down in its barrel for a couple of weeks after primary fermentation is done, and bottle aging can be as short as the three weeks that elapse between corking and uncorking.

Just so I'm not leaving you hanging like a neglected cluster of late-harvest Riesling, here's a little bit more information. The general purpose of bulk aging is to let the wine "find itself" postfermentation, which entails a couple of important things. First of all, a wine needs to fully complete its primary fermentation. Any wine that is still going through this initial stage, in my opinion, is not finished and bottling it too early will lead to fizziness and cloudiness in the bottle.

A wine also must lose any carbon dioxide it might have retained from its fermentations and it has to have enough time to settle out the lees. If you're so inclined, you could go through other steps like filtration or cold stabilization (more usual for white wines), but these are just icing on the cake. After a wine is inactive and settled out, the main determinant of when to bottle should be taste.

A gutsy red wine may need 12 months in the barrel to mellow out harsh tannins, whereas a delicate white wine can technically be bottled as soon as it falls bright. A zingy Pinot Grigio may actually be better in the long run if it's bottled up at 6 months of age rather than left to languish in barrel for a year. It's never a good idea to bottle too early, however, so err on the side of caution. But be aware that bulk-aged wine, if not cared for, can be at risk for oxidation or spoilage.

THE SOLERA SYSTEM OF AGING

While fans of fine Bordeaux and Burgundy table wines relish the vagaries that each vintage brings to the wines of those regions, consumers of ports and sherries prefer a consistent aroma, taste, and quality from year to year and are less concerned with drinking vintage-dated bottles. Therefore, instead of releasing all of a vintage into the marketplace once it is deemed aged, these aperitif or dessert wines are shunted into a solera system of aging, developed by the Spanish and Portuguese. This extended barrel-aging system produces wines of a constant average age and ensures a certain homogeneity of product over different vintages. It also promotes beneficial oxidation and imparts the unmistakable flavors of sherry wine.

The solera system may seem complicated at first, but it is an ingenious example of fractional blending. Here's how it works: Barrels of wine of the same type but different vintage are stacked with the oldest on the bottom and the youngest on the top. Let's say we've got eight rows of barrels representing eight vintages of wine.

Each year, as the harvest season rolls around, anywhere from 10 to 30 percent of the bottom (the oldest) barrels' volume is bottled as that year's product. The headspace that remains is filled with wine from the level above, and so on up the stack. The previous year's barrels on the top level are topped up with wine from the current harvest.

The average age of the wine in the bottom barrels rises with the years until it reaches a constant average age. With eight layers of barrels, our sample solera will produce wines that are an average age of 8 years old after 10 years of production (assuming that 25 percent is removed from the bottom row each year). There are some disadvantages, however.

◆ You need a lot of barrels and it takes a long time.

◆ One infected barrel could spoil the whole lot.

◆ It takes self-control. You can only draw off a certain amount of wine each year without losing the aging potential of each layer.

◆ You have to make the same stuff every year. There's no guarantee you'll be able to obtain a particular varietal every year for the next couple of decades. You could make the system work by creating similar wines, say, tannic, dry red wines from the classic Bordeaux varietals, every year and just hoping that the blend comes out okay, but who wants to take chances with all of those barrels of wine?

Q Why do people blend wines? Why not leave well enough alone?

A Though it sounds complicated (dealing with multiple batches as opposed to just one), blending varietals can make good sense. For one thing, a mix of quality wines with complementary characters is likely to be more interesting than the individual wines on their own. In some cases, a drinkable but uninteresting wine can be improved with the addition of a more robust or complicated type. Some people blend to impart a certain style. For example, 2 percent of a pH 3.20, non-malolactic-complete Riesling can give an exciting, racy lift to a malolactic-complete Chardonnay.

Here are a few general rules for blending.

Never blend a loser, i.e., make sure you're not ruining a good wine by mixing it with a bad one. That just brings down the quality of the whole batch, the exact opposite of what you're trying to achieve.

Pay attention to residual sugar and malic acid in the wines you're blending. If you put a perceptible concentration of sugar or malic acid into a wine that's completed primary and malolactic fermentation, you have an imminent referment on your hands unless you add more SO_2 and filter before bottling.

Be equally cautious with sulfur dioxide, because if you want the blend to go through MLF, even a little bit of SO_2 from a component wine could stop the malolactic bacteria in their tracks.

Satisfy your own taste. Remember that it's your wine. Don't be limited by the blends others have done — feel free to experiment with whatever sounds interesting to you.

■ ══════════ ■

Q What considerations should I take into account when blending two wines?

A Blending and amelioration (adding nongrape or wine adjuncts to a wine) are sound, time-tested arts employed by winemakers throughout history. Winemakers have been known to blend vastly different wines and to add sugar, juice, herbs, spices, and flower extracts to wines. These blending practices are intended to introduce, mask, or bring out certain characteristics in a finished product. Even home winemaking purists, those who believe that a beverage cannot be called wine if it has had nongrape material added to it, have been known to add a bit of brightly colored Syrah to their white Zinfandel to punch up the color.

Whenever you blend anything into a wine, it's important to remember that all sorts of instabilities, refermentations, and precipitations may occur. It's best to see what happens on a small scale before treating the entire lot. This may be tedious, but it's often the best way to avoid problems. Any time you introduce a foreign substance into a wine, including another wine, take a moment to think about the potential consequences. Two products that are stable on their own could potentially yield a very different product when combined. Because each wine, juice, or concentrate is made up of such an immense number of different compounds, it is nearly impossible to predict all of the interactions that two components might have.

Some wine-chemistry relationships can be anticipated, however. Tannins, for example, can precipitate proteins in wine. Thus, if you add commercial tannins to a wine in order to boost color complexity and astringency, you may find that you get an unsightly microlayer of protein at the bottom of your carboy. Similarly, adding a wine high in tartaric acid to a wine that is high in potassium may result in a precipitation of potassium tartrate crystals if the pH conditions are right.

As if that weren't enough to keep track of, you must also take into account the ubiquity of microbial life that can survive and even thrive in wine and grape matter. Many wine microbes are surprisingly hardy. Even when an initial yeast fermentation is complete and the wine is dry, there are many microscopic flora and fauna that can flourish in the seemingly nonfermenting environment. A microbial population that may be inhibited or dying out in one environment could find a new lease on life once another source of nutrients and sugars is introduced.

■ ══════ ■

Q Do you have any suggestions for combining red grape varieties?

A That depends on what you want to achieve and what blending components you have to work with. Each varietal is different, and looking to commercial trends will give you an idea of which grape varieties pair well with others.

For example, let's look at potential blending partners for the Zinfandel grape. Cabernet Sauvignon is by far the most popular blender added to Zinfandel by professional and home winemakers alike. This pairing makes sense, as Cabernet has the "guts" to stand up to a Zin but is able to lend more complex components like chocolate, tobacco and cedar aromas. Zin tends to be all about heat (it usually has 14 percent alcohol or higher), bright primary fruit (think ripe cherries and strawberries), and, if the winemaker chooses, a little bit of toasty oak to add some vanilla and spice notes. I find Zin to be a little bit simple and somewhat of a unilateral fruit bomb; a little Cabernet can add a note of distinction to what can be a monolithic (or just monotonous) wine.

Sangiovese and Nebbiolo (two lighter-bodied Italian grape varietals) reportedly also blend well with Zinfandel. These pairings make some sense if one recalls that Primitivo (grown for centuries in Italy) and Zinfandel are very close relatives. Using these wines to blend with Zinfandel would be more of a study in contrasts. The delicate aromatics of the Sangiovese and Nebbiolo might be blown out of the water by a really strong Zin, but if you are aiming for a more elegantly styled blend, this could work. Tasting different commercial wines that use the blending varieties you plan on making will also give you ideas and you'll have fun doing the research!

■ ══════════ ■

Q Is it good or bad to filter your wine prior to bottling?

A Filtering, if done at all, is a winemaking operation usually done right before bottling or as the wine is flowing through the bottling line. Commercial wineries, especially large ones, will often filter a wine before bottling and then pass the wine through another filter in the bottling line itself, as their goal is to insure that only clear wine, free of microbes, gets in the bottle and to the customer.

For the home winemaker, filtering is often less a question of quality than of cash flow or disinclination. The reality is that filtering is a fiddly bit of cellar work that involves a lot of expensive new equipment, quite a bit of self-education, and considerable trial and error. Some winemakers, even professional ones, just say "the heck with it" and skip filtration with no ill effects if their wines are dry, stable, and have settled to a satisfactory level of clarity.

If you're considering filtering, ask yourself what you're trying to achieve. A common reason to filter, especially for whites, is to achieve a stable environment in the bottle. You may not want your wine to go through malolactic fermentation, or maybe it's sweet and you don't want any ambient yeast cells conducting an illicit postbottling fermentation.

Another reason to filter is clarity. I can't tell you how much it spoils my experience when I'm judging a home winemaking competition and someone presents me with a cloudy Chardonnay. Homemade white wines should at least look clear, though if you rack cleanly and carefully, if your wine has gone through malolactic fermentation, and you're not worried about secondary fermentation in the bottle, you may not have to filter at all. Some of the most famous Chardonnay producers in the world don't filter their white wines, but it's certainly considered poor form to sell a hazy bottle.

Stability and clarity are good, right? Right, but not if you have to sacrifice quality. If you're forcing your wines through a very fine filter or using nasty paper-flavored pads that didn't pass the supplier's quality-control specs, you might suffer setbacks. Some winemakers believe that filtering strips wine of flavor, color, or aromatic compounds, no matter how you do it or what you use. There have been many studies on this point over the years. The only consensus seems to be that filtering can certainly change a wine's character in the short term, though I haven't found evidence to prove that over time it has a noticeable effect.

Red wines seem to change the most when filtered. Since they are dry, red wines are more stable than whites (most reds go through malolactic fermentation and are usually fermented dry). So it makes sense to filter reds only when necessary. Commercial red table wines are hardly ever brilliantly clear. If you shine a beam of light through them, you'll see a tiny bit of haziness. This is entirely normal.

Filtering never hastens the aging process; in fact, some argue that it hinders a wine's development. Whatever your aim, the rule is to filter only if you have to or really want to.

Q How does filtering work?

A The most common form of filtration used by small-scale wine producers is pad filtration. Pad filters are stacks of cellulose sheets that are mounted in a stainless-steel or metal frame or column. Wine or juice is forced by a pump or by air pressure through the cellulose pads and, depending upon the tightness of the cellulose matrix and the back pressure on the system, particles of a certain size will pass through while larger ones will get trapped within the matrix.

The designation "nominal" or a measurement like "0.45 micron" on a pack of filter pads refers to the size of particles the pad will let through. This pad is designed to prevent particles larger than the specified size (e.g., 0.45 micron) to pass through, though it's not guaranteed. This is the size through which yeast and bacteria will not pass but the wine will.

Q What is "sterile" filtering?

A I put the word sterile in quotes above because nothing in winemaking is ever really sterile. True microbial sterility is only achievable in the strictest hospital and lab settings when instruments are heated in special ovens to a certain temperature for a certain time. Even if you pass "dirty" wine through a 0.45-micron nominal filter into another container, and even if you cleaned that container really well, you'd never eliminate 100 percent of the microbes on its surface. The best that we winemakers can do, even in the commercial realm, is to knock down the microbial population to acceptable levels. What those levels are depends on each individual winery, its wines, and its goals.

A sterile filtration, by industry standards, uses a 0.45-micron filter that does not let microbes pass through, even those as small as bacteria. The process ensures that your bottled wine will be as stable as possible. Sterile filtration can be useful for commercial winemakers but may not be practical or affordable for most home winemakers.

The 0.5-micron filter sheet is a little bit looser than the 0.45-micron sheet and most likely would allow some microbes to pass, though it will usually completely clarify a wine and take out particles that would give a cloudy appearance. If I had a winery with 50,000 gallons of 1 percent residual sugar Chardonnay to bottle and sell, I would certainly make sure to final filter with the tightest pads possible and run it through a 0.45-micron in-line filter when bottling. Ruining thousands of customers' opinions about your products due to one little yeast cell is a scary prospect.

Home winemakers don't have to worry about achieving such stringent quality control parameters (or product recalls, lawsuits, or other risks of doing business), so filtering is much more of a choice. If you are very careful in your sanitation, and bottling processes and have a dry wine that's gone through malolactic fermentation and hasn't presented any problems like high VA or an obvious microbial infection, I'd say not filtering is an acceptable risk.

Q Are there phases of aging when a wine can taste and smell quite different than it did previously?

A While there is no single developmental time line for all wines, fruitiness in the mouth and in the bouquet does tend to drop out with time. Many young wines exhibit a marked fruitiness, but as time goes on, they sometimes go through periods described as "dumb phases." These phases can occur in bulk storage or later on in the bottle and depend on many factors.

A dumb phase is difficult to quantify, but the wine becomes somehow less expressive or less enjoyable than it once was. As every wine is different, it is impossible to predict when a wine might go through such a period or what complex chain of chemical reactions are causing the wine to taste and smell the way it does at any given moment. Polymerization of tannins, precipitation of anthocyanins, and oxidation of primary fruit phenolics all might contribute to this delicate and frustratingly hard-to-quantify phenomenon.

■ ═══════ ■

Q How can I eliminate fizziness in a finished wine prior to bottling?

A There are a few ways to degas your wine. The best solution depends on your particular situation. With a small amount of wine (a 5-gallon carboy, say), especially if it's not a delicate white wine (which could oxidize easily), you could try what I call the "cocktail shakedown method." Cap your carboy tightly and give it a good shake and then uncap it to let the motion drive some of the bubbles out of solution.

If your carboy is glass or is too full to rock and roll, rack your wine into smaller containers that can be shaken more effectively. Be careful with this method, however, as it does introduce some air into the wine. If you're trying to keep air contact to a minimum while shaking, I suggest gassing your shaking containers' headspaces with CO_2 or nitrogen in order to reduce the number of oxygen molecules sitting in the container before you go for it.

A better, less-oxidizing method of degassing is to sparge with nitrogen. (This method is also more time and money intensive.) Nitrogen actually helps other gasses come out of solution. To sparge with nitrogen, you need a compressed-nitrogen cylinder and regulator (try a local welding supply shop), narrow plastic tubing, and some kind of sparging stone (like a small fish-tank bubbler).

The idea is to attach the sparging stone to the tubing, the tubing to the regulator, and the regulator to the cylinder. Turn on the nitrogen and allow the sparging stone to bubble away in the bottom of your container until the carbon dioxide level is where you want it. For very small containers, this may take just 5 minutes. It is best to sparge in small time increments, let the wine sit overnight, and taste test again for carbon dioxide bubbles. If you still feel a lot of spritziness in your mouth, you may want to keep going.

This method does have a couple of downsides to it. For one thing, while using compressed gas in winemaking is no more difficult than using your barbeque's propane cylinder, compressed gasses always need to be handled carefully. For another, nitrogen can strip away aromatics. It is always a balancing act to determine just the right amount of sparging to accomplish your goals without stripping out ephemeral aromatic compounds.

Perhaps the easiest and most natural method of degassing is to just wait it out. If the wine isn't particularly cold (below 53°F, or 12°C), most CO_2 gas will naturally dissipate over a few months, especially if you are topping, stirring, or racking. Try extending your bottling time line a little bit. Bottling later might produce better wine than practicing extreme intervention just to hit a predetermined bottling window.

One caveat: Even if your primary and malolactic fermentations are complete, CO_2 could result from a wine microbe infection. Common culprits are bacterial strains such as *Lactobacillus* and *Pediococcus* or spoilage yeasts like *Brettanomyces*. These guys can survive happily on things you wouldn't necessarily think are digestible, like pentoses (5-carbon sugars as opposed to the more well-known 6), oak carbohydrates, and other unfermentable "sugars" that yeast don't really consume.

If you degas the wine and bottle it and still have spritziness (especially if the spritziness gets worse or bottles begin to burst), I recommend sending a sample to a wine-testing laboratory for microbial identification. No amount of degassing will solve the problem of a microbial population happily eating away at your wine and producing its own constant supply of carbon dioxide gas.

■ ══════════ ■

Q What is wine conditioner?

A Not widely used in the professional winemaking world, most wine conditioners contain both a sweetener (usually sucrose) and a preservative/yeast inhibitor (usually potassium sorbate). It is added to a finished wine just before bottling to put back some sweetness without the risk of refermentation. The sorbate is supposed to keep the yeast at bay so you end up with a sweeter wine that does not referment.

Be careful to look at the ingredients on the wine conditioner, as sometimes there isn't enough preservative to prevent a refermentation in the bottle. In fact, I've found "wine conditioner" that is only a mixture of sucrose syrup and potassium metabisulfite, which will add a tad of SO_2 but do very little to inhibit yeast (which require upwards of 50 mg/L free SO_2 in order to slow down or refrain from hungrily snapping up any fermentable sugar in sight).

Also consider that while potassium sorbate inhibits yeast growth, it won't kill yeast or stop an ongoing fermentation altogether and does nothing to protect your wine from bacteria and other spoilage organisms. And another caution: Especially in high doses or in combination with a malolactic fermentation, sorbate can contribute to a funky geranium-like off odor in wines.

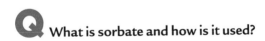

Q What is sorbate and how is it used?

A Sorbate comes from sorbic acid — it is sometimes sold in powdered form as potassium sorbate — and is authorized for winemaking use in almost every country (notable exceptions being Switzerland and Austria). It is fungistatic (inhibits yeast) and, in higher concentrations, fungicidal (fatal to yeast).

Sorbic acid is not very soluble in water, tastes slightly acidic, and has no effect on bacteria. It inhibits a refermentation from occurring when sugar is added back to a wine prior to bottling, or can stop fermentation prematurely to retain a certain level of residual sweetness.

Q Can I use sugar substitutes such as stevia to back-sweeten a wine before bottling without fear of it refermenting in the bottle?

A I've heard of many home winemakers winning awards with stevia-sweetened wines, so it's worth a try! *Stevia rebaudiana* is a perennial herb native to South America; the sweet plant extract used as a natural sugar substitute is gaining in popularity with home winemakers. It apparently dissolves instantly if used in its powdered form, remains stable in solution, doesn't cause off flavors, and, as far as I know, is nonfermentable, so no yeast or bacteria will be able to eat it and cause fizziness or sediment in the bottle. Stevia is used in quantities of 50–150 mg per 750 mL bottle, depending on the level of sweetness desired. Since it's not fermentable, folks who have experienced secondary fermentations in the bottle may want to try stevia for sweetening rather than sugar, honey, or a wine conditioner.

Another popular sweetener that's coming into its own as a home winemaking adjunct is sucralose, commercially known as Splenda. If you're considering putting your wine on the market, remember that it's not legal in the United States to use these alternative sweeteners and bottle up your product as "table wine." If you're not on a commercial track, then you can have as much fun experimenting as you want!

CHAPTER 8

All About Bottling

Q What are the basics of bottling?

A Bottling may appear to be complicated, but it's really not. At its easiest, bottling wine simply involves siphoning the finished product into the bottles (leaving about 2 inches of headspace), inserting a cork into the hand corker, positioning the bottle under the corker, and pulling the lever. It's always wise to buy some extra corks and practice with an empty bottle before you do it for real.

Wine bottles can be purchased at home-winemaking stores, or you can simply wash and recycle your own bottles. Most supply stores also rent hand corkers and sell corks. You should only buy corks that are tightly sealed in plastic bags, because exposure to dust and microbes can spoil your wine. A 59-gallon-barrel (223 L) batch of wine will yield about 24 cases, or 288 standard-size (750 mL) bottles of wine.

Q How do I know when it is time to bottle?

A Make sure all fermentation is done, both primary and any secondary or malolactic fermentation, and the wine is clear. It's never a good idea to push to bottle a wine that is still trying to find itself (i.e., if there is still noticeable microbial activity or if the wine is very cloudy). In these cases, a little time will do wonders, as long as the free SO_2 levels are maintained in the 25–30 mg/L range, depending on the wine, and containers are either totally topped up or their headspace is being flushed with carbon dioxide gas to inhibit microbial activity and oxidation.

Once these basic conditions have been met, a wine's readiness for bottling depends entirely upon what kind of wine it is. A dry, floral, delicate Riesling may be ready to bottle once it falls bright, has been racked, and has lost most of its CO_2 after primary fermentation. A robust Syrah, on the other hand, may need up to two years in barrel, during which time the tannins will become more complex, the mouthfeel will round out, and the wine will approach a smooth and balanced equilibrium. Each wine is different. Experimentation and experience with your own particular wines are the only ways to tell when a wine is ready to bottle.

Q Do I need to prepare corks before bottling?

A None of the professional winemakers I know treat their corks before bottling. We buy them from the manufacturer in vacuum-sealed, oxygen-free bags. Though impossible to sterilize because of the pores in which fungi and bacteria can still be lurking, corks direct from the factory should be as clean as you can possibly expect. It's when the factory's bags are opened and repackaged in winemaking supply shops that you run into problems, as the corks can dry out, be exposed to microbes, and collect dust.

In the home-winemaking world, however, debate centers on how to treat corks before they're fed into the hand corker and forced down the neck of a bottle. I think the whole boiling and soaking routine is a holdover from the old days of winemaking. Back then, corks were not very pliant and had to be softened by heat. In addition, the water acted as a lubricant to help the corks get into the bottle. In those days, corks were not very clean to begin with, so boiling was also an attempt at sanitation.

Natural corks today have a coating comprised of silicone and paraffin wax. This coating helps protect the cork somewhat, but most important, the paraffin provides the corks with a little tackiness (as in stickiness, rather than fake pink flamingos) so that the inserted cork doesn't slip all the way down into the neck of the bottle.

These newer corks are a breeze to use if you have a good hand corker. If you do find that you need to soften them or use a little added lubrication, make a sulfite solution and soak them for 15–20 minutes. (See box on page 54 for recipe.)

Common cork types

Q What is "cork taint" or "corked" wine, and what does it smell like?

A "Corkiness" is an aromatic defect in bottled wines caused by molds (related to the ones that make penicillin) that reside in the bark of cork trees. Even after cork is harvested, processed, and shipped, it can still contain a high concentration of these little guys. If the molds come into contact with chlorine anytime during the winemaking process (either through use of chlorine-containing cleaning compounds, which you should never use, or more passively through chlorinated city or county water supplies), they crank out a stinky compound called 2,4,6-trichloroanisole. Most people can detect chloroanisoles at extremely low thresholds (in the parts per trillion range) and classify the smell as "swampy," "moldy," or "mildewy."

■ ════════ ■

Q What are the best ways to prevent cork taint?

A There are several simple things you can do to avoid cork taint.

♦ **Pay attention to detail** when purchasing, storing, and using corks. Buy your corks from a dealer with a high turnover rate. Store them in a cool, dark, dry place, and never open the bag until you are ready to cork your wine.

- **Never use chlorine** to sanitize anything that comes into direct contact with your wine. Chlorine helps activate the formation of trichloroanisole, which creates the musty odors on natural cork, so keep chlorine compounds away from siphon hoses, bottling equipment, fermenters, and the like.
- **Consider testing your water supply** for chlorine and use filters to remove it before you use any tap water in winemaking.
- **Alternatively, use synthetic corks.** Since they are not made from a living substance, synthetic corks are free of mold issues. They come in the same sizes and shapes as natural corks, and you can use the same bottling equipment and corkers as you do with natural corks.

Q **What are the advantages and disadvantages of different kinds of closures such as natural and synthetic corks, screw caps, and others?**

A The principle of natural and synthetic corks is the same — a plug of compressible material is squeezed into a tight cylinder and forced into the neck of the bottle. The expansion of the cork, which ideally fits perfectly tight and uniformly snug against the bottle neck, causes an elastic-static seal that should keep wine from evaporating out and air from getting in.

It is a common misconception that wine needs a natural cork so that it can "breathe" during the aging process. The vast majority of the chemical reactions that take place to develop a wine's "bottle bouquet," as well as the changed textures we associate with properly aged wine, are reductive reactions that take place in the absence of oxygen. The final "dose" of oxygen a wine needs is received during the bottling process. Any air that sneaks into the bottle after it is corked causes the wine inside to prematurely oxidize well beyond what is needed for balanced bottle aging.

The closure debate that is currently raging in the wine industry seems to come down to six of one or half a dozen of another — natural corks often have better compression and expansion behavior than synthetics, but natural corks are prone to cork taint. Synthetic corks are becoming more and more popular as commercial and home winemakers alike seek to avoid the 5–15 percent of bottles that can be ruined due to cork taint. Unfortunately, some synthetic corks actually leak worse than traditional wine corks; they also can be tough to insert and can form imperfect seals, leading to loss of free SO_2 during aging and higher rates of premature oxidation.

Many wineries are switching to screw caps, which have none of the above-mentioned problems of corks. In fact, screw caps are considered by many to be the perfect wine-bottle closure in technical terms, but a perceived lack of "tradition" or "romance" keeps many commercial wineries from switching over completely.

For home winemaking, I think we should all take a page out of our home-brewing beer buddies' book. Why not try crown caps? The greatest Champagne houses in France lay their delicate, effervescent, and expensive product down for the aging and riddling process in bottles topped not with the familiar mushroom-cap cork but with the same kind of workaday crown cap we pop off a bottle of homebrew. They only finish the bottle with a cork before sending it out the door for sale.

■ ══════ ■

Q Are there set rules or guidelines for what bottle shapes and colors traditionally go with what wine styles?

A The bottle conventions followed by many commercial wineries owe more to tradition than scientific reason. The distinctive bottle shapes French winemakers chose for their regional products centuries ago continue to be associated with their place of origin. Today, though, the French buy their wine bottles from international glass suppliers along with everyone else.

There are four main bottle shapes in North America that are named for the types of wine that have traditionally been put in them. The two most widely used are the Burgundy and Bordeaux styles, followed by Hock- and Champagne-type bottles.

Burgundy   *Bordeaux*   *Champagne*   *Hock*

The Burgundy bottle shape has pronounced but sloped shoulders. One usually finds Chardonnay and Pinot Noir (the classic varietals of Burgundy) bottled in this shape. It is also being used increasingly for Syrah, Viognier, Pinot Blanc, and other popular grape types. The color traditionally associated with this bottle shape is called "dead-leaf green." When empty, the bottle displays an olive-gold green hue, though many wineries are experimenting with other colors for this glass shape. I've seen a Pinot Noir rosé bottled in a clear (called "flint" in the industry) Burgundy bottle to show off the lurid pink color of the wine.

A Bordeaux bottle is the familiar tall type with pronounced shoulders in which most Napa Valley Cabernet Sauvignons or Bordeaux-type blends are bottled. For reds, the glass color is a dark forest or antique green. White wines (Sauvignon Blanc is one of the famous white-grape types of Bordeaux) are often bottled in flint glass.

The Champagne bottle is the familiar heavy-bottomed, thick-lipped, dark-green bottle used for the world-famous beverage. The Champagne bottle shape is the only one that has a compelling scientific justification behind it. The thicker glass and high punt (the indentation on the bottom of the bottle) make it structurally sound enough to withstand the 5 atmospheres of pressure usually present in Champagne or sparkling wine.

The Hock bottle is often used for sweet or dessert wines. Hock is an old name for German wine, specifically from the Rhine Valley area. After the 1600s, when Germany figured out that the aromatic and acidic Riesling grew particularly well in this region, Hock became synonymous with a Riesling-based sweet wine. Though now obsolete for describing wine, the term still refers to the traditional container. The Hock bottle is much taller than it is wide and has a consistent, nearly triangular slope from the bottle lip all the way down to the base. The glass color is usually antique green or brown, but lurid hues of bright green and blue are also considered traditional for this shape.

Modern home and commercial winemakers, however, are no longer limited to these traditional bottle shapes. The ones mentioned were the only options available to the wine producers of each winemaking region, but that was two centuries ago!

A Wine by Any Other Name

Referring to a wine as "Burgundy" or "Bordeaux" is appropriate only when the wine itself is actually from those regions in France. Thus, calling a wine from California "California Burgundy" is not only a misnomer but is, in fact, internationally illegal. However, I have yet to hear any complaint about using French wine-growing regions in describing bottle types.

Q **Do flange-top bottles serve any useful purpose or are they an affectation on the part of wineries?**

A Ah, yes, the beloved flange tops. These are the bottles that look normal except for an extra lip of glass about the size of a metal washer on top. The corks are set inside the bottle neck, just below the glass lip. Rather than being dressed a capsule like most wine bottles, they are topped with a little disc of plastic or wax.

The usual justification is that the top helps you pour the wine without dripping down the side of the bottle, but I frankly think it's just one more packaging trend like neon-colored synthetic corks.

Flange-top bottle

Add in the fact that thrifty and environmentally conscious winemakers can't reuse these kinds of bottles very easily, and there's very little to recommend them. Myself, I'm not a fan.

■ ══════ ■

Q What is the proper way to wash and sanitize wine bottles?

A You might be surprised to learn that most commercial wineries don't actually wash or sanitize their bottles before filling them. At most, when the empties are dumped from the glass company's case box onto the conveyor belt, the bottles are automatically turned upside down and receive a quick blast of nitrogen or carbon dioxide, mostly to blow out any little pieces of debris that may have fallen into the bottle during the manufacturing process.

Most wineries, however, use brand-new bottles, not recycled ones as many home winemakers do. Recycling bottles is a practical and thrifty idea, especially for home winemakers. It's cheaper, easier, and obviously better for the environment to recycle wine bottles year after year, but of course, those bottles must be thoroughly cleaned before they are used. If possible, use nonchlorinated water; chlorine can contribute to corkiness during aging. (See What are the best ways to prevent cork taint?, page 235.)

Here is a scaled-down bottle-washing scheme.

1. Rinse immediately upon emptying and hang upside down to dry.
2. Cover and store in a clean, dry place.
3. Rinse out twice with unchlorinated water, making sure to shake water around in the bottles to remove dust.
4. Rinse with a sulfite solution.
5. Rinse with clean water and drip-dry.
6. Bottle away!

■ ══════════ ■

Q Do corks have to go completely in the bottle, and if so, how do I get them there?

A No, the cork doesn't need to be all the way into the bottle in order to form a sufficient protective seal. However, the less cork you have inside the bottle, the greater the chance that the seal will become ineffective with time. After a few hours on a hot day in the trunk of the car, the cork could pop all the way out due to the expansion of the liquid inside the bottle.

If you want to try to force the corks back into the bottle by hand, then you can certainly try that, but some corks just won't go in. If you want to bottle your wine well and not worry about it while it's aging, it's best to use a good hand corker and insert the whole cork into the bottle neck.

Advice on Corkers

Save your shoulders some wear and tear and rent a floor-standing corker rather than try to mess about with an awkward hand corker. The floor-mounted models are sturdier and do the job much faster. They often can be rented at winemaking or brewing supply stores; I even know of a few winemaking clubs that have bought a corker for all of the members to use.

Q **What causes bottles to leak even if they seem to be properly corked? Is there a way to stop a bottle from leaking?**

A Corks leak when the seal between the cork and neck of the bottle isn't complete. Interestingly, glass is classified chemically as a liquid, even though we think of it as a pretty solid material. I've inspected many truckloads of wine bottles from many different manufacturers, and it's not unusual to find bottles that are out of round or slightly squashed on one side. I once had to send back an entire truckload of bottles because one out of every ten was so football-shaped it wouldn't even take the label properly! Add the fact that synthetic corks often have a harder time than natural corks re-expanding into an imperfect space, and the chance of leakage may increase.

Is there a way to stop up a leaky bottle? Extracting the cork and recorking the bottle with a new one may help, but if the problem is with the bottle shape, there's not much you can do other than decant the wine into a different bottle and recork it. Or you could just drink it!

■ ══════════ ■

Q Where can a small winery buy corks for larger-format bottles?

A As lovely as these 3 L (101 ounce) bottles are, it can be a problem finding appropriate corks for a neck that size. Luckily, most glass suppliers to the wine industry are

Standard bottle sizes

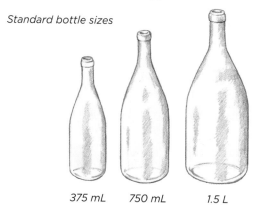

375 mL   *750 mL*   *1.5 L*

familiar with these bottle sizes and will usually ship large corks, even in small batches of 20–50.

My advice is to speak to the proprietors of a friendly home winemaking shop or even a homebrew shop, as they frequently stock winemaking supplies. They should have a cork supplier they work with and may be able to arrange a special order for you. Working with a retailer might actually save you money because you could piggyback your request on a larger order. You might even get better-quality corks if the company ships your local retailer a fresh, sealed bag for that large order. Sometimes, even in the commercial winery sphere, if you're an individual with a small order, cork companies will just send you a few loose corks in a cardboard box, completely open to the ambient air!

Large-format corks are a bit of a rarity and are not produced as often as the standard-bottle cork sizes. Because there is little demand, even in the world of commercial winemaking, large corks are often stored for longer periods of time and under less-than-ideal conditions, sometimes in partial bags that have been opened for a small order. This being the case, it's rather tough to tell how old (and therefore how dried out) a cork is. The drier the cork, the more difficulty you'll have compressing it into the bottle neck and the harder it will be for the cork to expand back into the neck. As you can imagine, old, dried-out corks can lead to bottle leakage or contribute to premature oxidation.

That being said, there's no reason you shouldn't bottle your wine in large bottles, especially if you've got the kind of wine that people would be drinking in a year's time anyway. Just be aware that cork closures have their limitations and corks for larger-format bottles are even more limited. If you can't get a piggyback order for your few large corks through a local winemaking supply shop, I suggest you try calling some of the folks who supply corks to the industry. They might not be willing to sell you only one or two corks, but it is certainly worth a shot.

Q **How do I add a wax coating to a finished bottle of wine?**

A There's nothing that gives a bottle that swashbuckling air so much as a drippy, waxy, melted seal. Luckily, it's easy to do. Once you find the right kind of wax, that is. Some folks use beeswax, but I find that the smell is a little too much for me. Beeswax can also be very soft and it comes off the bottle too easily. Candle wax looks too much like candle wax, and paraffin is out of the question. Happily, many winemaking supply retailers carry the correct kind of wax in a variety of colors.

Here is the technique I use.

1. Melt the wax blocks in a small, deep saucepan, or save your saucepan and use a coffee can, on top of your stove over medium heat. Melting can take a long time, close to two hours. Covering the pan helps the wax

melt more quickly. Do not try using a higher setting! (Another heating alternative is a store-bought home deep fryer. It'll get hot enough to do the job, will heat evenly from all sides, and will not cause a fire if used properly.)

2. Make sure the corks are completely flush with the lip of the bottle (so no air bubbles will be trapped underneath) and dip the neck of your bottles in as far as you like. For a 750 mL size, I like to cover the cork and go about half an inch more.

3. Take the bottle out of the wax and let it dribble down the sides as it cools. It will cool relatively quickly, so re-dip if you're not getting enough dripping to suit your tastes. As with anything new, it always helps to practice a few times on some old, recycled wine bottles before trying it with your real product.

Beware of Hot Wax

This is hot wax you're working with and it can hurt you if it comes in contact with your skin. These waxes work so well for bottles specifically because they have a higher melting point than most other waxes. Some of these waxes are also flammable. Please check with the manufacturer, as using a gas stove to do this might be asking for trouble.

CHAPTER 9

Smelly Wine and Other Tough Problems

Q What can impart a vinegar taste to finished wine?

A Sounds like an attack of your friend and mine, the acetic acid bacteria, or *Acetobacter*. Unfortunately, if you've got a lot of vinegar, or acetic acid, present in your wine, there's not much you can do about it other than attempt to blend it out by dilution with wine of a similar quality. (See chapter 8 for more on blending.) While some companies in the wine industry offer a "filtration" service, in which the acetic acid is removed by reverse osmosis, this process is prohibitively expensive for small-scale producers.

There are quite a few things that you can do in the future, however, to lessen the chance that *Acetobacter* species will threaten subsequent batches. It helps to understand a little bit about what you're up against. These bacteria live in wineries, on the equipment and in the air. In fact, you're probably breathing in some right now. Unfortunately, when these little guys come in contact with wine and oxygen, they produce acetic acid, the stuff that creates that vinegary smell and taste. Even the best of us come up against *Acetobacter* once in a while.

Unclean equipment can be a contributing factor, although it is very difficult to ever entirely eradicate bacteria from the winemaking environment. All we can do is find ways to live with them while keeping them in their place. Acetic acid bacteria need the following things to survive: oxygen, a hospitable environment, and a food source. The following guidelines should help reduce the chances that *Acetobacter* will find, infect, survive in, breed in, and make acetic acid in your wines.

- Keep equipment scrupulously clean at all times.
- Keep containers as full as possible, as acetic acid bacteria thrive in half-empty containers with plenty of air.
- If there must be headspace in a barrel or carboy, blanket the surface of the liquid with carbon dioxide or nitrogen gas, if available.
- Keep pH as low as your style will allow to inhibit microbes.
- Use sulfur dioxide as an antimicrobial agent, keeping free SO_2 between 20 and 35 mg/L, depending on the pH. Higher-pH wines need more free SO_2 in order to inhibit bacteria.
- Store your wines in a cool, dry area. Lower temperatures and dry air discourage not only acetic acid bacteria but molds and fungi as well.
- Watch wines that have low alcohol levels (less than 10 percent). Alcohol acts as an antimicrobial agent to some extent, and wines with low alcohol levels are especially susceptible to attack by bacteria.
- Keep finished wine, or wine that has just finished fermentation, especially clean and topped up. They are extremely vulnerable to *Acetobacter* attack since the protective layer of carbon dioxide produced during fermentation is no longer present.

- Immediately clean up spills wherever they occur, and keep the tops of barrels, carboys, and fermenters especially clean and free of residue. *Acetobacter* are often transmitted by insects like fruit flies, so don't provide them with a chance to thrive in your winery.

■ ══════ ■

What can I do with finished red wine that has a yeasty taste?

Yeasty, toasty overtones are often a part of the early red winemaking process and will sometimes go away with time. I wouldn't necessarily see a yeasty aroma as a defect — it certainly isn't one of the classic spoilage aromas like hydrogen sulfide (rotten eggs). However, if you don't like it, there are some things you can do to avoid it next time you make wine.

Using riper fruit, which ensures that you get lots of aromatic goodies in the fermentation, will help your finished wine have a fully developed nose and flavor, diminishing the über-yeasty quality of the bouquet. It's also possible that you're confusing a yeasty smell with the buttery smell of a complete malolactic fermentation caused by diacetyl.

If your wine is already bottled, there's not much you can do about it. I would try letting it age a little more and see if the aroma changes with time. Chances are that it will. If your wine is still in its bulk storage container, you can always try blending it with a wine of similar quality that has a less yeasty aroma. Try something with a more fruity character; a big hit of fruit on the nose could go a long way towards masking an overly yeasty bouquet. Though I never advocate blending a loser and dragging down the quality of the wine being blended in, in some cases you will achieve a wine that is better as a blend than its individual components were on their own.

Q What could cause a rosé to turn from pink to an orange color?

A The most common problem associated with pink winemaking is loss of color due to oxidation. All wines experience color changes as they develop and, in the case of red wines, will lose some color over time. As color molecules bind to each other, they fall out of solution as a fine dust at the bottom of the bottle, decreasing the overall color of the wine.

Oxygen present in the wine can also bind to these color compounds, and over time their appearance to the human eye can change from the purple-blue end of the spectrum to the yellow-orange side of the spectrum. This oxidation happens in all wines, but pink wines are particularly susceptible because they have fewer color compounds and the loss is much more noticeable.

To prevent the loss of color, avoid oxygenation in the wine after the primary fermentation is complete. At this time, the natural protective layer of carbon dioxide that forms during fermentation begins to dissipate, leaving the wine more vulnerable to oxidation and subsequent color loss. Because the completion of malolactic fermentation tends to hasten the conversion of color compounds into the red-orange spectrum, I do not recommend taking rosés through this process.

■ ════════ ■

What could cause an aroma and taste of rubber and burnt toast?

Unfortunately wines can contain so many sulfur-containing defect aromas (what you're "tasting" is probably really an aroma) that it's difficult to diagnose a possible cause for your specific situation. Sulfur is a ubiquitous element in wine, present in amino acids, characteristic varietal aromas, and even yeast cells themselves. "Good" sulfur can turn ugly when it gets metabolized or chemically changed in such a way that it turns into a stinky volatile sulfur derivative, the most common of which is hydrogen sulfide. The study of these compounds is an enological field in active evolution, and much research is in progress to try to identify more compounds, determine their causes, and effect practical remedies.

While it's not possible here to delve into the detail this subject entails, I can discuss some of the most common causes of sulfur-derived defects you're likely to come across and, in some cases, can try to control. There are a few that immediately come to mind.

The first is overoaking your wine with darkly toasted chips. This is the most benign diagnosis and the easiest to fix. Before you ever add oak to your wine in levels over 1 g/ L, it's wise to run bench trials to see what level of oakiness you like. Take small samples of your wine and add oak chips at varying rates. Taste the wine and see what level you most enjoy. If this is too involved, play it safe and go with a low rate, below 1 g/L (260 mg/gallon).

To fix a wine that is overoaked, the best course of action is to remove the oak from the wine (if using beans) or rack the wine back into a neutral container and let it sit for about a month. Sometimes a wine, especially a very young one, that displays over-oaked character will bounce back as it ages and as some of the aromatic oak components blow off and/or either bind up into nonaromatic compounds or precipitate out of solution.

If removing the oak doesn't help, the next thing to try would be to blend away a stinky wine with a nonstinky one. Though this goes against one of my cardinal rules of blending, to not blend a loser with good wine, some winemakers actually like a very low concentration of this kind of burnt-toast smell; in low enough doses and in the right wine, it could contribute to aromatic complexity.

The second possibility is the presence of one of the following sulfur-containing spoilage compounds: hydrogen sulfide, disulfides, or thiols. There are numerous potential pathways for these stinky compounds to contaminate your wine. Sulfur spraying in the vineyard too close to the harvest date can create hydrogen sulfide, whereas pesticides that contain thiocarbamic acid can cause smelly dimethyldisulfides and methane thiols.

Yeast can also spit out elemental sulfur in the form of hydrogen sulfide when stressed, so other causes might include insufficient nitrogen levels during fermentation, high fermentation temperatures, low fermentation temperatures, a too-rapid fermentation, or anything that will stress your yeast. Most often, hydrogen sulfide smells like rotten eggs and mercaptan (which can evolve from untreated hydrogen sulfide over time) smells kind of oniony, but I've seen them both develop into burnt-rubber (and burnt-toast when you've got oak in a fermentation) aromas in finished wines. Sometimes an addition of copper sulfate (see page 262 for technique) can help as the copper can bind up some of the offensive compounds.

A more obscure cause of your aroma could be exposure to light. (Some winemakers call this "sunlight flavor" or "sunstruck" aroma.) Ultraviolet light triggers the oxidative photo breakdown of cysteine and especially methionine (sulfur-containing amino acids naturally present in all wines), producing volatile thiols (like dimethyldisulfide) that render a wine completely undrinkable.

White wines are much more light sensitive than reds, as certain seed catechins (present in red wines in much greater concentration) can preferentially absorb UV radiation, essentially protecting the amino acids from breakdown. This is one reason why it's always a good idea to bottle white wines in colored bottles and to store your wines in a dark place.

Commercial wineries that sell white wines in clear bottles are relying on (a) their wines being stored appropriately in transit and at the store and (b) the wines being sold quickly enough to not develop this defect over time. This is another reason why it's never a good idea to buy a bottle of wine that's in someone's shop-front window! Again, a small addition of copper sulfate can sometimes help to deal with this particular aroma.

Since most winemakers don't have access to the laboratory equipment like gas chromatographs or high-performance liquid chromotographs that it would take to identify exactly which smelly sulfur derivative they're dealing with, sometimes we have to try a couple of home remedies as treatment to see what makes an improvement. The following two questions deal with prevention and treatment of wines that smell awful. Do remember that, when it comes to stinky defects in our wines, the old saw about an ounce of prevention really does apply here.

Q What can I do to prevent my wine from smelling like rotten eggs?

A That rotten egg odor is a classic sign of hydrogen sulfide, the bane of winemakers everywhere. Though yeast produce a certain level of hydrogen sulfide (H_2S) in every fermentation (it's a natural by-product of multiple metabolic and chemical pathways), it's no fun when high concentrations of this noxious odor spoil an entire batch of wine.

Perhaps the easiest way to prevent high H_2S levels in fermentation is to not use vineyard sprays that contain elemental sulfur dust, especially within three weeks of harvesting grapes. If even 1 microgram of elemental (unbound and pure) sulfur is present in juice or must, yeast cells can produce enough H_2S to be perceptible. If you buy grapes from someone, ask what they've sprayed the vineyard with, if anything, and when they sprayed.

Another common cause of high levels of H_2S is low available nitrogen during fermentation; yeast will produce perceptible hydrogen sulfide if they are under nutritional stress. Yeast need at least 250 mg/L total nitrogen to conduct a healthy fermentation. Challenging fermentations like high Brix (over 25°) situations may require upward of 300–350 mg/L.

Some yeast strains require more initial nitrogen than others, so refer to the manufacturer's specifications for the particular kind of yeast you're using. Before inoculating, I always adjust the yeast-available nitrogen (YAN) of my must levels to at least 250 mg/L using yeast foods. (You have to send out juice samples to a commercial wine lab in order to measure YAN, which is a total of the free amino nitrogen as well as the ammonia content.)

This will help the yeast get what they need to survive, thrive, and conduct a clean, H_2S-free fermentation. Do be careful not to overfeed fermentations, as any leftover nitrogen sources the yeast don't eat can be food for spoilage organisms like *Brettanomyces* yeast as well as some bacteria.

If you can't measure your nitrogen levels or can't send samples out to a lab, you can always wing it. One technique is to add some diammonium phosphate (DAP), which supplies the must with ammonia to give the yeast a nitrogen source. Try adding 1 g (0.035 ounces) of DAP for every 10 L (2.6 gallons) of wine (keep in mind that 3 pounds of grapes produce about 1 L of wine). Do not add diammonium phosphate after the must drops below 3–5° Brix, as the yeast membranes can no longer take it up due to increasing alcohol toxicity.

It's also a good idea to avoid the yeast strain Montrachet 522, which is a notorious H_2S producer. There are certain types of yeast that are genetically predisposed to generate a lot of hydrogen sulfide during the course of their fermentation. There are also certain yeast strains that produce low amounts.

It's also important to make sure your wine has enough air during active fermentation, as oxygen helps yeast avoid being stressed. Similarly, once the wine is dry, it's usually a good idea for the first racking of a wine, after primary fermentation is complete and the wine is settling down for the first time, to be an aerative one. This helps keep certain sulfur-containing compounds in the wine from changing into stinky versions of themselves or from combining into smelly odors.

Racking a new wine off its heaviest primary lees in the first week after fermentation has stopped is very important because a dense, deep, mucky carpet of lees (in young wine they consist mainly of dead and dying yeast cells) can develop hydrogen sulfide in its interior and can seep up into the wine to ruin the entire batch if not racked soon enough.

■ ══════ ■

Q **Are there ways to treat a wine that smells like rotten eggs?**

A If your wine is still fermenting and the Brix is above 3–5°, add a little diammonium phosphate (about 1 g/10 L) to give the yeast a needed nitrogen boost. If your fermentation is below 3–5° Brix, aerating the juice or must (splash-racking from container to container once or twice) can do the trick. This is because the formation of sulfur-derived off odors, of which hydrogen sulfide is the most common, is essentially a reductive process. Giving the wine oxygen shifts the reactions back the other way, away from the formation of reductive compounds.

If the wine is very young and is still on its primary fermentation lees, it's a good idea to rack it off them, as compacted lees can engender hydrogen sulfide and a wealth of other sulfur-derived odors. The aeration in the racking will help as will getting the dry wine off the lees.

If you stir your container and keep the lees suspended, however (usually by stirring every week), you can attempt to keep your wine on its primary fermentation lees, as one would in the Burgundian-style production of white wines. The key is to not let the lees form a deep, compacted layer at any time.

Lees lose their ability to form reductive compounds over time (it is thought because of the decreasing activity of sulfite reductase), so if you can stir the lees once a week for about the first month or two of a wine's life, you'll probably safely pass through the lees-reduction danger zone. The good thing (if there is any good thing) about hydrogen sulfide is that, early on in a wine's life, it can often be treated and will disappear quickly.

Unfortunately, hydrogen sulfide is harder to get rid of once a wine gets more than a few weeks old. In this case, copper sulfate ($CuSO_4$), a copper-containing salt that is legal to use in small amounts in most countries, can be a winemaker's best friend. See the box on the next page for specific steps in treating your wine with $CuSO_4$. If left untreated, hydrogen sulfide can evolve into mercaptans and disulfides, which can be more difficult to remove with $CuSO_4$.

USING COPPER SULFATE (CuSO₄)

In concentrations higher than those recommended
for use in wine, $CuSO_4$ can be poisonous to humans,
so it should only be used if you can measure it out with
absolute accuracy. $CuSO_4$ — 25.47 percent of which is
copper — is also legal in North America as long as
residual levels don't exceed 0.5 ppm as copper. $CuSO_4$
is available as crystals or liquid (most stores stock a
10 percent, 1 percent, or 0.1 percent solution).

◆ $CuSO_4$ liquid or powder should not be inhaled or
  ingested.
◆ Wear safety goggles and rubber gloves when
  handling.
◆ Store safely away from children and pets!

To see if $CuSO_4$ will help the off smell in your wine
(not all stinky wines will respond), I advise conducting
a quick bench trial with a 0.1 percent $CuSO_4$ solution as
follows. Keep in mind that a $CuSO_4$ solution is only 25.47
percent copper. We are calculating for an end concentration of copper here, not $CuSO_4$ solution.

If you can't buy $CuSO_4$ solution in as low a concentration as 0.1 percent, you can dilute what you've purchased
if you have volumetric pipettes or flasks.

1. Label three glasses: "control," "0.25 mg/L copper,"
   and "0.5 mg/L copper."
2. Measure 100 mL of wine into each glass.

3. Measure out 0.1 mL of 0.1 percent $CuSO_4$ solution into the "0.25 mg/L copper" glass and 0.2 mL of solution into the "0.50 mg/L copper" glass.
4. Swirl each glass, let them sit for about 5 minutes, then smell each. DO NOT TASTE THEM!

If the smell of the wine improves substantially with the "0.25 mg/L copper" glass, you could try to add even less to another test glass to see if you can get the same aroma improvement with less $CuSO_4$. In the case of $CuSO_4$, which can sometimes change the mouthfeel or strip aroma from wine, if you can get away with adding less, do so.

To apply the treatment to the total batch, apply the preferred rate to your volume of wine (for example, if you liked what 0.1 mL/100 mL of a 0.1 percent $CuSO_4$ solution did and you have 10 L of wine, you will need to add 10 mLs of solution). Stir the solution well into your wine and let sit for at least 48 hours before racking off. A slight precipitate is entirely normal.

As each wine is different, there is no one $CuSO_4$ answer for every situation. In some instances, even the "0.50 mg/L copper" level of $CuSO_4$ addition doesn't help a rotten egg wine, in which case your best bet is seeing what time will do for the wine, blending it away, or getting rid of it altogether. This is a depressing prospect for every winemaker, but the reality is that there are some sulfur-derived aromatic defects that just can't be cured, no matter what we try to do.

Q What causes a butter flavor in wine?

A The buttery flavor and aroma that we sometimes experience in a finished wine usually come from a malolactic fermentation by-product called diacetyl that is described as tasting like movie-theater popcorn butter or fresh cream. Though a small amount of diacetyl can be formed by yeast during fermentation, by far the largest appreciable amounts will be produced during malolactic fermentation. Malolactic fermentation occurs when certain species of bacteria (generically known as lactic acid bacteria) eat the naturally occurring malic acid in grape juice, turning it into lactic acid.

I refer to diacetyl as a by-product because the winemaking goal of encouraging malolactic fermentation typically is to reduce the total acid content slightly (malic acid is twice as acidic as lactic acid) and to render the wine free of malic acid, which could be a later food source for any bacteria that happened to be in the wine after it is bottled.

Encouraging a wine to go through malolactic fermentation (sometimes called the "secondary fermentation") is up to the winemaker. Many winemakers choose instead to inhibit malolactic fermentation (by adding SO_2 or filtering to remove the bacteria) for stylistic reasons. Many wines, especially crisp, acidic whites like Riesling, Pinot Grigio, and Sauvignon Blanc, are better if they maintain their natural acidity levels. These wines, many wine judges might argue, would similarly be worse off for expressing a buttery, diacetyl aroma.

What can you do if you've got an overly buttery wine? There aren't any treatments that erase this character once it's in a wine, so this is definitely a case where blending is really the only option. If you can cut the buttery wine with something of similar quality that isn't showing a lot of diacetyl character, you might find a good balance.

It should also be noted that adding toasted oak chips to a buttery wine or storing it in new oak barrels can reinforce and even amplify the perception of diacetyl by contributing creamy, vanilla, or *dulce de leche* aromas. A small amount of diacetyl can add complexity to a wine, especially to full-bodied reds, but too much can certainly be overpowering. (See page 169 for more on malolactic fermentation.)

Q **What can cause a sediment like fine sand to appear in a wine?**

A This is a case of the common "tartrate fallouts." The sediment you're seeing is probably tartrate crystals (potassium bitartrate salt). This happens to the best winemakers in the world (you know, the folks who get $150 per bottle); it's entirely natural and to be expected, so you don't have to worry about trying to correct it if it doesn't bother you too much.

Grapes are naturally high in tartaric acid. Finished wines are full of dissolved tartaric acid, which helps them maintain the "pucker" and the refreshing "zing" that so many of us enjoy in red and white wines alike. Tartaric acid is often added before a nongrape wine is fermented because sometimes the fruit used to make other types of wines doesn't have enough natural acid.

Temperature changes, blending, additions like bentonite, or movement during bottling and filtering can change the delicate dynamics of a wine so that some of the dissolved acid actually crystallizes into a solid. Once the particles become large and heavy enough, they fall to the bottom of the bottle, where they look like fine sand or, if there is a lot of tartaric acid and it forms especially large crystals, shards of broken glass.

The variables that determine how many tartrate crystals a wine will throw in its lifetime are multifold and hard to fully understand. In wines with high tartaric acid content, low temperature, and high ethanol content, you'll generally see more tartrates falling out over a long period of time. This means that the potassium bitartrate is not soluble in the wine.

Since time and temperature are the two easiest parameters to control for the home winemaker, storing a wine at the lowest temperature possible (above the freezing point) for as long as possible (say, a month) will force out the greatest amount of crystals. Follow this homemade "cold stabilization" by siphoning the wine off the sediment and you'll be able to bottle a wine that will throw a minimum of sediment in the future. (See page 205 for more on cold stabilization.)

This is a pretty benign problem that winemakers have been dealing with ever since wine was first made from grapes. The crystals are tasteless, odorless, and will do you no harm if you happen to swallow them. (See the next question for more on tartrate precipitation.)

■ ———————— ■

Q How can I best rid my wine of tartrate crystals?

A Temperature changes, especially cooling (like putting your leftover wine into the fridge overnight), seem to be the main culprit in precipitating tartrate crystals. The cold temperatures shift the chemical equilibrium of the wine's potassium bitartrate salts from being soluble to forming solid crystals that, when large enough, fall to the bottom of the bottle, where they look like fine grains of sand or tiny pieces of glass.

Commercial wineries (to avoid consumer complaints as well as to make the product look nice on the shelves) force this precipitation to happen before bottling by preemptively chilling and then filtering their wine. After being held at around 35°F (1.7°C) for 24–48 hours, sometimes with seed crystals of potassium bitartrate mixed in to help accelerate the process, the wine is then filtered at the 0.45-micron level (or 0.45 "nominal") to remove the crystals. The treated wine is then bottled and sent to market with a significantly reduced likelihood that it will throw a potassium bitartrate precipitate while sitting in someone's fridge at home.

Unfortunately, home winemakers don't usually have the industrial chilling systems and the filters needed to effect a proper cold stabilization. Fortunately, potassium bitartrate crystals are a purely cosmetic issue that small-scale and home winemakers don't need to lose sleep over. Potassium bitartrate precipitation doesn't significantly affect a wine's aroma, color, taste, flavor profile, or even its ageability, so cold stabilization not a necessary step.

If you still are worried about the crystals you have and those that might crop up in the future, I can offer a scaled-down cold stabilization of sorts, though it's really only a distant approximation. By at least chilling the wine down as close to 35°F (2°C) as possible and for as long as practical for your individual situation, you'll most likely accelerate whatever possibility of precipitation your wine may have. And by subsequently filtering, you'll be able to remove whatever crystals have been formed (if any — some wines don't make them).

How best to get a batch of wine cooled down? It depends on your individual situation and how much wine you're dealing with. I've heard of northern-dwelling winemakers who leave their barrels out in an uninsulated garage all winter, utilizing the months-long time line coupled with low temperatures. If you make supersmall batches and only have one or two 1-gallon jugs, you could try keeping them in the fridge for a few weeks.

Keep in mind that your storage container itself may not like supercold temperatures. I for one would be wary of exposing my oak barrels, not to mention my wine, to outside temperatures that fluctuate daily, as big swings in temperature are to be avoided during long-term aging. As long as you carefully filter the wine off of any sediment that has formed, you will reduce the amount of crystals that the wine will form in the future.

Even a proper commercial cold stabilization procedure won't guarantee against future tartrate crystal precipitation, and a homegrown cold stabilization is less likely to. Since cold stabilization is a purely elective step done for cosmetic reasons by larger wineries, I would argue that unless you've got a wine that is really pumping out an unsightly precipitate, it's best to just dispense with a cold stabilization step altogether.

■ ═══════ ■

Q How can I cut down on sediment after the batch is bottled?

A It sounds as though you bottled your wine a little too early, before it had a chance to move completely through its unsettled or "adolescent" phase and fall bright.

Unfortunately, once your wine is bottled, there's not much you can do with it unless you want to uncork all the bottles, pour them back into an aging container, and let the wine settle out. This is ill-advised because you'll be exposing your wine to oxygen and bacteria; you're probably better off letting the wine stay where it is and decanting it carefully before drinking.

You can, however, try to prevent this from happening next time. Home winemakers are more likely than commercial winemakers to experience sediment in their bottled wines. This is due to a number of possibilities, some of which are outlined here.

Use of nongrape fruits. If you are using fruit other than grapes, hazes or sediments may occur at seemingly strange points in the winemaking schedule. It's usually not just a question of acidity, pH, or oxidation; some fruit simply doesn't lend itself to winemaking without a lot of human intervention. I suggest using pectic enzymes to break up some of the long-chain carbohydrate compounds that can mess up a nongrape wine's stability. Fruits like apples and pears are rich in pectin; they often throw pectin hazes during aging and in the bottle.

Protein instabilities. All wines contain at least a little protein, which can manifest itself in the form of a fluffy flocculated sediment or just a slight haze in the wine. Add bentonite at a rate of 2–4 g/gallon (500–1,000 mg/L) to help pull out proteins, let settle, and rack the clear wine off before bottling.

Microbial instabilities. Be aware of microbial contamination at every step of the winemaking process and your wine will be healthier and throw less sediment. If you want to invest in a filtration rig (or persuade some friends to buy one together) and filter your wine before bottling with 0.45-micron membranes or with 0.45 "nominal" pads, you can greatly reduce your chances of having microbial issues (and their associated sediments) in the bottle. Microbes living in bottled products are almost always going to cause some haze or flocculation.

Tartrate precipitation. The sediment you're observing could be sandlike tartrate crystals (potassium bitartrate salt). (See previous two questions for more detail.)

Racking regimes. Most commercial wines are racked at least three or four times during the production process and then are aged in barrels or tanks for at least 6 months before bottling.

Aging conditions. Home winemakers often store their wine in garages, basements, and other areas where it can be difficult to control the temperature. Make sure your wines are not subject to large temperature swings to minimize tannins and other compounds from changing chemically and ending up as sediment.

Lack of patience. Pros, especially those that have years working with the same vineyard under their belt, know that they have to wait at least 18 months before even attempting to bottle up a supertannic Alexander Valley Cabernet Sauvignon. It's hard for home winemakers, especially those who are just starting out and may be unfamiliar with their raw material, to anticipate just how much time a wine may need to totally settle out in its bulk aging container before bottling. And sometimes it's just so hard to resist bottling a batch up and handing it out for Christmas gifts!

■ ══════════ ■

Q What can cause an oily film to form on top of a dry wine in storage?

A It sounds like an infection of film yeast, which, before the population gets too high and more noticeable, often manifests itself as an oily plaque on the surface. These heterogeneous populations of yeast (undoubtedly with some bacteria mixed in) are aerophilic and therefore live on top of the surface of wine in storage containers where there is air in the headspace. Though the wine may smell and taste fine at the time, film yeast, if allowed to grow, can contribute spoilage aromas and flavors in finished wine, especially if they are allowed continued access to oxygen.

Luckily film yeast are relatively easy to control. Your two best weapons are fully topped-up containers and adequate sulfur dioxide levels. Depending on the pH of the wine and the time until bottling, most winemakers agree that during storage, red wines need 25–30 mg/L of free SO_2. Because the antimicrobial and antioxidant properties of SO_2 are pH-dependent, higher-pH wines need higher levels of free SO_2

to stay healthy. Most microbes, especially bacteria but also yeast, tend to thrive at a higher pH.

Once you've got a film yeast infection in your wine, it's impossible to completely remove it without filtration and moving to another, clean container. If you don't have a filter, however, you can knock down the yeast population quite a bit by following these steps.

1. Try to carefully skim the surface of the wine to remove the film, if you can.

2. Adjust the free SO_2 levels in the container. You may want to go a bit higher than you normally would for this addition, perhaps up to 40 mg/L free SO_2 if your usual is 30 mg/L.

3. Top that container as full as you can. This will severely reduce the wine's exposure to oxygen, which is what caused the yeast to thrive in the first place.

Some winemakers will even go so far as to fill a spray bottle with a 10 g/L potassium metabisulfite solution (wear a respirator mask when handling) and pump a few squirts twice a week on the surface of the wine. I've heard anecdotally that this does keep the film from re-forming, even if it's just on that 1-inch square in a carboy's neck.

The good news is that the film won't reappear when the wine is bottled, provided that the closure provides a good seal. Remember, however, that prevention, in the form of keeping containers topped up and maintaining adequate free SO_2 levels, is always easier than intervening farther down the road.

Q What could cause an acetone off odor in a finished wine?

A The odor you're smelling is probably acetaldehyde, the most common aldehyde compound found in wine. Acetaldehyde results when ethanol (alcohol) is oxidized by yeast or, more commonly, bacteria. The odor you notice is usually caused by a high bacterial population coupled with an oxidative environment and, as such, often occurs in wine left untopped in the cellar.

It also can be caused by high temperatures during fermentation. Temperatures higher than, say, 90°F (32°C) place stress on the yeast cells, which may then produce a solventlike aroma. This odor tends to be less apparent when the wine is very young, but may reassert itself when the wine has had a chance for its newly fermented character to mellow out in the bottle.

If you want to try to fix the smell, there's a chance that adding sulfur dioxide will help; add it as long as your wine is dry and finished with primary as well as malolactic fermentation (if desired for your wine). Keep in mind how much SO_2 you've already added to this wine. High levels of SO_2 (the legal limit in most countries is around 300 mg/L total sulfur dioxide) can usually be picked up in the aroma of a wine, and you may like that less than the acetaldehyde.

If you don't want to add any more SO_2 to your wine, you can try to blend it with another wine of similar quality without the strong acetaldehyde aroma. Though I never advise throwing perfectly good wine after a bad one, some wine-makers feel that a little acetaldehyde, like a teeny bit of acetic acid, can actually add complexity to a wine. I caution against trying to eliminate what's normally seen as a spoilage character in a wine, but you should know that there are options for dealing with excess acetaldehyde in your wine, as long as there isn't so much that adding sulfur dioxide or blending with another wine doesn't help.

■ ══════════ ■

Q Can I save a finished, bottled wine that ends up very flat?

A I'm assuming that by "flat" you mean a taste that is unexciting and uninspiring, in which case the culprit is usually a lack of acidity. Happily, we can adjust acid levels to get them in a good range for our wine style. This is best done in the juice or must stage, before fermentation, when the added acid (usually people add tartaric acid) has a chance to assimilate and harmonize during the fermentation.

The last thing you want to do, however, is to mess with wine that's already in the bottle; once a wine is in the bottle, it's as though you've closed the door on its early development. Upon going into the bottle, a wine should have all of the chemical underpinnings like alcohol, acid, and tannin to see it through its bottle-aging stage. My spouse, a photographer, relates bottling wine to developing a roll of film. Once you develop that negative, you can touch up the print, but the essential character of what the photo can be is already solidified. It's almost impossible (and usually inadvisable) to try to turn back the clock.

If you really are unhappy with your bottled product and consider it undrinkable, before you start throwing good wine after bad, you may just want to scrap this batch and start over. However, if you think that your "flat" wine could be a good blend base but just needs a little perking up, you could try blending some of your other wines in with it, one that has what you think your base wine lacks.

Though one of my cardinal rules is "never blend a loser," if you truly think your bottled product is worth saving, finding a missing puzzle piece from your cellar stock could work. Whenever you blend, take into account that unforeseen instabilities or refermentations may crop up. If the added wine has perceptible residual sugar, for example, you may start a refermentation. After blending, be sure to adjust your free SO_2 levels, filter if necessary (if you have the equipment), and rebottle. (See chapter 8 for more questions on blending.)

Before making any major blending decisions, do some test blends. With graduated cylinders or volumetric pipettes, measure out different quantities of each wine, blend them together, let them sit in covered glasses overnight (plastic wrap works just fine), and taste them the next day. The idea is to discover what proportions work best in terms of taste and logic for the amount of wine you have on hand.

A hint for noncommercial producers that is perhaps a bit unorthodox but that can work wonders is to purchase a bottle or two of good wine to blend with the flat wine. This way you won't have to dip into your precious homemade stock, you have a multitude of choices, and you might be impressed with what a few percentage points of great wine can do to perk up a lot of mediocre (or flat) wine.

This little trick is illegal if you're selling your wine in the marketplace and it really should be a last-ditch effort, as it degrades the natural authenticity of your wine.

My most important bit of advice is to keep careful wine-making notes so that you know what works, what doesn't, and how to avoid mishaps in the future.

■ ━━━━━ ■

Q What can make a wine fizzy?

A First of all, you need to make sure that the initial fermentation is actually finished.

Because hydrometers have a difficult time measuring minute amounts of residual sugar, an even better way for home winemakers to check residual sugar levels is to send samples out to a wine lab for enzymatic analysis. A simpler method is to buy the Clinitest tablets that diabetics use to detect sugar in their urine. To do the test, you simply drop a tablet into a sample of wine. The wine will change color, and you compare the color against the chart provided in the kit.

Note: Never put your tablet-treated wine sample back into the mother batch. The chemicals that produce the color change are toxic and should not be ingested. Dispose of each sample after use.

In addition to incomplete fermentation, there are several other possible causes of fizziness.

Refermentation is likely if you've blended in a wine that's not completely dry itself or have topped up with a sweet wine. This scenario can happen with red, white, or rosé wines and is not necessarily a bad thing, if planned for and handled in a controlled manner. In fact, refermentation is what puts the sparkle in sparkling wines.

The process occurs when the wine has not gone completely dry and residual yeast (or ambient yeast picked up during a racking or filtration) wake up and ferment what's left, creating the fizziness you've experienced. If you bottle the wine with a small percentage of residual sugar and use crown caps, like the caps on a beer bottle, then you capture the carbon dioxide in the bottle — as opposed to having it dissipate through a carboy's airlock. With the right base wine, and with a carefully measured percentage of residual sugar, this extra fizz can make a ho-hum wine sizzle.

Malolactic bacteria can release carbon dioxide even in a dry wine. Malolactic bacteria float around freely in the air we breathe; even though you didn't inoculate for them, they can land in your wine and begin munching on the malic acid there. Many winemakers actively encourage this secondary fermentation because of stylistic reasons (it can round out the mouthfeel and produce buttery aromas some find pleasing) or because it stabilizes the wine for bottling by preempting any bugs that might attack the residual malic acid when the wine is in the bottle.

Not all winemakers want their wines to go through malolactic fermentation, however, and use sulfur dioxide, usually administered in the form of potassium metabisulfite, to inhibit it. Maintaining levels of free SO_2 around 25–30 mg/L (depending on the pH — some high-pH wines need higher levels) will help keep malolactic fermentation under control if it is not desired.

Nonmalolactic bacteria can also cause fizziness and spritziness. If you know your wine is bone-dry, has gone through MLF, and is sulfited but is still spritzy, you may have other spoilage organisms in your wine. The possible culprits include *Brettanomyces* (a yeast that can survive in dry wines and often lives on nonfermentable 5-carbon sugars like those found in oak) or certain strains of *Oenococcus* or *Lactobacillus*.

The only way to remove many of these organisms from your wine is to perform a 0.45-micron filtration. These filters are increasingly available for the small-scale winemaker.

An ounce of prevention is worth a pound of cure. Rather than performing a major intervention by filtering infected wine that may be irreparably spoiled and need to be dumped anyway, follow these steps to avoid unwanted fizziness.

◆ Practice good sanitation.

◆ Inoculate your wine with yeast (and malolactic bacteria, if used) strains appropriate for your must and juice.

◆ Exclude oxygen and ambient microbes from your finished wine.

◆ Maintain adequate levels of free SO_2.

Q How can I improve the color of my reds?

A The most important factor is making sure your fruit is ripe. Most reds reach optimum color around 24–26° Brix. Overripe fruit, however, doesn't help color. If you let the clusters hang too long, some of the color-containing compounds start to degrade. Once you are sure the color is as developed as it can be on the vine, do your best to build up and then keep that color in the finished wine.

Tannins, when coupled with oxygen during fermentation, help stabilize the color compounds (that's why it's a good thing to aerate your must). For a low-tannin varietal like Pinot Noir or Nebbiolo, a favorite trick of mine is to ferment on 1–2 g/L oak beans or chips. The added tannin helps to boost and stabilize the color, while the extra heat from the fermentation means you're getting the most out of the chips.

Another option worth considering is adding maceration enzymes formulated to promote color extraction and stability.

■ ━━━━━━━ ■

What can I do with a wine that ends up too high in alcohol?

Blending with a lower-alcohol wine is really the best option for home and small-scale winemakers as long as the wine you're adding makes sense for stability, balance, and your winemaking style. However, if you don't have enough suitable wine to lower the alcohol to a point you like, try making it into a dessert wine. Home winemakers can apply the following remedy.

When faced with something like a 17 percent alcohol monstrosity, I would sweeten, fortify, soak a cheesecloth "tea bag" of herbs and spices in the batch, and maybe acidify with tartaric acid to taste. You might try sweetening the wine with grape juice and then punching it up with some orange peel, dried cranberries, and a little cinnamon. Let the wine sit in a small oak cask until it falls bright and then bottle it up! Just make sure that you hone your picking call next time and measure your juice or must well before you pitch your yeast.

Of course, commercial wineries have all sorts of high-tech (and highly expensive) ways to remove alcohol at their fingertips, like reverse osmosis or distillation, but doing these kinds of treatments only makes sense if you need to adjust thousands of gallons of wine. For small-scale producers, it's always better to adjust alcohol in the field or in the fermenter by not picking overripe fruit in the first place and by adjusting alcohol to appropriate levels with water before fermentation.

CHAPTER 10

Evaluating, Serving, and Enjoying Your Wine

Q Why should I evaluate my own wine?

A Evaluating your wines and keeping track of those evaluations is the only way to develop a sense of what does and doesn't work for your particular winemaking situation. By recording your sensorial impressions (color, smell, taste, mouthfeel) of the wine and keeping track of the hard numbers (Brix, TA, pH, free SO_2), you develop a personal history of your winemaking. Winemaking in the dark is no fun. Even if you like to ferment by the seat of your pants, you'll most likely find it very useful to have a concise record of your past successes (or failures) to guide your future efforts.

One wine-evaluation system many winemakers like to use is based on the University of California-Davis 20-point scale. Developed by some of the world's premier wine scientists in the 1960s, the 20-point scale allows winemakers to maximize objectivity while retaining pertinent hedonic information about their wines in a sound and reproducible manner.

As professional winemaking has developed over the past several decades, the University has refined this scale to reflect current tasting methodology, which is designed to distinguish between wine flavors rather than evaluating particular characteristics. This technique is called descriptive analysis. However, for the home winemaker, the older scale still serves as a relevant and useful tool. (See the following two questions for more on evaluating wine.)

Q **How does the UC-Davis 20-point scale work?**

A The basis of this system is that various wine characteristics are assigned a numerical value. The characteristics measured by the UC-Davis scale are color, clarity, aroma/bouquet, taste/balance, sugar, acidity, body, tannin, and general quality. If the wine being judged measures up to a particular characteristic, it is awarded a certain number of points. If, for example, it has the brilliant clarity that is desirable in a wine ready to be bottled, give it 1 point. (Half points are generally not used in scoring wines, but feel free to improvise.) As you award points, record your impressions of the wine and take notes for future reference.

COLOR (1 POINT)

The first noticeable trait of wine is its color. Hold it up to the light or tilt it away from you against a white piece of paper on the tabletop to observe the true color of the wine against a neutral background. In your notebook, describe the color in your own words. Whites range from practically colorless to a golden yellow; reds span the entire red/blue range of the spectrum from almost violet to a deep brick red, depending upon varietal and age of the wine.

The color point is awarded to wines that clearly fall within their color boundaries. If a new white wine is deep gold in color, bordering on brown, chances are it has been oxidized and should probably rate a 0. Similarly, if your Cabernet doesn't have as much color as it should, don't award it full credit. Make a note to beef up your red wine maceration program.

CLARITY (1 POINT)

Though it's rare for commercial wines to have a clarity problem, it's pretty common for homemade wines to be not quite as brilliantly clear or sediment-free as their store-bought counterparts. When awarding the clarity point, feel free to be a little lenient. You might refuse the point only if the sediment or haze can't be corrected with decanting or bottle aging and is a true defect, even by home winemaking criteria. Again, record in your notebook the character of the haze or sediment, if there is one.

AROMA/BOUQUET (5 POINTS)

Do your tasting in the morning, when taste buds are at their best. Also make sure the tasting room is free from other smells.

Give your glass a big swirl to liberate the aromatic compounds in the wine and then bury your nose in it. Block out the rest of the world and concentrate on the information that your brain is receiving from your sensory organs. Are you reminded of specific smells? If so, write them down. Overzealous wine critics aside, most wine experts try to define aromas in concrete terms like "blackberry" and "bell pepper" rather than with meaningless phrases like "a cunning hint of saucy effervescence."

By using simple, everyday language that everyone can understand, you keep the doors open to practical discourse and shut out the dated air of exclusivity that seems to cling to the ritual of wine tasting.

Besides trying to define the aromas (the Aroma Wheel's categories can help you here), note the overall aroma picture. Do off odors render the wine undrinkable? Then award it a 0. If the wine has a slight whiff of hydrogen sulfide or a bit of a chemical smell but is still drinkable, it should be awarded a 1. A unilateral wine with no distinguishing aromas rates a 2, while a flawless wine with a pleasant aroma characteristic of its varietal deserves a 3.

The process gets a bit trickier when it comes to 4s and 5s. The deal is this: Aromas are the smells the wine gives off when young and fresh. Bouquet (often referred to as "bottle bouquet") is the collection of smells and sensations that a soundly made wine develops as it ages. If your five-year-old Syrah is defect-free, shows varietal character, and has a nice bouquet, go ahead and give it a 4 or a 5. Similarly, if your Sauvignon Blanc isn't made to age and you think it smells exactly like a finely made Sauvignon Blanc should, give it full points.

TASTE/BALANCE (5 POINTS)

Take a swig of your wine and swish, swirl, and slosh it around in your mouth. The point is to saturate your entire mouth with wine to channel the volatile components to your sensory receptors for maximum appreciation. A wine earns top marks in this category for being free of unpleasant or out-of-place flavors, for being true to type and age, and for being balanced. Even though that's a pretty subjective term, a wine is balanced if no one characteristic sticks out and if all the elements seem to work together well.

Be careful not to confuse this or the aroma/bouquet category with the general quality category at the end. These more specific categories are designed to remove some of the subjectivity while you concentrate on awarding points for "making the grade" and not for personal opinion — yet.

SUGAR (1 POINT)

This one is simple. If you wanted your Muscat to have about 3 percent residual sugar and it tastes like it does, award your wine a point. If, on the other hand, your goal was to make a dry Zinfandel and it's obviously got a little bit of sugar left, than score this category a 0.

ACIDITY (2 POINTS)

There's a bit more leeway in this category. It all depends, again, on the type of wine you're making. If you have pretty high acid with a lot of tannin, alcohol, and oak to back it up, then your wine deserves both points. On the other hand, if your wine is too high or too low in acid for its overall composition, award it 1 or a 0, depending on how far off the mark it is.

BODY (2 POINTS)

Body is the sensation of fullness or roundness in the mouth that texturally differentiates wine from water. If a wine has good body and feels substantial, it should be awarded both points. If it is lacking in the body department, give it a 1 or 0. Be careful not to confuse body with sugar content. Sugar can give a wine a sense of fullness that is actually a matter of taste sensation rather than texture.

TANNIN (1 POINT)

Tannins give wine, especially red wine, that sense of grittiness or puckering that you can feel on your tongue, cheeks, and teeth. Though it could go under the body category as a textural quality, it belongs in its own group because its presence (or absence) can make or break a wine.

Award a wine 1 point if the level of tannin is appropriate for the wine you've made. For example, if your six-month-old Cabernet has enough tannin to knock your socks off, it's not necessarily a defect. If you mean to age it to mellow it out, by all means award it a 1. Similarly, if you've made a white wine without a lot of tannin, which is appropriate, also award it a 1. If, however, your red wine is lacking oomph, give it a 0 and make a note to yourself to beef up your maceration strategy, to add more oak, or to add some tannic acid.

GENERAL QUALITY (2 POINTS)

Finally, here's your chance to record your overall impressions of the wine. I know, I know, it's hard not to be biased. But if you like the wine so much that you wish you could make it again next year, give it a 2. If you can think of many areas you'd like to improve upon or if that style of wine just isn't your bag, feel free to give it a 1 or even a 0.

It's nothing to be ashamed about if you make a wine that you don't fancy; it's called a learning curve. Next time you'll make something different and probably better, and you'll have a bunch of carefully recorded notes to help.

INTERPRETING AND USING THE RESULTS

An outstanding wine will score usually between 17 and 20 points, with some weaker and some stronger areas. If your wine scores lower than a 17, check out the areas where it seems to need a little help, and if improvements can be made for next time, make note of them. Be careful not to fall into the wine magazine trap of being too absolute in your judgments; if a wine scored an 18, it doesn't necessarily mean that it's that much "worse" than a wine that scored a 19 or 20. The 20-point system rates many different things, and the numbers are truly meaningless without your notes and comments alongside them.

Now that you know how to truly assess wines and keep records the way the pros do, you can tell the wine snobs to take a hike and swirl your glass with a little of your own savoir faire.

Calculating Wine Calories

An easy calculation to find out how many calories you imbibe is to take the alcohol percentage (always listed on the label of commercial wines), multiply it by the number of ounces you are drinking, and multiply the result by 1.6. For example, if you're drinking 5 ounces of wine that is 12 percent alcohol by volume, you'll be consuming approximately 96 calories.

IT'S ALL IN THE GLASS

Though you don't need to invest in hundreds of dollars' worth of imported crystal, there's no doubt a good glass can increase the pleasure of the experience of tasting and evaluating your wine. Here are some pointers when it comes to selecting the best wineglass for the job.

Size. Those gargantuan wineglasses the size of a fishbowl need to go — I've seen ostensibly well-behaved customers at fancy restaurants crash elbows and almost take out their neighbors with one hearty swirl. Three and a half inches in diameter is the biggest a red wine bowl needs to be. A lip of 2 inches across tapers that bowl to a nice amount of nose room.

Red   *White*   *Champagne*

White wine glasses tend to be scaled smaller than reds because red wines can take more air. Depending on the age of the wine (older wines should sometimes be sheltered from excessive air exposure), reds can actually improve with a good aeration. A bigger bowl means more surface area and a bigger air-to-wine ratio.

On the other hand, I reject what I see as a ploy by the stemware industry to sell more glasses, and most days I use the same good-sized glass for reds, whites, and dessert wines. If you want to serve more than one wine at dinner, feel free to use multiples of the same glass. You can save money and storage headaches by buying one size in bulk.

Shape. Speaking of expensive stemware, many would have you believe that you must have a different glass for every single varietal. That's like saying that you need a different fork for every type of pasta you serve. While no one's arguing with the obvious fact that a martini glass or shot glass makes a pretty poor wine-tasting vessel, there's absolutely no reason you can't enjoy a Sangiovese in the same wineglass from which you imbibe a Bordeaux. Just make sure the rim is a smaller diameter than the bowl of the glass to ensure that those nice aromas wafting up from the wine will get trapped in the glass's headspace (or shall we say nose-space?).

The one "special" wineglass you really need is a Champagne flute for sparkling wine. The tall, narrow geometry of the glass helps the wine retain its effervescence; those 1950's throwback saucers do nothing but slop over your wrist when you toast and clobber the bubbles out of your bubbly in no time (wait for it) flat.

Thickness. Though one of my favorite wine experiences was sipping young Argentine Malbec from thick-lipped, recycled jelly jars (maybe the spectacular outdoor setting in the Argentine Andes helped), it's generally true that a thin-rimmed wineglass elevates the wine-tasting experience.

A sonorous fine crystal can up the aural ante, and an ultrapremium watermark (notice how prominent these are getting on glassware these days?) might impress your guests, but I think thin crystal or glass stemware increases our pleasure quotient simply because there's a lot less glass to interfere with the wine.

Color. Colored wineglasses can be fun, but for evaluating wine, it's critical that the material be clear. The same goes for cuts, patterns, or bubbles in the glass — if you want to evaluate your wine, you have to be able to see it clearly. What we see has a huge effect on how we perceive what we put in our mouths.

At the UC-Davis Department of Viticulture & Enology, when a researcher wants his or her tasting subjects to focus only on the aroma, flavor, or mouthfeel of a wine, the wines are presented in black glasses that make it impossible for a panelist to discern anything about a wine's color.

Enospeak

Sometimes the overheated strings of descriptors popular among wine critics do less to actually describe the wine than to befuddle the average winemaker. Some of my personal favorites follow.

◆ In-your-face gobs of jammy fruit
◆ A cinnabar robe, denoting superannuation, which, if this specimen were left unimbibed, would unquestionably deteriorate precipitously into decrepitude
◆ Legs like a centipede crossed with a gazelle
◆ A graceful but hesitant aroma, not unlike a young fawn poised on the edge of a bucolic meadow
◆ Subtle aromas of violets, damask roses, and road tar
◆ Oodles of character, hints of rare steak
◆ A Shelleyesque aspect of melancholy — this is a gothic wine that needs Prozac and a spa day
◆ Tight-grained French Alliers oak and a delicate suspicion of that certain je ne sais quoi

And one that I feel justly expresses many a wine out there in the market place:
◆ Whacked upside the head with an oak 2 x 4

Q What can cause a wine to taste different when left in a glass over the span of a few minutes?

A An important and interesting thing about wine is that it changes over time. The concept of letting wine breathe — exposing it to air by decanting it into another, usually larger, container without a stopper — is to bring about what is hoped will be positive changes in the aroma, taste, and texture. Sometimes, when hit with a slug of oxygen, wines (especially older wines or ones lacking in tannin structure) rebel and either keel over and die or turn nasty and acetic. Some wines that are prematurely oxidized in the bottle have a hard time accepting any more oxygen.

A corollary explanation is that it wasn't so much the wine that changed as your senses. Our taste buds are not a constant in the great world of wine tasting. Our perceptions of tastes can change according to mood, time of day, or even background music. Did you nibble a chocolate bar or grab a cookie off the baking sheet on your way through the kitchen? Sugar on the tongue always makes the next sip of wine taste more sour — that's why "dessert" wines have a hefty amount of sugar to be able to stand up to sweets.

■ ═══════ ■

Q What is the point of opening a bottle and letting it breathe before drinking it?

A Not all wines need to breathe upon opening. This is one of the oldest and most pervasive misconceptions about wines. This myth is perpetuated by Hollywood movies, outdated books on wine connoisseurship, and the culture of wine snobbery in general. Sometimes, however, a little air in a freshly broached bottle can be helpful. Once the cork has been removed from the bottle, oxygen immediately begins reacting with the wine's components, oxidizing some and beginning chain reactions that go on to further change others. It is perfectly normal to prefer a wine after it's been open for a few, or even many, hours. It happens to me all the time.

While it's true that oxygen will always have some effect on the wine the minute it's opened, there's no guarantee that the effect is worth the wait. Most wines are perfectly delicious upon opening, and white wines almost never need to breathe before drinking. In fact, older wines with anti-oxidant compounds that long ago polymerized and oxidized may become tired and completely lifeless after hours of breathing.

Allowing a wine to open up or blow off any weird in-the-bottle aromas is common and can be a definite positive, especially for young red wines. If you want to introduce these desired effects of oxygen immediately upon opening the bottle, decant the wine and let the oxygen start working. The important thing is that you discover how to treat a particular wine in order to maximize your enjoyment of it.

The best way to enjoy any wine and to walk the fine line between "to breathe or not to breathe" is this: Open your bottle about 15 minutes before you plan on serving it. This gives any egregious aromas that may be present a chance to blow off. Then pour the wine for your guests and let them enjoy its aromas and textures as they change and develop over time. I can't emphasize enough that each wine is different and some will exhibit greater change than others. This is something that's terribly hard to predict from wine to wine and sometimes even bottle to bottle among the same lot.

■ ══════════ ■

Q Can I use a spare refrigerator for long-term wine storage?

A By all means, put that extra fridge to good use and store some of your collection in it! Extra refrigeration is a boon to just about any winemaker, wine collector, or home brewer — just ask hard-core brewers how much they love their lagering fridges. The critical point is to adjust the temperature to a steady 53°F (11.7°C). This can be done with external thermostats available at most home-brew shops.

Storing wines in too cold an environment can cause untoward potassium bitartrate crystal precipitation, and some experts even suggest it will ruin the wine in the long run. Chilling wines just before serving is fine, of course, but don't store wines at these temperatures for too long. Note that commercial wine-storage refrigerators are built to help regulate humidity, while the air in regular food refrigerator is drier. A refrigerator isn't an overly arid environment, but if you're worried about humidity, pick up a hygrometer (humidity meter) and try to keep your refrigerator as humid as a

Storing Your Wine

Wine is best stored under constant conditions with 52–55°F (11–13°C) and 70 percent humidity as the goals. I recommend storing cork-finished bottles on their sides to keep the cork moist. Screw-capped or crown-capped wines do not need to be stored this way, but inevitably are because they also fit nicely into our preexisting wine racks.

Try to store your wine in a spot where the temperature and humidity don't vary greatly, as big changes in conditions have the potential to damage a wine. Many people store wine in an interior closet that stays the same temperature as the surrounding climate-controlled house or down in a basement, where the temperature remains more constant.

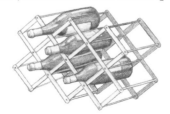

proper wine-storage cabinet. Metering systems and humidification tools can be purchased from the same companies that sell those fancy cabinet-like wine-storage units.

■ ══════════ ■

Q **Why do some Chardonnays taste oaky and buttery while others don't have those qualities at all?**

A Even though many critics pooh-pooh Chardonnay as being always buttery and oaky, there are, as you note, two stylistic schools of thought. One emphasizes a big, buttery, oaky, nutty character, while the other favors a spare, steely, minerally style that is fruit centered, crisper, and more acidic, but no less elegant.

The style you decide to emulate obviously depends upon your personal preferences, but will also be dictated by your starting materials. Very ripe, flavorful juice that has sufficient acid (at least 6.5 g/L) will be able to stand up to oak and malolactic fermentation, producing an age-worthy wine that will marry well with these enriching, character-highlighting treatments.

If your juice is not particularly flavorful, is less than 23.5° Brix, or is lacking an acidic punch, go for the lean, brisk style that is achievable with this kind of fruit, provided that you add enough acid to get the pH below 3.5 and the titratable acidity above 6 g/L. Juices of this nature, and many concentrates, become lost under all of the oak and yeast-autolysis richness associated with the first style.

The key to the second style is to preserve the fruit character and not mask it with oak. Fermenting at cooler temperatures in stainless steel (or neutral barrels), discouraging lees exposure, and using neutral oak for long-term aging are techniques employed by professionals who make this style of Chardonnay. For those who are looking to weave a more complex (though some would say more garish) tapestry with their Chardonnays, options include barrel fermentation with warmer ambient temperatures, long-term lees contact, malolactic fermentation, and protracted aging with newer French or American oak.

Q Is Shiraz the same as Syrah? And what can you tell me about Petite Sirah?

A The Syrah (sih-RAH) grape originated in Asia Minor and is called Shiraz by the Australians, presumably after the city in the Middle East near where the grape is thought to have originated. It is the most acclaimed red grape of the Rhône Valley in France and is also the most-planted Rhône grape in the United States, Australia, and beyond.

Versatile and adaptable, Syrah grows in a variety of climates, from the hot, sandy soils of the Sacramento River delta in California to the cool, high-altitude vineyards of the Andean foothills in Argentina. Its planting diversity leads to a wide variety of wines being produced, including the lyrical Syrahs of California's Santa Barbara County and the fat, oaky, jammy Shiraz-Cabernet blends of southern Australia. Whatever the style, typical Syrah descriptors include dark fruit, earth, smoke, and pepper.

Though Syrah can grow in a wide variety of locales, it does need some coolness and yield control to develop its full potential. It tends to show water stress as it ripens and, if not carefully watched, can shrivel too much as the cluster goes through the last weeks of ripeness. This contributes to another typical Syrah problem: high pH. Seeing pH values of 3.7 or higher when the sugar content is just at 24.5° Brix is not uncommon. It's a tough call for a winemaker to make — wait for the ripe flavors, mature seeds, and browning stems, or pick sooner and keep that pH in the realm of normalcy. For this reason, it's nice if you can find fruit from a cooler area where sugar accumulation is slower and the flavors, aromas, and tannins have time to catch up before the pH gets too high. If picked correctly (with all things in balance), a good Syrah can compete with some of the best Pinot Noirs and Cabernets in the world for ageability, style, and complexity.

Petite Sirah (peh-TEET sih-RAH), also called Durif (duhr-EEF), is a different grape than Syrah, although the name hints at this varietal's origin. Many consumers and even winemakers are still in the dark about Petite Sirah/

Durif. Now grown mostly in California, this varietal originated in France, where it started life as a man-made cross between Syrah and a grape called Peloursin, developed by a Dr. Durif. It has dark color, an intense, peppery aroma, and a huge portion of tannins. Using it in blends the world over, especially in California and Australia, many winemakers discover that a little bit goes a long way. The word "petite" doesn't really seem to be a good way to describe this grape — there's nothing small about its teeth-staining color and big tannins. A pure varietal Petite Sirah should be bottle aged for at least a year to become approachable!

■ ════════ ■

Q Why does red wine give me a headache but white wine doesn't (assuming I haven't had too much of either)?

A The "red-wine headache" is one of those wine discussions that lies somewhere between legend and reality. However, there are some real answers. I'll lay them out and you can decide for yourself. Many people mistakenly assume that red wines contain higher levels of sulfites than white wines. The opposite is actually the case, because most winemakers add more SO_2 to white wines than to reds. White wines need more protection from oxygen than red wines do, and SO_2 acts as an antioxidant. (See Can I make a sulfite-free wine?, page 102.)

A few people (about 0.01 percent of the population) lack the digestive enzyme sulfite oxidase and truly are allergic to sulfites or lack the ability to digest them. These folks can't process sulfites, commonly found in foods like lunchmeat, sausage, cheese, dried apricots, and even beer. A headache can be one of the symptoms of sulfite allergies, but this is most likely not the cause of your malady.

Biogenic amines, a group of naturally occurring fermentation by-products that includes histamine and tyramine, are more and more thought to be the cause of the classic "red-wine headache." Biogenic amine concentrations in wine depend on microbial activity. The higher the cell count during a lactic acid or other bacterial fermentation, and the longer the fermentation goes, the higher the eventual biogenic amine levels in the wine.

Biogenic amine levels are higher in red wines, which are more likely to have gone through malolactic fermentation and experienced extended maceration, both situations in which *Acetobacter* and other bacteria have a longer time to act on the wine. Biogenic amines can cause vasoconstriction and vasodilation, both common headache triggers in the general population.

Whether it's biogenic amines, sulfites, or something else, the bottom line is that you should go with what feels best. If red wines give you problems, there are plenty of great white wines to try!

THE MOST POPULAR GRAPE

The most commonly planted grape in the world isn't Cabernet Sauvignon or even Chardonnay. The title goes to Airén (eye-RHEN), a white grape traditionally used in making brandy that covers the regions of La Mancha and Valdepeñas in Spain. Totaling almost a million acres worldwide, Airén is leaving its history of bland, insipid wines behind as modern technology, improved refrigeration, and more conscientious winemaking are resulting in light, fragrant, and fruity wines. It is sometimes blended with the better-known Tempranillo (a red grape) to create a light-bodied red called Clarete.

Grenache, called Garnacha in Spain, is the runner-up and is an important grape there as well as in France and in the United States. Grenache is a vigorous grower, even in hot, dry, windy climates, and like Syrah, it tends towards lots of green growth and needs devigorating soils to keep it under control.

This versatile grape is a natural partner to Syrah, and the two are featured in many popular Rhône blends, like those from the famous Châteauneuf-du-Pape.

It also makes a tart, flamingo-pink rosé from Tavel, one of the most celebrated pink wines in all of France. A bit of a "drink me now" wine, especially when made into a rosé, but paired with the earth, truffle, and meaty character of a Syrah or even Mourvèdre, it can age and develop extremely well.

Q **What amounts of carbohydrates, sugars, and calories are found in dry white and red wines?**

A That's a good question, and one that is easily answered. Whether made from a kit, from nongrape fruit, or from grapes, a typical 5-ounce (approximately 150 mL) glass of a dry wine with an alcohol content of 12 percent typically has about 100 calories and between 1.5 and 3.0 grams of carbohydrates (as tallied by proponents of low-carb diets such as Atkins). The number of calories and carbohydrates depends on the alcohol percentage of the wine, the residual sugar content of the wine, and the amount that you drink.

All of the calories in wine come from carbohydrates. Most of these carbohydrates in dry wine are in the form of ethyl alcohol. A much smaller percentage of the carbohydrates and calories could come from straight, unfermented sugar, as a wine perceived as dry can contain between 0.2 and 0.4 percent unfermented sugar.

There are many kinds of wines out there, and to accurately count the number of calories per glass of wine, you need to know some of the chemical stats about it. However, the "100 calories per glass of dry wine" rule is a good general guideline. (See page 291 for more on calculating wine calories.)

CHAPTER 11

Fruits and Roots:

Country and Kit Winemaking

What are some keys to making good wine from a commercial kit?

Kits are an easy way for novices to break into winemaking at home. The ingredients are all in place, everything is measured out, and there are specific instructions to guide you. Even so, there are a few things the beginning kit winemaker should pay particular attention to for success.

Read the directions. I know this sounds like a no-brainer, but a kit is designed so that following the directions produces the best possible result. First-timers should definitely follow instructions to the letter, and even experienced winemakers should keep tweaking to a minimum.

Stir the ingredients thoroughly. Those concentrates, powders, and additives will sink right to the bottom if not mixed properly.

Make the proper volume. There's no way a 6-gallon (23 L) kit can be stretched to make 10 gallons (38 L) of wine. The proportions would be completely off and you'd be left with an insipid, flavorless beverage that would be prone to spoilage due to the low alcohol content. Add only the amount of water called for in the directions.

Take good notes. Even though you are following someone else's instructions, take notes as you go along. Keeping a record of what you do every time you make wine teaches you what works and what doesn't.

Practice thorough sanitation. Just because you have a detailed instruction booklet, don't forget to keep your winemaking common sense about you. Good sanitation is just as important for winemakers making 6 gallons (23 L) in their garage as it is for professionals making 5,000 gallons (19,000 L) in a winery.

■ ══════════ ■

Q What is the shelf life of wine kits?

A If your kit is more than a year old, check the quality of the juice in the kit. If it smells oxidized, looks browned, or seems otherwise less than perfect, don't use it. There's an old saying in the wine business, "Wine waits for no one." This holds true for kit winemaking, so even though you aren't forced to harvest your grapes at a given time of year, you still want to make sure that your ingredients are of the highest quality.

■ ══════════ ■

Q It seems like a lot of additives come with wine kits. What are they for and is it necessary to use all of them?

A Your question is complex. In fact, it could lead to pages upon pages of response if I elucidated upon every possible additive that might show up in a wine kit. Even though a kit might contain unfamiliar ingredients, there isn't anything that is going to harm you if used according to the manufacturer's directions. You may feel overwhelmed by the multiple packets and powders with strange names, but be assured that they are put there for a reason.

Successful kit winemaking is really all about following the directions to the letter, especially for beginning winemakers. The manufacturers carefully calculate the composition of the included concentrate and then package up everything you'll need to make the wine to their predetermined style.

This is where winemakers sometimes try to get a little tricky. Most winemakers I know are constant tweakers, not that they're freaks or weirdos (though some are proud to tell you they are), but that they always like to try something new and push the boundaries on style and technique. This can lead some to experiment with kits, from simply adding half the recommended amount of oak beans to being unorthodox enough to combine the concentrate packs from two different kits and fermenting them in a big double batch. The former tweak is harmless, as oak character is something of a personal choice, while the latter requires a bit more experience to know what you're doing with a blend of something like Viognier and Albariño.

The bottom line is that all of those little packets and vials in a kit are there for a reason — to make the wine the way the kit was designed. Following is a description of some of the most common kit ingredients and why they're included in each kit.

- **Yeast** is included with the kit because it's critical. You can't leave out the yeast and expect to make wine. Yeast packets are also packaged to match the kits and shouldn't be substituted with other strains.

- **Acid packets or acid blends** lend an acidic tang to the wine and also help keep the pH in balance appropriate for the wine style. A lower pH (higher acid) is often required for white wines or sweet wines, whereas full-bodied reds tend toward higher pHs and, as a result, will have a smaller dose of acid to add, if any at all. Some juices or concentrates come preacidified to the right level, so an acid addition isn't necessary.

- **Sulfites** are included as a preservative and antioxidant. Because yeast cells naturally produce sulfur dioxide as a result of an alcoholic fermentation, it's impossible to make a sulfite-free wine. It is highly recommended to use the kit's sulfur dioxide (usually included as powdered potassium metabisulfite), or you risk losing your wine to spoilage or premature oxidation.

- **Tannin powders** are derived from oak or from the grapes themselves. They can lend a pleasing astringency to a wine, usually a red. Tannin powders aren't necessary for the microbiological health of a wine and aren't as important from a chemical point of view as, say, sugar and acid, but they can contribute to the complexity of mouthfeel.

- **Sorbates,** usually in a soluble form like potassium sorbate, are used to inhibit yeast. It's likely that the sorbate listed on a kit's label is there in case the kit is for a wine with residual sugar, in which case the sorbate can protect against refermentation. Sorbate is an extremely common chemical preservative that's used in the food and beverage industries worldwide. It tends to have an odor described by some as "celery" or "pineapple" and isn't usually used in the making of fine wines, which rely on sterile filtration to prevent bottled sweet wines from re-fermenting.

To be on the safe side, I recommend that novice winemakers use the potassium sorbate according to the kit directions, especially for a sweet wine with residual sugar. If you try to make sweet wines without potassium sorbate, fermentation can restart and might cause the bottle to explode.

◆ **Oak powder or chips** are more and more often a part of winemaking kits. This is perhaps the one kit component that you can safely not use, as its absence won't affect the microbial stability or safety of the wine. However, oak can contribute a sizeable amount of tannins and mouthfeel-enhancing components, and there's no doubt that a well-integrated oak aroma improves some wine styles.

◆ **Bentonite** is a naturally occurring clay that has been used in winemaking for centuries. It pulls proteins and other positively charged items out of finished wine and juices, letting them settle to a layer of sediment at the bottom of a carboy or tank, helping to clarify as they go. Bentonite is harmless and can be cut out of the program if desired — just be aware that you might need to spend a longer time settling your juice or wine and that you might encounter protein hazes later on.

♦ **Kieselsol** is a proprietary name for a fining agent belonging to the class of silica dioxides and has an action very similar to that of bentonite. Silica dioxides electrostatically bind with positively charged proteins in wine and initiate flocculation and settling. Not using the fining agent means that you'll have to spend a longer time settling your wine, and you may end up with a protein haze after it's bottled. It is unusual to have bentonite and Kieselsol packaged in the same kit, as they have very similar results.

■ ═══ ■

Q How can I best save an open container of grape juice concentrate?

A Dump the remains into a freezer-safe storage container and stick it in your freezer. The high sugar content might prevent all of the liquid from freezing, but the cold will slow down any chemical reactions or microbial growth that could degrade the concentrate. Try to use it within 6 months if you can, just to be sure the quality of those delicate aromatic compounds remains intact.

Q Should kits go through malolactic fermentation?

A This is one of those instances where making wine from a kit is not the same as making wine from fresh grapes or juice. If the kit doesn't include a malolactic bacteria culture or a step in the recipe for its successful completion, then the wine isn't meant to go through MLF. Malolactic or secondary fermentation lowers the overall acidity of the final wine. It also can produce buttery-flavored wines when that character isn't desired and sometimes can produce off odors or make a wine that's not acidic enough.

The majority of kits are preadjusted with an acid blend that might contain a lot of malic acid. If you inoculate the wine for malolactic fermentation before you add your post-primary fermentation hit of SO_2, you may lose a good part of your total acidity and the wine will taste flat and uninteresting.

Even worse, most kits have trace amounts of sorbate added to the concentrate to extend their shelf life, and many kit recipes ask you to add sorbate upon completion of primary fermentation. If malolactic bacteria were added at this time, they would convert sorbate into hexadiene, resulting in a smell like rotting geraniums, not a favorable aroma.

I suggest following the kit's instructions with regards to malolactic fermentation. Going off the map with a kit wine is a little tricky because you don't know the exact composition of the starting material.

Q

How do you make wine out of nongrape material?

A

Any nonpoisonous vegetable or fruit can be fermented — if it has sugar, yeast will eat it. Your choices are only as limited as the variety of fruits and vegetables growing in your garden. A cursory glance through any home remedy book or cookbook from a century ago will show you that our forebears brewed up alcoholic beverages from whatever their gardens and orchards happened to produce. Many modern hobbyists pursue the historical, if sometimes a bit eccentric, practice of making wine from garden-grown ingredients.

Often called country wines in the United States and Canada, these nongrape beverages are as interesting to drink as they are to make. Most country wines, especially those based on herbs, vegetables, or flowers, require some form of added sugar in order to produce enough alcohol for a stable end product. Most recipes call for added table sugar, grape-juice concentrate, dried raisins, or the like in order to produce a final alcohol content of 8–12 percent. If you want to create a dessert wine, which may have a final alcohol content of 16–22 percent, then you will need to start with an even greater amount of initial sugar. (Of course, wines with this much alcohol must be fortified. Regular yeast is not capable of fermenting to that level of alcohol.)

Though wine scientists still can't agree on a consistent Brix-to-potential-alcohol calculation (vintage, varietal, and other factors all come into play), you can make a good estimation. To arrive at the starting Brix needed, divide your desired end alcohol percentage by 0.55 for a table wine and 0.57 for a higher-alcohol dessert wine. For example, if you want to make a 12 percent alcohol dry wine, you need a starting Brix of around 21.8°. For a 17 percent alcohol dessert wine, your starting Brix will be much higher at 29.8°.

After you've determined your starting Brix, take a look at what you've got out in the garden that appeals to you. You basically treat the material the same as you would grapes, though most vegetable or flower recipes call for boiling or steeping the material for a period of time.

For hard or stemmy material, like carrots, boil around 2 cups (0.5 L) material in a gallon (4 L) of water for 20 minutes or until soft. For soft, leafy material, like rose petals, bring a gallon (4 L) of water to a boil, remove from heat, add 2 cups (0.5 L) of material, and steep for 15 minutes, covered. Then add the sugar, acid, and any other additives (tannins are common to increase mouthfeel) to the liquor.

Sweeteners, whether you're using juice concentrate, honey, or maple syrup, have different concentrations of sugar, so you will have to experiment to find out how much of a given sugar source will yield your Brix target. For sweetening and acidifying any wines from materials that are new to you, I always recommend doing bench trials or adding the sugar source gradually while measuring the must's gravity.

Fermentation should proceed as it would with any other fruit wine — some winemakers take solids out before fermenting and ferment the juice like a white wine, while others leave all the fruits, roots, or veggies in the fermenter. Leaving the solids in for the ferment will contribute more color and could help extract more interesting aromas or flavors.

Watch out, though, because much garden-grown starting material is strongly (or strangely) flavored, and you might end up with too many "interesting" things in your finished wine. Feel free to fish out solids during the fermentation if you feel your wine is taking a wrong turn; since the liquid has absorbed all the sugar and much of the flavor and aromatic goodies already, you should be able to do this safely.

Aging and racking should be similar as well; do expect some peculiar flavors and aromas! One word of caution with vegetables and some fruits — you might need to buy some pectic enzyme from your supply store, because some fruits and veggies (strawberries and apples come to mind) contain a lot of pectin that can cause instability in the bottle later on. Other high-pectin fruits include currants, citrus fruits, cranberries, and plums.

■ ══════ ■

Q **How can I prevent a country wine from turning out flat or watery?**

A It's important to make sure you've got enough sugar, acid, tannin, and aromatic and flavor compounds to result in a flavorful beverage that is both stable (more than 10 percent alcohol) and somewhat zippy (more than 6.0 g/L total acidity). These numbers are relatively easy to shoot for and can be adjusted up or down depending on how your initial fruit comes in. Always use a juice with an initial sugar content in the realm of 22–24° Brix to be sure of producing a final alcohol level of more than 10 percent by volume. Initial total acidity profiles should start around 6.0–8.0 g/L, as some of the acid will drop out of solution during the fermentation process.

Flavor and aroma are a bit more subjective, of course, and are largely personal decisions. Before buying your fresh fruit, sample a few good mouthfuls. Is it delicious? Does it make you salivate and want more?

If you're stuck with not-so-great starting material, you can attempt to tart it up a bit by adding a little grape-juice concentrate before the primary fermentation. An added benefit is that you'll also be adding extra nitrogen, amino acids, and other goodies that yeast need to conduct a healthy fermentation.

■ ═══════ ■

Q What are some guidelines for aging and storing country wines?

A Two general guidelines for aging wines from fruits, vegetables, and herbs are to cellar any wine at least three months before opening the first bottle and to consume it within 3 or 4 years. Many fruit and vegetable wines

lack the natural acidity, alcohol content, tannin, and phenolic concentration of grape-based wines, all of which contribute appreciably to the longevity and graceful aging of the wine.

That being said, there are some things you can add to or change about your country wines if you want them to better withstand the test of time. To make a delicious and age-worthy wine, most fruits and vegetables need extra help from adventurous winemakers who are willing to adjust their musts in order to start off with one that is properly balanced. Your best strategy for success is to shoot for an initial sugar content of at least 22° Brix, a pH of 3.10–3.65, and a TA of 6.0–8.0 g/L.

If you can't measure the acids, at least measure the sugar with a hydrometer and adjust the must with an acid blend of tartaric and malic acids to taste. You want the initial must or juice to taste just a bit sweeter and tarter than juice you'd be comfortable drinking at the breakfast table. Adjusting the acid and the sugar will give you more alcohol in the finished product and more "zing" on the palate, as well as added protection against premature aging.

If your wine is going to be darker in color, like a blackberry wine, you may want to add some additional tannin or phenolic compounds to the must before you ferment. These will help the wine have a pleasing mouthfeel, body, and "grip," or pleasing sensation of astringency on the tongue, and will also provide invaluable protection against excessive oxidation in the bottle.

Tannin mixes can sometimes be purchased in home wine-making stores as commercial powders and potions, but the most natural way to add them is to use red grape juice or grape-juice concentrate. Buy these from a home winemaking supply store, not from the supermarket, as those frozen cardboard tubes of Concord grape juice have often been treated with high levels of potassium sorbate, a preservative that inhibits yeast growth — okay for supermarket juice but not good for wine!

Using grape juice or grape-juice concentrates also adds sugars, acids, and nutrients that yeast need to perform a happy, healthy fermentation. This is one of the reasons why so many herb, flower, fruit, and vegetable recipes call for grape juice as the base.

Finally, it is important to age your wine bottles in the right conditions.

Place bottles on their sides so the cork can remain moist. Dried-out corks pull away from the sides of the bottle neck, creating a pathway for wine to leak out and oxygen (as well as microbes) to leak in.

Keep your wine away from sunlight, as ultraviolet rays can penetrate the bottle and damage the contents. Aside from accelerating oxidation, sunlight can actually cause certain sulfur (not sulfur dioxide) molecules to be released into the wine, resulting in skunky aromas.

Store your wines at a consistent temperature. This is perhaps the most important step. Find a place where the temperature is 55–65°F (13–18°C) and remains stable.

FORGET THE GRAPES!

Some uncommon or unexpected plants that can be used in country wine recipes instead of grapes include rose hips, dandelions, coffee, hawthorn flowers, basil, black tea, celery, carrots, rhubarb (just the stalks; the leaves are poisonous).

Note: I don't want to give the impression that you can make a complete wine out of the above materials. Most of them need a hefty dose of grape concentrate, or table sugar at the least, to make a stable beverage, and they really should be considered more as flavoring agents.

Avoid the following poisonous plants for winemaking: foxglove, hemlock, ivies, jimsonweed, lilac, mistletoe, nightshades, poison ivy, poison oak, poppies (though you can use the dried seeds).

You should also steer clear of: cabbages or cruciferous vegetables of any type (sulfur components make them too stinky); bulbs (edible bulbs like leeks and garlic contain sulfur; most others are poisonous); ferns (except for fiddleheads); fungi (not enough carbohydrates to ferment and many varieties are poisonous); geraniums (high geraniol content leads to overpowering off odors).

Q How can I best add berries and other fruits to grapes when making wine?

A For noncommercial winemakers, fermenting fragrant, tasty nongrape fruit with grape juice or must is not only fun but also makes sense from a technical point of view. Very often, the grapes that are available to home winemakers (backyard "mystery" grapes, second crop, or odd hybrids) lack acids, sugars, aromatic compounds, or tannins. Adding a complementary fruit can really make up for these deficiencies while adding a welcome punch of flavor.

Wines made solely from regular fruit, however, don't always have the oomph that we're looking for in a good table wine — the color may not be stable or the mouthfeel isn't rich. At other times, all-fruit juice lacks the proper acid balance or the nutrients necessary to support a healthy fermentation. So fermenting wine grapes and regular fruit together can produce pleasing wines that benefit from the best of what both fruits have to offer.

When deciding what combination of fruit and grapes to try, consider the result you want to attain. Do you want additional color and tannin, or do you need extra acid? Dark fruits (berries or plums, for example) will enrich color and tannin, while citrus fruits contribute a lot of acid. Are you looking to explore new aromatics? Try strongly scented fruits like blueberries or even flowers (elderflowers or rose petals) to beef up the aroma.

If you're aiming for a Cabernet Sauvignon-type wine (dark-colored, dry, full body, good tannin structure, final alcohol of 13.5 percent), I recommend using at least two-thirds Cabernet Sauvignon grapes. If you don't, the other fruit may overpower the grapes. Adjust your must to typical winemaking specs (23–26° Brix, 3.5–3.6 pH, 6.5–8.0 g/L TA) and ferment as usual.

After fermentation, taste carefully before you press, because the nongrape fruit might give you something unexpected, such as too little tannin. It could also contribute too much tannin — for example, if you used small blueberries with a high skin-to-juice ratio. Press gently; berries are rich in pectin and often generate a high percentage of solids. It's also important to keep an eye out for anomalies when you settle and rack. As the wine ages, watch for pectin hazes and use appropriate fining agents to clear the wine when necessary. Age your wine in the same way you would any of your dry red table wines and enjoy!

■ ═══════ ■

Q Why do many country wines seem less clear than grape wines?

A Certain fruits just do not work well for winemaking. Many fruit winemakers have a difficult time getting their fruit to "behave." It's usually not only a question of acidity, pH, or oxidation; some fruit just requires a lot of intervention. Apples and pears, for example, are rich in pectin and often will throw pectin hazes during aging and in the bottle. I suggest using pectic enzymes to break up some of the long-chain carbohydrate compounds that can mess up a fruit wine's stability. Similarly, a settling agent like bentonite should almost always be used in fruit wines to help the wine clear up well after fermentation is over.

One way to mitigate the effects of using nongrape fruits is to add a little grape concentrate to your must or juice, or to ferment half grapes and half other fruit. This way you still get some fun fruit flavor while allowing your fermentation to develop within more suitable parameters for a stable and balanced wine.

Q **What could cause a bitter/tart taste to develop in a cherry wine?**

A It seems you've got an overload of phenolics. In the future, press your fruit more gently, either with a basket press (available in most home winemaking stores) or by hand with a large sieve and a stirring spoon, depending upon the volume that you're dealing with. The key operating concept here is "gently." Cranking the seeds and skins of your wine through a grinder extracts way too much of the bitter seed and skin tannins from the fruit into the wine.

To fix a current batch, you can try fining to remove some of the tannins. Two fining agents I suggest you try (one or the other) are egg whites (albumen) and polyvinyl polypyrrolidone (PVPP).

Albumen is one of the oldest and most widely used fining agents in both home and commercial winemaking (and is also cheap and readily available). It's typically added to red wines (or very tannic fruit wines like yours) in concentrations of 0.125–0.5 mL/L, a very wide range, to be sure. Lightly beat the egg whites with a whisk, add to your container of wine, stir gently, and let settle for a few weeks or until you can see that the mixture has flocculated to the bottom. Once this occurs, rack the wine into a clean container and proceed with your aging or bottling program.

PVPP is a synthetic polymer powder available at your local home-winemaking store. Seen as more of an "interventionist" or "use only when needed" fining agent because it can sometimes scavenge color and change the mouthfeel, PVPP absorbs bitter phenolic compounds and then settles out to the bottom of the wine vessel. The legal limit for use in the United States is 7.9 g/L, a relatively high dose. In my experience, it is typically added to wine in concentrations of 0.5–3.0 g/L and then left to settle as per fining with egg whites or bentonite.

Some winemakers choose to filter PVPP out of their wines, while others just let it settle out and then rack off the treated wine into another container. Either way, the above numbers are general guidelines, and it is always best to test small amounts of wine first to find which concentrations work best for your particular wine. In the case of PVPP, even though you may lose some color and a little body, it's better than having too much bitterness.

■ ══════ ■

Q What could cause a lot of colored sediment to fall out over the first year of bottle age in a country fruit wine like blackberry?

A What you're seeing is a classic example of what happens to all wine eventually. Even the best wines suffer a loss of color, tannin, and other goodies over time as the chemical equilibrium of the wine forces these compounds and others out of solution and turns them into an unsightly glop that collects at the bottom of the bottle. Here are some questions to ask yourself.

Am I storing my wine properly? Extreme heat or cold or even drastic shifts in temperature can cause tannins and anthocyanins (the astringent compounds and the color compounds in wine, respectively) to change their chemical structure so that they no longer remain soluble in the wine. Make sure your wines are not subjected to large swings in temperature during storage. I keep my wines in the crawl space under my stairs, a spot that stays a pretty constant temperature year-round.

Am I racking my wines enough? If you don't go through at least three or four rackings before you bottle your wines, you could greatly enhance the chance of sediment ending up in your bottles, even if the wine appeared clear enough originally. Most commercial wines are racked at least three or four times during the production process and then are aged in barrels or tanks for at least 6 months before bottling.

Am I introducing any extra proteins? Some types of yeast nutrient are high in protein content and need adequate time to settle out before the bottling process. Proteins have a nasty habit of pulling anthocyanins out of solution and in fact are often used as a prebottle fining agent to "soften" wines by doing just that. Beware of recipes and procedures that don't allow adequate settling time — and subsequent racking time — after the addition of proteinaceous agents and other additives.

Am I using appropriate fruit? Some kinds of fruit just don't make good wine. You might want to try using at least a 50:50 ratio of grape-juice concentrate to blackberry juice. I suggest using Zinfandel or Merlot juice with dark berry fruit wines. This will provide a healthier environment for the yeast and compensate for many of the problems that can occur when fermenting with 100 percent nongrape fruit juice while maintaining a blackberry flavor and aroma profile.

Q **What changes red stains to blue when water is used to clean containers that held the juice of elderberries and other dark berry fruits?**

A Quick chemistry refresher: If something is acidic it is said to have a low pH and if something is not at all acidic (basic), it has a high pH. The pH scale ranges from 0 to 14, with the middle point being the pH of water, which is neutral at 7. Acids (vinegar, fruit juices) have a pH lower than 7 and bases (bleach, baking soda) have a pH higher than 7. Wines typically measure around 3.5 on the pH scale.

How does this relate to your residual elderberry juice turning blue if you add a lot of water to it? The red pigments of grapes, strawberries, elderberries, and other fruits remain red only in an acidic environment (like wine). If you shift the pH of the pigment's environment to make it less acidic (therefore more basic), the chemical structure changes to reflect light in the blue-green spectrum instead of the usual red-purple spectrum.

By diluting the elderberry stains with a large amount of water and making the environment much more basic, you're crossing over that color-switch point and causing the pigments to change from red to blue. The pH scale is a logarithmic function, and pH 7 (the pH of the water) is much more "basic" than pH 3.5, even if pH 7 is officially "neutral."

CHAPTER 12

Different Sips:

From Sparkling to Strong to Strange

Q Can you describe the process of creating a sparkling wine?

A Ah, the tiny bubbles. Sparkling wine is one of my very favorite beverages, one that I often sip even during harvest when, believe it or not, most winemakers are so sick of having their hands in the *vino* all day that they turn to other tipples. You may have heard the old saw that "it takes a lot of good beer to make a lot of good wine." Well, in my case it takes a lot of sparkling wine to keep me going through harvest when the last thing I want to do is relax at the end of the day with a big, tannic, alcoholic Cab. Those little bubbles can get expensive though, so if you're like me, you need to craft your own steady supply.

As you might suspect, making a Champagne-style wine (we can't legally call it Champagne unless it comes from that area of France) is a little trickier than making everyday table wine. With the professional *méthode champenoise* (may-TOHD shahm-peh-NWAHZ) technique, the second fermentation takes place in the same bottle you buy at the store. This is tough to do for small-scale winemakers without all of the professional equipment, but you can use a modified procedure to achieve somewhat similar results.

Sparkling wine, when produced on a small "garage winery" scale, generally takes about 9 months from start to finish, including making the base wine. There are three separate processing stages. Each stage has its own list of equipment and ingredients.

Caution, Yeast at Work!

During the winemaking process, yeast cells eat sugar and convert it to alcohol and carbon dioxide gas. If that gas is shut up in a sealed bottle, it can build up internal pressure to dangerous levels. With sparkling wines, where you purposefully introduce sugar to a finished wine and then referment it in a sealed bottle, you need to be very aware of pressure buildup; sparkling wines average about 6 bars of pressure!

Sparkling wine should only be stored in extra thick and sturdy Champagne-type bottles and sealed with a crown cap, not a regular wine cork. When handling bottles in storage, wear protective eyewear and gloves in case of an explosion. Keep stored sparkling wine bottles away from pets and small children. Be aware that with an increase in ambient temperature, bottles may be predisposed to breakage and explosion.

Stage One: The first step is to reinoculate your base wine (the cuvée) by introducing some sugar and yeast into it.

Stage Two: When the cuvée is cloudy with gently fermenting yeast, bottle it. This gives the wine its sparkle. The yeast continues to ferment the added sugar in the sealed bottles, producing alcohol and a small amount of carbon dioxide. The carbon dioxide gas dissolves into solution and the yeast cells die out, leaving a thick layer of lees (spent yeast cells) on the bottom of the bottles.

Stage Three: To prevent spoilage problems or off odors from the lees, chill the wine and decant it into another bottle to which you've added the dosage (doe-SAHJ), a final addition of distilled alcohol, wine conditioner, and some of the original cuvée. This stage is necessary to take sparkling wine to its long-awaited finish. By chilling the original bottles and then carefully pouring the sparkling wine off the lees into the new bottles, you clarify the wine and balance its body and texture a bit so it's ready to drink.

The wine conditioner provides the wine with a touch of sugar, but don't be surprised if you don't taste it in the final product. Base-wine cuvées used to make sparkling wines are high in acid, so the resulting sparkling wine is as well. The high-acid content makes sparkling wine so crisp and refreshing that it takes just a little extra sugar to balance out the final taste profile of the wine.

■ ══════ ■

Q Can I carbonate wine using a beer-kegging system?

A A true Champagne-style sparkling wine is produced by the classic *méthode champenoise,* where a second fermentation is actually conducted in the bottle. Though less authentic and arguably less quality-oriented, artificial carbonation can be used by the home winemaker to give a little fizz without fermenting in the bottle. All you need is a standard homebrewing kegging system consisting of a Cornelius-style 5-gallon stainless-steel keg, a CO_2 tank with a gas regulator, and the hoses and fittings to connect it all up. You will also need a counterpressure bottle filler. This is the basic beer-kegging system used by thousands of home-brewers across North America. It can be purchased at most homebrewing supply retail shops.

The following process was adapted from *Techniques in Home Winemaking*, by Daniel Pambianchi. As with the

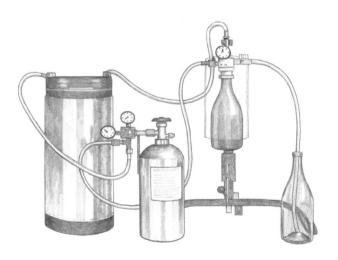

Carbonation system

production of any sparkling wine, wear appropriate eye and face protection when working with pressurized equipment. It is also critical that you use sparkling-wine bottles that are designed to withstand the pressure of carbonation.

CARBONATING

1. Put your chilled fermented base wine into the sanitized keg and close the lid.
2. Attach a hose between the CO_2 tank and the "In" valve on the keg.
3. Turn the main control knob on the tank until you hear gas running through the hoses into the keg.
4. Using the regulator gauge as a guide, adjust the tank pressure to 40 psi, and begin to shake the keg. This allows the CO_2 to mix with your wine and begin the carbonation process. Keep shaking the keg for about 10 minutes.

BOTTLING

1. Hook up the filler with a hose to the "Out" valve on the keg.
2. Connect the bottle pressure gauge on the filler to the CO_2 tank.
3. To fill the bottles, first open the gas valve to allow CO_2 gas to fill up the bottle. Then open the wine valve as you close the gas valve.
4. Slowly open the filler's control valve to allow wine to fill the bottle.

5. Use a plastic stopper or a crown cap to seal the bottle. The best part is, you can drink these wines right away!

■ ══════════ ■

Q What is the best way for a home winemaker to make fortified wines?

A Fortified wines have had alcohol added to them, usually in the form of neutral grape spirits (brandy without the oak aging). Fortification can happen at different stages in the winemaking process. This is one of the many variables that winemakers can alter to affect the outcome of the final product.

Port-style wines (typically red) are allowed to ferment down to about 6 percent alcohol from a starting point of 25–35° Brix before alcohol is added to arrest the fermentation. The yeast die off due to ethanol toxicity (this naturally occurs for most yeast above about 15–16 percent alcohol) and the remaining sugar is unconsumed, resulting in a sweeter beverage. After the fortified must is pressed, the product remains stable due to its high alcohol content.

Other fortified wines are simply products of a normal gone-to-dry fermentation to which alcohol is added to boost the ethanol percentage, either for stability or stylistic reasons (a higher alcohol content often contributes a fuller mouthfeel and longer finish).

Yet another class of fortified wine isn't really wine at all in that there is no fermentation involved. An example close to my heart is Angelica, a beverage popularized during California's mission era. Easily made, it is simply a half-and-half mixture of juice from the Mission grape and whatever grape brandy one happens to have around. With its high alcohol content acting as a natural preservative, the mission padres undoubtedly found this an easy-to-store and assuredly easy-to-drink tipple.

To make a fortified fermented wine with some residual sugar, simply add brandy or other spirits to the fermenting juice, which arrests the fermentation by killing off the yeast with the high alcohol content, while the desired amount of sugar remains in the fermenter.

For port-style wines from concentrates, you would perhaps not dilute the concentrate as much (leaving it at 25–30 percent sugar as opposed to the usual 22–24 percent), then inoculate with a commercially available sugar-tolerant yeast. Fortify to stop the fermentation when the sugar is down to about 6 percent or according to taste. You can also purchase special port-style kits. Just follow the instructions closely on these kits.

 How is a white Zinfandel made? Is it a different grape than red Zinfandel?

A White Zinfandel is actually a rosé made from the just-pressed juice of the red Zinfandel grape. Instead of fermenting the grapes and juice together as with most red wines, this wine is pressed right away. Without the prolonged contact with the skins, the resulting color is light pink and the flavor is much lighter.

Ironically, the white Zinfandel craze, which helped create a new interest in Zinfandel, started out as an attempt to make a better dry red table wine out of a grape that had long been dismissed as an uninteresting varietal suitable only for hot climates. Bob Trinchero, the winemaker at Sutter Home Winery in the Napa Valley, decided in 1972 to try to make a rich, dry red table wine from Zin grapes grown in the cooler Amador County region of the Sierra Nevada foothills. To make the wine even more concentrated, he bled off a portion of the juice from the crushed grapes and allowed the must to ferment normally.

When he noticed that the juice he had drawn off had a lovely pink color and a nice flavor, he decided to ferment it like a white wine. The resulting dry, tart rosé turned out to be popular with winery employees and a few locals. During a subsequent harvest, the Zinfandel juice didn't entirely ferment to completion, leaving that year's rosé with a little bit of residual sugar. That product became a tasting room sell-out as well as an international success. Today, it is one of the top-selling wines on the market.

Q Are there special yeast considerations when making mead?

A Mead is a fermented beverage based on honey. As long as you dilute the honey appropriately, you'll have a sugar solution that most wine yeast strains should happily ferment to dryness or to whatever point you choose to arrest fermentation with cold temperatures, added alcohol (yes, you can make a fortified honey wine), or sulfite additions. It's always a good idea to add yeast extract, nutrient, or hulls, however, because honey lacks many of the essential nutrients that yeast need to survive.

Q What are some herbs or fruits that can add interest to a mead?

A Take a page out of this beverage's long and glorious history and do what the ancients did when they wanted to mess with their meads — dose it with any edible herb, spice, or floral mixture that suits your fancy.

For a traditional northern European flavor, go for a mix of mint, melissa, and borage (with maybe a little thyme thrown in for fun). A summery floral mixture might include chamomile flowers, lavender flowers, orange peel, and a little sage or marjoram leaves for interest.

Fruits go well with honey, especially cranberry, raspberry, peach, and apple. Simply use fruit juice or concentrate in place of part of the honey called for in the recipe. Make sure the starting sugar concentration is correct according to the level called for in the recipe. Add some extra table sugar or juice concentrate to bump up the sugar if it is lacking.

Q What is the best way to add spices or herbs to my wine or mead?

A There are several different ways to introduce herbs, spices, or flowers to a fermentation, though some general rules apply for using plant additives. Dried plants have more concentrated flavors than fresh plants, so use less dried plant material than you would fresh. Stick with what you know. Don't use any weird or wacky plants if you are not familiar with them. Pick up an herb guide at your local bookstore, or go to a reputable source on the Internet if you have any questions about which plants are safe to use.

Start conservatively. Just as with oak, overuse of any flavoring agent can easily overpower everything else in your batch of wine or mead. As for actual techniques, one of the easiest methods is to simply drop a handful or two of fresh material (or a tablespoon or so of dried) into your fermenter. The heat and the alcohol will extract some of the new material's character and the mead will definitely be different for it.

When fermentation is over and you're ready to transfer the mead off of its gross lees for the first time, simply leave the organic matter behind in the fermentation vessel. You may need to rack through a strainer if the spices are floating in the mead. This separation is important, because by the end of a 10-day fermentation, the plants probably have given their all, and as they continue to break down, they may actually start to rot, which will detrimentally affect your mead.

You could also use the tea bag method, which is exactly what it sounds like. Tie up your plant material of choice, fresh or dried, in a small cheesecloth sack with a couple of sanitized marbles and suspend it in your finished mead. (See page 191 for more on this method.) That way you don't have to rack anything to separate the plant material from the mead, and it's very quick and easy to remove the herbs if you feel the mead is getting too strongly flavored. For flavoring anything past the initial fermentation stage, I recommend using dried plants, as they tend to be freer of molds, fungi, and wild yeast and bacteria than fresh plants, and they are less likely to rot or throw off a haze.

You can also greatly add to your entire beer, mead, and winemaking repertoire by creating a battery of essences to doctor up anything from an entire barrel to a bottle to a single glass of your favorite brew. You'll need a collection of little infusion jars of about ¼-cup (59 mL) capacity — clean, dry baby-food jars or glass spice jars with tight-fitting lids are ideal. Fill each small jar with a few tablespoons of a single dried herb or spice (or a mixture — be creative!), fill the jar with vodka or another neutral spirit, and screw on the lid tightly.

Leave the jars on a shelf and agitate one to three times a week in order to extract the aromatic goodies from the herbs. After a month or so, you'll have a strong-smelling spirit that can be added in small amounts to batches of beer, wine, or mead. Again, be conservative when adding these essences to your concoctions — they can be strong! Start with an ounce (29.5 mL) and add more to subsequent batches if the flavor is not strong enough.

Essential Fun

A fun thing to do with these essences is to take several bottles of wine or mead, add a different essence to each, and see how the flavor develops over time. My favorite essences to make at home and have on hand are: clove, cinnamon, lemon peel, orange peel, grapefruit peel, rose, star anise, rosemary, ginger, honeysuckle, apricot (from dried apricots), and peppermint. And don't forget, they're also really useful in cooking and in making creative cocktails. Rosemary, for example, makes a great martini.

Q Is there a way to add vanilla flavors to wine without using wood?

A Vanilla (natural or artificial) is a lovely flavor and aromatic component of many foods and beverages, and it makes perfect sense for home winemakers to consider it as a wine additive. Since hobby winemakers aren't constrained by the table wine laws that forbid the addition of nonwine essences like vanilla, they should feel free to experiment away.

A compound called vanillin is responsible for the distinctive aroma that is often associated with oak aging, especially of Bordeaux varietals like Cabernet Sauvignon, Merlot, and Cabernet Franc. Vanillin is one of the 6-membered benzene-ring molecules (remember high school chemistry?) that, because of their structure, are very aromatic; they exist in a gaseous state and waft up into our noses when agitated, as when we swirl a wineglass. Commercial vanilla extract is high in vanillin, or compounds that smell remarkably like it, and I can see how a small amount could be used in unoaked wines to mimic some of the effects of aging in an oak barrel.

Real vanilla beans are extremely pungent, however. Dropping a vanilla bean, or even part of one, into a wine could overpower it. It's unwise to risk an entire lot on an unmeasured addition. Similarly, as grapes and barrels vary, so do vanilla beans. It's impossible to predict how much flavor or aroma one type of bean might impart over another.

An easy way to add natural vanilla aromas and flavors to your wine is to make a homemade extract. Fill a small, airtight glass container with a neutral ethyl alcohol such as rum or vodka. Add as many vanilla beans as you can either fit in the jar or afford. Set the jar in a warm or sunny spot, agitate every other day for at least 2 weeks, and soon you'll have your own homemade vanilla extract! (Because the beans are so strongly flavored, it takes less time to make vanilla extract than the essences described earlier.) You can use it drop by drop in your bench trials, as well as for mixing cocktails, making beverages, or baking cookies.

Whether you make your own or use a commercial brand, the main challenge to using any aroma- or flavor-boosting compound is how to do it in such a way that the results are pleasing to the winemaker. My main advice is to be conservative. Commercially available vanilla extracts are potent liquids and, as any cook knows, a little goes a long way. As when adding anything that could potentially make your wine objectionable if you overdo it, I recommend conducting the additions on a small scale first.

"Small" will depend on the size of your lots and the scale of measuring equipment you have. Since most home winemakers don't have micropipettes that can measure out microliters — as opposed to milliliters — of a liquid, I suggest trying a drop of an additive in, say, 200 mL (7 ounces) of wine. Give that a sniff and a taste and, if you like the addition at that rate, you can feel comfortable applying it to the rest of your batch of wine.

It's always better to take the test drive a little further just to be sure. Seal that sample of wine in an airtight, topped-off container like a baby-food jar overnight. Give it another sniff and taste test the next day and see if you're still happy with the results.

Don't forget to check the clarity of the wine sample as well. Sometimes adding anything — whether it's a fining agent, oak chips, or a flavor extract — can cause imbalances and instabilities in wine that will result in a haze or a precipitate. If this is the case and you still want to proceed with the addition, keep in mind that you will have to rack, fine, or filter in order to remove the particles before you bottle your wine.

Remember that aging in oak barrels not only imparts vanilla flavors but also contributes to the overall wine structure and character through micro-oxygenation and interaction between the wood's and the wine's myriad components. Oak tannins, lignins, and other carbohydrates, all of which can significantly impact a wine's flavor, aroma, and mouthfeel, are also extracted while a wine ages in oak barrels. You won't achieve that spectrum of flavors simply by adding vanilla extract to your wine. The delicate interaction of the wine with the oak, lees, and air all play a part in how a wine evolves over time.

Q Can I make wine out of Mountain Dew or Sprite by adding yeast and letting it ferment?

A I've never heard that one before, but that doesn't mean it isn't possible. It's just that when I think of commercial soda, my winemaking Magic Eight Ball says, "Signs Point to No." Here are a few reasons why these beverages, though full of fermentable sugar, to be sure, make far-from-ideal bases for wine.

pH. These drinks are far too acidic to support a healthy yeast population.

Carbonation. The osmotic pressure from the carbonation would kill the yeast.

Nutrition. Soft drinks contain none of the nutrients (such as amino acids and other nitrogen sources) necessary for yeast growth and reproduction.

Character. Last (but not least), soda pop drinks, especially the ones you've mentioned, have no natural tannin, aromatic compounds, or phenolic compounds to give structure, flavor, and body. We expect wine to taste a certain way, and sodas supply few, if any, of these compounds.

If you deacidified the soda, degassed it to make it flat, and then added nutrients, you might be able to ferment it into something alcoholic. Whether it would then be drinkable is a decision that I will most happily leave to you.

Q **Sake and other cereal wines are made out of rice. Could I make wine out of beans?**

A I suppose the biochemically correct answer is yes — anything that has fermentable carbohydrates could, under the right circumstances and with the right microbe as the fermentative agent, be metabolized into ethyl alcohol. However, it's pretty unlikely that you'd be able to convince a wine judge that the resultant liquid should be entered in the "table wine" category. You're correct that mankind's never-ending search for a palatable and potent beverage has led to some pretty creative brews.

The Japanese long ago perfected the delicate art of making sake and, as rice isn't a readily fermented starting material, to this day they inoculate a starter portion of each batch with a special mold called *koji-kin,* or *Aspergillus oryzae.* The *koji-kin* live on and eat into the rice kernels, transforming the long-chain carbohydrate molecules into smaller sugar molecules that the yeast can then digest and turn into alcohol.

Certain bush-dwelling African tribes utilize a different enzymatic process to make a beverage from their local grain; they liberate the fermentable sugar by chewing up and spitting out the grain into the fermentation vessel, letting their salivary enzymes do the work that mold spores do in making sake.

I even heard a rumor of a UC-Davis graduate imbibing a beer that was made from pasta! No matter where we roam, we always seem to be looking for something fermentable that we can turn into a pleasurable alcoholic beverage.

I have to question using beans to make wine, however. I'm not at all sure that one could fashion something even vaguely palatable with beans as the only source of fermentable sugar. Beans just don't contain that much sugar. Even though they probably have enough carbohydrates (sugars) to start a yeast fermentation, there aren't enough to supply sufficient alcohol to make a proper wine, which, even in home winemaking terms, usually has at least 9 percent alcohol.

Secondly, beans, as we know, are an excellent source of protein. Rice and other starches, which are almost entirely comprised of carbohydrates, are not high in protein, which makes them favorable for beer or "grain wine" production. A high-protein, low-carbohydrate environment is not ideal for yeast, which need sugars to survive. Furthermore, proteins can cause hideous stability issues in finished wines. A high protein content can lead to hazes, ropiness, and sliminess — all things one prefers to avoid.

Thirdly, beans lack many of the organic acids and aromatic compounds that make wine the fine beverage that it is. Grapes and other fruits are natural sources of tartaric, citric, and malic acids, and these molecules give wine its depth of flavor and aroma. Beans don't smell like anything in particular, and I would argue that a fermented bean liquid would be more like a beer than a wine.

Not to rain on your parade even further, but you would probably have problems finding yeast that would be able to live in a bean liquid or paste. I imagine that the environment would have high pH due to lack of acid and be low in carbohydrates due to lack of sugars and therefore much more conducive to bacterial growth than yeast growth.

———————

Q **If I made a coffee wine, would the caffeine survive the fermentation process?**

A Coffee wine, eh? I've heard of using strong black tea as a tannin additive and of using coffee in brewing recipes for a supercharged stout, but I've never heard of making coffee wine. I'm not an organic chemist, but I believe the caffeine would tend to stay around in the wine to a degree. I don't think yeast would metabolize the caffeine, though you might lose some in the progressive rackings. It could also precipitate out of solution under certain conditions, but I would count on having some residual caffeine left in the wine. The level of caffeine, of course, would depend on how much coffee you used in the recipe — just as your average cup of joe will be stronger with more ground beans, so will your wine. Happy fermenting with your java!

———————

GLOSSARY

Acetaldehyde. (Also called ethanal.) The most common aldehyde compound found in wine. Acetaldehyde results when ethanol (alcohol) is oxidized by yeast or, more commonly, bacteria and is the main cause of any acetone off odor found in wine.

Acetobacter. A group of bacteria that convert wine to vinegar (ethanol into acetic acid) through an aerobic (oxygen-present) fermentation.

Acid blend. A generic name for any commercially available blend of acids (usually citric, tartaric, and sometimes malic) sold for the acidification of homemade wines.

Acid titration. Measuring the acid content of wine by adding a base of known concentration until all of the acid is neutralized as shown by an indicator that turns pink when the end point is achieved. By measuring the amount of base it takes to neutralize a wine's acid, we can calculate a wine's acidity.

Aeration. The process of incorporating air into a wine, must, or juice, either by splashing while racking, swirling a wine-tasting glass, or simply by stirring a container very vigorously. This is sometimes done to "blow off" undesirable aromas such as hydrogen sulfide or to give an initial dose of oxygen to a fermentation just getting under way.

Airlock. See *fermentation lock*.

Ampelography. The ancient science of identifying grapevines by their physical characteristics.

Anthocyanins. (See also *phenolic compounds.*) Polyphenolic compounds responsible for wine color.

Antioxidant. A compound such as sulfur dioxide (SO_2) that retards the effects of oxidation in wine (browning, sherry-like aromas).

Astringency. The dry, puckery sensation caused by tannin in wine. The tannins actually denature the salivary proteins, causing a rough sandpapery feel in the mouth.

Balling. (See also *Brix.*) A scale graduation for a hydrometer used in reading the specific gravity of liquids or their sugar content.

Baumé. (See also *Brix.*) Another way to express density of a solution.

Bentonite. A powdery clay that attracts proteins and is used as a fining agent to heat stabilize and clarify wines.

Bottle aging. Aging wine in the bottle for a few weeks to several years after it has been bottled.

Brettanomyces (Brett). A genus of yeast that can impart a mousey, plasticlike, or metallic flavor to wine. *Brettanomyces* is almost always considered a spoilage organism, though some winemakers, especially in Europe, appreciate a small amount of this character in their wines.

Brix. The amount of sugar in a wine as measured by a hydrometer. It is the ratio by weight of dissolved solids (expressed as sucrose) in 100 g of 20°C water. For example, a 23° Brix must has the equivalent of 23 g of sucrose in 100 g of water.

Bulk aging. Aging that occurs after fermentation but before final bottling.

Bung. A stopper for the opening of a cask or barrel.

Campden tablets. A convenient way of delivering sulfites to wine. One tablet usually contains 0.44 g of compressed potassium metabisulfite or sodium metabisulfite, though concentrations can change from product to product.

Cap. The fruit skins, stems, and pulp that float to the surface of the must during a fermentation.

Carboy (demijohn). A glass or plastic container, typically of a 5-gallon volume, that is used for fermenting juice, carrying out secondary fermentations, and long-term storage.

Chaptalize. To add sugar to a wine or juice.

Chill proofing. See *cold stabilization*.

Clearing. The natural settling out of small particulates and suspended matter in finished wine, either over time or with the aid of a fining agent like bentonite or egg whites.

Clinitest tablets. Originally intended for diabetics' self-monitoring of the sugar content of urine, Clinitest tablets are also useful for determining dryness (absence of sugar) in wines.

Cold soak. Leaving the grapes in the primary fermenter at a low temperature for a certain period of time — sometimes hours, sometimes days — before inoculating with the yeast or until the must begins fermenting on its own.

Cold stabilization. The exposure of wines to very cold temperatures prior to bottling, primarily to precipitate any tartrate-salt (potassium bitartrate and calcium tartrate are the most common) crystals that could come out of solution later in the bottle. Considered more of a cosmetic quality-control step than a necessity for home winemakers, almost all commercial white wines go through this process.

Copper sulfate. Used for the treatment of wines affected by a rotten egg smell (hydrogen sulfide and other sulfur-derivative spoilage compounds). $CuSO_4$ is poisonous in high concentrations and should only be used if it can be measured and controlled carefully.

Cork taint (corked wine). Wine that has a pronounced musty smell, like old, decaying cardboard. The aroma primarily comes from 2,4,6-trichloroanisole (TCA), a chlorine-containing metabolite of certain mold species that live in the crevices of wine corks and cannot be completely eradicated, even after corks are treated in the factory.

Country wine. A colloquialism describing wine made from herbs, flowers, or fruit other than grapes.

Crusher/destemmer. A common piece of winery equipment, used to remove the grape berries from stems. Some machines have removable rollers that turn them into destemmers only, making crushing optional.

Crushing. Generally, the act of turning fresh grapes into must. More specifically, crushing entails passing the destemmed grape berry through a series of rollers to release more juice for fermentation.

Cuvée. French term for the specially blended base white wine that is put through a secondary fermentation in the production of sparkling wine. It can also refer to a blend of different wines in general.

Degas. To release extra gas in a finished wine, before bottling, to prevent fizziness.

Degrees Brix. See *Brix*.

Diacetyl. A buttery-smelling aromatic compound produced by lactic acid bacteria during malolactic fermentation. Generally desirable in subtle levels in red wines, it is also seen as a positive in some white wine styles like oak-aged Chardonnay, but not in fresh, floral, and fruity whites.

Dosage (doe-SAHJ). The process of adding a sugar solution to sparkling wine before final corking.

Dry. When a wine has no sugar left after fermentation, either from a chemical standpoint (usually considered as less than 0.2 percent sugar) and/or a sensory standpoint (the wine is no longer perceptibly sweet).

Dumb phase. A time when the wine becomes somehow less expressive or less enjoyable than it once was. As every wine is different, it is impossible to predict when a wine might go through such a period or what complex chain of chemical reactions are causing the wine to taste and smell the way it does at any given moment.

Enology. The science of wine and winemaking.

Enzymes. Proteins that catalyze a chemical reaction by serving as an intermediary. Commercially prepared enzyme powders and solutions can be used to break down pectin or hydrolyze grape skins to release more color into a wine.

Ethanol. See *ethyl alcohol.*

Ethyl alcohol (ethanol). A product of yeast fermentation that is found in all alcoholic beverages. Yeast produce around 0.56 percent ethanol for every degree Brix in the initial must.

Extended maceration. (See also *maceration.*) A procedure wherein the fermented wine is left on the skins for a certain period of time after primary fermentation. Extended maceration is believed by some winemakers to enhance mouthfeel, tannin extraction, and color development.

Falling bright. A somewhat old-fashioned winemaking expression that means "clearing." It is generally thought preferable to allow a wine to clarify naturally rather than put it through the fining or filtering process. "Falling" refers to the settling out of floating particles that could cause cloudiness, while "bright" refers to the clarity.

Fermentation. (See also *malolactic fermentation.*) In general terms, any microbially brokered metabolic breakdown or digestion. In winemaking, the chemical process by which sugar in a liquid is broken down by yeast into alcohol, carbon dioxide gas, and other by-products, including aromatics and compounds that contribute to mouthfeel.

Fermentation lock (airlock). A plastic or glass device that fits over the top of a carboy or into the bung hole of a barrel to keep out air while allowing any gas produced by wine to escape.

Film yeast. A type of yeast that lives on the surface of wine in storage containers where there is air in the headspace.

It causes an oily film to appear on the surface of the wine, which, if left untreated, will lead to spoilage aromas and off flavors in the wine.

Fining. The process of adding an agent such as bentonite or egg whites to help clarify and stabilize the finished wine. This operation is done before bottling to prevent cloudiness or flocculation in the bottle.

Flocculation. The aggregation of solids or particles that settle out in wine, either in barrel, tank, or bottle. Another word for precipitation.

Fortification. Adding alcohol in the form of a distilled spirit like brandy to a finished wine before bottling. Traditionally, ports and sherries, which contain about 18 percent alcohol, are made this way.

Fractional blending. The blending of wines of the same type but different vintages to produce wines of the same average age. The solera system, used by some traditional sherry producers in Spain, is a fractional blending system.

Free run. Juice that flows from the first pressing of the grapes or finished must. The free-run juice or wine is often low in solids and phenolics.

Fruit forward. A descriptor meaning that the fruit is very prominent in the aroma and taste of a wine.

Glycerin (glycerol). A carbohydrate (sugar) that is not a substantial food source for most wine yeast strains, glycerin is naturally produced in small quantities during most fermentations.

Grip. A nontechnical term used by some winemakers to describe astringency and the feeling of tannins in the mouth. A wine that has good grip is showing appreciable tannins in a pleasurable way.

Gross lees. The heaviest sediment that remains after the primary fermentation is complete; it is the initial settling out of must or juice postfermentation.

Heat stabilization. A practice more common in the commercial winemaking realm than in small-scale or home winemaking. A wine that is "heat stable" should not produce a visible protein haze when a filtered sample is kept at 100°F (37.7°C) for 24–36 hours. Heat stabilization is not necessary for wine quality or wholesomeness; a heat stable wine is just less likely to throw an unsightly haze over its life.

Hydrometer. An analytical device that measures the relative density of a solution; used to measure the amount of sugar (in Balling or degrees Brix, Baumé, or specific gravity) in a juice or wine.

Inoculation. The process of introducing yeast into the grape juice or must in order to initiate fermentation.

Kieselsol. A proprietary name for a fining agent belonging to the class of silica suspensions that act like bentonite.

Lactic acid. An acid present in wines that have gone through a malolactic fermentation. Lactic acid is less acidic than malic acid.

Lactic acid bacteria (malolactic bacteria). (See also *malolactic fermentation*.) Any bacteria that metabolizes malic acid into lactic acid in wine. The most common strains, which survive in up to 10 percent alcohol, include members of the genera *Oenococcus, Lactobacillus,* and *Pediococcus.* Some strains of lactic acid bacteria can produce large amounts of acetic acid as well as off odors that smell like rotting meat.

Lees. The spent yeast cells and other solids like grape skin particles that accumulate on the bottom of winemaking vessels after the fermentation is complete and the yeast has died out.

Maceration. (See also *extended maceration.*) The process through which wine grape (or other fruit) skins, seeds, and pulp are mixed in with the fermenting juice to extract tannins, color compounds, and aroma from the grapes.

Malic acid. (See also *malolactic fermentation.*) A naturally occurring grape acid that decreases with ripening. It is one of the principal components of a wine's total acidity and flavor profile and can contribute a valuable freshness to white and rosé wines.

Malolactic bacteria. See *lactic acid bacteria.*

Malolactic fermentation (MLF). (See also *secondary fermentation* and *lactic acid bacteria.*) The transformation of malic acid into lactic acid by specific strains of bacteria. Results include a slight deacidification of the wine, production of carbon dioxide gas, turbidity, and flavor and aroma changes. Usually described as "buttery" or "creamy," this aromatic profile is especially desirable in quality red-wine production as well as in some whites, such as Chardonnay.

Mouthfeel. A wine-tasting term that describes the sensation of wine in the mouth. A "round" mouthfeel is generally desirable. Referring to the feeling of fullness, viscosity, and astringency, this is a subjective and relative term. The residual sugar, acid levels, tannin levels, alcohol concentration, and glycerol content all affect how a taster will describe the mouthfeel of a wine.

Must. The soupy mass of squished skins, seeds, and pulp that are fermented together when making red wine or wine from nongrape fruits. If the pulp and other solids are pressed off before fermentation, as in making white wines, the raw material is simply called "juice."

Oak adjuncts. Noncoopered oak that is used during fermentation to help stabilize color and add tannins and in finished wines to contribute an oak-aged character. Sometimes called "oak chips," oak adjuncts are available in various sizes (from sawdust to staves) and toast levels (from light to dark).

Oaking. Using oak adjuncts to give oak characteristics to a wine being fermented in nonoak barrels or storing wine in new barrels to impart an oak character.

Oechsle. One of the many scales developed in Europe centuries ago to measure the density of liquids. Considered obscure (but still present in the odd winemaking manual), the measurement is mostly only used in Germany, Austria, and Switzerland. Originally calibrated at 17.5°C (63.5°F), it is now expressed as a density of solution at 20°C (68°F).

Overoaked. A wine that has more oak aroma and flavor than is appropriate for its style.

Oxidation. The reaction of juice, must, or wine with oxygen. Typical negative side effects of such reactions are browning of wine and juice and "cooked" flavors and aromas. Limited amounts of exposure to oxygen are actually healthy for young wines, because yeast need oxygen to grow during the initial stages of fermentation.

Pectin. Complex carbohydrate chains naturally occurring in fruits; can contribute to the viscosity and also the haziness of a wine. The chains can be dissolved by pectic enzymes, which are sometimes used in winemaking when dealing with nongrape fruit.

pH. In simple terms, pH indicates a wine's relative acidity. It isn't so much a measure of the acid present as a measure of the level of dissociation in solution. The pH level predicts to a great degree the finished wine's taste, aroma, mouthfeel, and ageability. The higher the pH, the higher the chance of bacterial contamination and spoilage.

Phenolic compounds. Sometimes called polyphenols or polyphenolics, this large complex group of molecules includes such specific wine components as tannins and anthocyanins. Polyphenols (chains of phenolic compounds linked together) interact with oxygen, with each other, with sulfur dioxide, and with a myriad of other wine components, making them one of the key "architect" molecules in wine.

Pitch. To add yeast to the must or juice in order to begin fermentation.

Pomace. The crushed fruit or grapes left after the juice has been extracted (in the case of white wines) or the fermented wine has been pressed (in the case of red wine).

Potassium bitartrate. (See also *cold stabilization.*) A solid salt (tartaric acid combined with potassium, both naturally present in juice and wine) that creates the primary physical instability in bottled wines. Potassium bitartrate crystals often form and precipitate out of solution in aging and bottled wines. Harmless if ingested and primarily a cosmetic concern for commercial winemakers, the formation of crystals is accelerated by increasing alcohol content or lower temperatures.

Potassium metabisulfite. (See also *Campden tablets.*) Sold as a powder or compressed into tablets, potassium metabisulfite inhibits molds and bacteria and serves as an antioxidant and general cleansing agent.

Potassium sorbate. A persistent fungistat sometimes added to wine to inhibit yeast and to grape juice concentrates to prevent fermentation. In usual wine concentrations (around 200 mg/L), it can have a pineapple-like smell and in wines that are ML complete, it can take on a geranium odor. Most commercial wineries choose to exclude yeast in sweet wines by sterile filtration rather than adding potassium sorbate.

Press cake. Another term for pomace, especially when still in the press and compressed into a solid cake.

Press cuts (press fractions). The first press cut is the free run, or the juice or wine that runs freely out of the press, with no mechanical pressure. With increased pressure, more juice or wine emerges from the press, and with it, tannins, phenolics, and other potentially interesting (and potentially negative) compounds. Winemakers take press cuts (separating out the free run from further press wine) in order to evaluate them separately for quality.

Press wine (hard press). The wine that emerges from the press under very hard pressure. It usually has a higher pH and is higher in tannins and bitter compounds than the free run and the first pressings. In some wineries, press wine is discarded or blended into a cheaper wine of lesser quality than the top tier, higher quality products.

Primary fermentation. (See also *malolactic fermentation* and *secondary fermentation.*) The vigorous first fermentation, called the alcoholic fermentation, in which yeast convert sugar in the juice or must to alcohol and carbon dioxide.

Punt. The indentation in the bottom of a bottle; for sparkling-wine bottles, it is an important structural element that strengthens the bottle against internal pressure.

Rachis. The stems of grape clusters.

Racking. Moving juice or wine from one container to another; usually implies taking the clearest top portion of the liquid and leaving the sediment behind.

Refermentation. (See also *fermentation, malolactic fermentation,* and *secondary fermentation.*) An additional fermentation in wine after the primary alcoholic fermentation has taken place. When unintended, it is seen as a defect.

Refractometer. A hand-held tool that measures sugar levels in juice by bending light through a prism in a way that correlates to the refractive properties of the juice. Because carbon dioxide gas can interfere with accuracy, refractometers do not work on fermenting juice or must.

Residual sugar. Any sugar left in the wine after the fermentation has stopped and the yeast have completed their life cycles and died out. Sometimes residual sugar is desired, as in sweeter white wines or dessert wines. A wine with no residual sugar is considered to be dry.

Ropiness. A spoilage condition that resembles slime, raw egg whites, or mucous. It is caused by an extreme microbiological contamination that produces long-chain carbohydrates (polysaccharides) and dextrans, hence the ropiness. Thought to be caused by a wide range of bacteria, ropiness is more of a risk in higher pH wines. Ropiness cannot be fined or filtered out, so the wine must be disposed of.

Roundness. (See also *mouthfeel.*) Describes the body of the wine or the sensation of fullness in the mouth that texturally differentiates wine from water.

Secondary fermentation. (See also *malolactic fermentation* and *refermentation.*) A bit of a misnomer, secondary fermentation can refer to two things: a true second alcoholic fermentation that follows completion of the first and is usually purposely started by adding yeast and extra sugar to the finished wine to make CO_2 for a sparkling-wine effect; or malolactic fermentation, which is not a yeast-brokered fermentation but one that is completed by bacteria. Done for stability (to rule out later MLF in the bottle) or stylistic reasons (to reduce the wine's acidity, resulting in creamy or buttery aromas), malolactic fermentation can be carried out in the barrel right after the primary fermentation is complete.

Second crop. Later-developing, smaller, and more acidic secondary grape clusters located farther out on a grape-vine's canes and on lateral shoots, away from the primary fruiting zone. Commercial wineries avoid making wine with second-crop grapes, but many home winemakers use them as they are cheaper.

Second-run wines. Wines made by adding sugar, water, and other adjuncts to fruit that has already been pressed or fermented. A home-winemaking practice only.

Sorbate. (See also *potassium sorbate*.) Sorbic acid usually found in soluble form like potassium sorbate that is used to inhibit yeast.

Sparging. Physically introducing gas under pressure (usually nitrogen or carbon dioxide) to a wine or juice. Sparging a wine with nitrogen removes carbon dioxide, whereas sparging with carbon dioxide helps exclude oxygen and protect a wine during cellar movements.

Specific gravity. A measurement of relative density, it is the ratio of the density of juice or wine to the density of distilled water at 68°F (20°C). Since it is a ratio, there are no units. A juice or wine more dense (with sugar, for example) than water will have a specific gravity over 1.000. Since alcohol is less dense than water, completely dry wine with no residual sugar will always have a specific gravity less than 1.000.

Splash rack. (See also *racking*.) To move wine from one container to another using techniques that incorporate air into the wine as it pours into the receiving vessel. Splash racking can often drive off hydrogen sulfide in young wines.

Stuck fermentation. A fermentation that stops before the desired level of sugar consumption is reached and is caused by the yeast slowing down and eventually dying. Most common problems include alcohol toxicity due to overly high initial Brix, insufficient yeast-available nitrogen (YAN), fermentation temperatures that are too high or too low, and competition with other yeast and bacteria.

Sulfides. Volatile sulfur-containing aromas in wine that usually smell like rubber, burnt toast, or rotten eggs, in the case of hydrogen sulfide. Sulfides, especially at low levels, are often mistaken for *gout de terroir* or "earthy character," but in high concentrations, these strong odors can ruin a wine.

Sulfites. (See also *sulfur dioxide* and *potassium metabisulfite*.) A class of sulfur-containing compounds used as an antimicrobial agent, as an antioxidant, and as a preservative. Sulfites generally refer to the salt of sulfur dioxide when bound to other compounds.

Sulfur dioxide (SO_2). In the form of potassium metabisulfite crystals, liquid sulfur dioxide, or sulfur dioxide gas, SO_2 is an effective antioxidant and antimicrobial agent that has been used for millennia in winemaking. Yeast naturally produce about 10 mg/L SO_2 during the course of a fermentation, so it is impossible to produce a wine free of SO_2.

***Sur lies* (soor-lee).** French for "on the lees." The process of aging wine on the lees.

Sweet wine. Any wine that contains perceptible residual sugar. Sugar is perceptible, depending on the individual taster and the composition of the individual wine, at about 0.3–1.0 percent; a wine is often considered "off dry" at this stage. True dessert wines, like ice wines and the famous Château d'Yquem, often have 7–10 percent residual sugar.

TA. See *titratable acidity.*

Tannin. Large-molecule, astringent phenolic compounds found in grape skins, seeds, and stems, as well as in oak barrels and oak adjuncts, that make your mouth pucker and feel dry when you drink red wine. Tannins are extracted from the grapes during the maceration process and from oak during aging.

Tartaric acid. The most abundant natural acid in wine, it is not digested by any microorganisms during fermentation, so stays with the wine through bottling unless chemically removed or by precipitating as potassium bitartrate.

Tartrate crystals (tartrate fallout). See *potassium bitartrate.*

TCA (2,4,6-trichloroanisole). Noxious swampy- or musty-smelling molecule excreted by certain molds in the presence of free chlorine molecules. The main culprit when a wine is described as "corked."

Terroir. A French term meaning "soil" that also speaks to the entire set of growing conditions where a wine originates. While most international winemakers and viticulturists discuss macro- and microclimate (encompassing the physical realities of *terroir* like soil type, drainage, and aspect), PR and marketing professionals have seized on *terroir* to communicate not just the geological and geographical but also the metaphysical and spiritual provenances of its quality.

Titratable acidity (TA). Sometimes erroneously called total acidity, titratable acidity is the amount of acid that can be neutralized to an end point by an added base. TA indicates acid concentration but not acid strength.

Titration. An analytical method used to determine titratable acidity. A strong base of a known concentration is added to a sample of must, juice, or wine in measured amounts. An indicator chemical effects color change at the point when the base has neutralized all of the available hydrogen ions in the acids. The titratable acidity can then be determined in relation to how much base it took to neutralize all of the acids in the wine.

Topping up. Adding wine (the same wine or a similar wine) to a vessel to minimize headspace and reduce the chance of oxidization during bulk storage and aging. Critical to prevent VA formation, premature oxidation, sulfur dioxide loss, and a host of quality defects.

Total acidity. (See also *titratable acidity* and *volatile acidity*.) The empirical sum of all acids in a wine, both titratable and volatile.

Volatile acidity (VA). The part of the total acidity of a wine that can be evaporated or distilled away from the fixed acidity. Important in winemaking because volatile acids, of which acetic acid is by far the largest contributor, contribute to off odors. Elevated VA often results from an *Acetobacter* infection but can also result from a sluggish fermentation, stressed yeast cells, or many other microbial pathways.

Wild yeast. Sometimes referred to as "native" or "feral," wild yeast are naturally present on grapes, on winery equipment, and in the air itself. Some wineries rely on these itinerant microorganisms to start their wine fermenting, but since these yeast strains are far from uniform in population and fermenting ability, using them instead of inoculating with a proven pure culture can present a serious risk.

Yeast. One-celled fungi that grow naturally on grape skins and convert sugars to alcohol and carbon dioxide gas. Yeast is the organism that changes grape juice to wine. Special strains of yeast, bred for alcohol tolerance and healthy fermentation characteristics, are used in fine winemaking the world over.

Yeast-available nitrogen (YAN). A number that reflects the concentration of free amino nitrogen and ammonia (another source of nitrogen) levels in the juice. Most fermentations require 250–350 mg/L YAN to go to healthy completion.

Yeast food (yeast nutrient). A precalculated commercial mix of vitamins, minerals, and amino acids added to juice or must to ensure a clean, complete fermentation. Adding it to nongrape wines is essential because many fruits lack adequate nitrogen levels to support healthy yeast growth. Adding too much can leave unused nutrients available for the taking by unwanted spoilage organisms.

RESOURCES

Information

For wine recipes and detailed information on choosing the right yeast, visit *www.storey. com.*

WineMaker Magazine
www.winemakermag.com

Wines & Vines Magazine
www.winesandvines.com

University of California-Davis
Department of
Viticulture & Enology
530-752-0380
www.wineserver.ucdavis.edu

Aroma Wheel
© Ann C. Noble
www.winearomawheel.com

Books

From Vines to Wines, Jeff Cox, Storey, 1999

The Home Winemaker's Companion, Gene Spaziani and Ed Halloran, Storey, 2000

Techniques in Home Winemaking, Daniel Pambianchi, Véhicule Press, 2002

Calculations

Fermsoft
www.fermsoft.com
Check under "products" for several types of converters.

Turbo Yeast
www.distillery-yeast.com/ distillery_tips/converters/ converter.htm
Hydrometer scales and others

WineMaker magazine
www.winemakermag.com
Sulfite calculator, wine log

Suppliers and Wine Labs

Barrel Builders
800-365-8231
www.barrelbuilders.com
Barrels, oak chips, cellar tools

GusmerCellulo
www.gusmerenterprises.com
Equipment, supplies, malo-lactic bacteria

KLR Machines, Inc.
707-823-2883
www.klrmachines.com
Crush/cellar equipment

Lallemand
www.lallemandwine.com
Yeast, bacteria, nutrients

Lesaffre
www.lesaffreyeastcorp.com
Yeast supplies

Mel Knox Barrel Broker
415-751-6306
www.knoxbarrels.com
Ingle barrels, odd sizes

Saury
707-944-1330
www.sauryusa.com
French oak barrels

StaVin
415-331-7849
www.stavin.com
Premier oak products

Scott Laboratories, Inc.
800-821-7254
www.scottlab.com
Supplies, grape-processing
equipment, analysis

Seguin Moreau
707-253-3408
www.seguinmoreau.com
French, American, and
Hungarian barrels

Tonnellerie Radoux
800-755-4393
www.tonnellerieradoux.com
French, American, and Hungarian barrels

Vinovation
707-824-7905
www.vinovation.com
French oak chips, equipment,
lab services

Vinquiry
707-838-6312
www.vinquiry.com
Analytical services,
consulting, supplies

White Labs
www.whitelabs.com
Yeast and fermentation
services

Wyeast
www.wyeastlab.com
Yeast supplies

INDEX

Page numbers in *italic* indicate illustrations; those in **bold** indicate tables.

sulfur dioxide (SO$_2$)
(continued)
  smells, sulfur dioxide (SO$_2$)
    for, 274
"sunlight flavor," 256–57
Superfood, 141
sur lies ("on the lees"), 21,
  148–49
suspended solids and
  hydrometer, 38–39, 40–41
sweeteners for
  back-sweetening, 229–30
  country wine, 316
  wine, 180–81
synthetic corks, 236–37
Syrah (Shiraz), 59, 68, 91, 92,
  93, 94, 205, 239, 301–3

T

TA. *See* titratable acidity
tannin-peptide hazes, 193–94
tannin powders in kits, 311
tannins
  color and, 281
  country wine, 319–20, 325
  evaluating, 290
tartaric acid, adding, 16
"tartrate fallouts," 265–69
taste, 284, 288–89, 296
tea bags, adding plant
  material, 191, 340–41
Techniques in Home Winemaking
  (Pambianchi), 333–35

temperature, importance to
  fermentation, 154, 155, 157,
  158–59, 160, 165–66, 172,
  256
  hydrometer, 37, 39, 40, 41
  yeast, 154, 155
Tempranillo, 305
terroir, 26, 91
time line, winemaking, 15–18
titratable acidity (TA), 16, 26.
  See also acidity
  country wine and, 319
  error sources, titratable
    acidity assay, 126–28
  measuring levels, 112–13
  pH and, 112, 114, **114,** 123–
    25, 126
Titret tests, 106–7
toasted vs. charred oak
  barrels, 194–95
toasting levels of oak, 192
topping (topping up), 17,
  202–5, 208, 233, 251
Torrontés, 30
Torulaspora delbrueckii, 147
total acidity. *See* titratable
  acidity (TA)
treating corks, 233–34, *234*

U

University of California-Davis,
  24, 150, 284, 285–91, 294